P9-DNJ-310

The New Deal and the States

Federalism in Transition

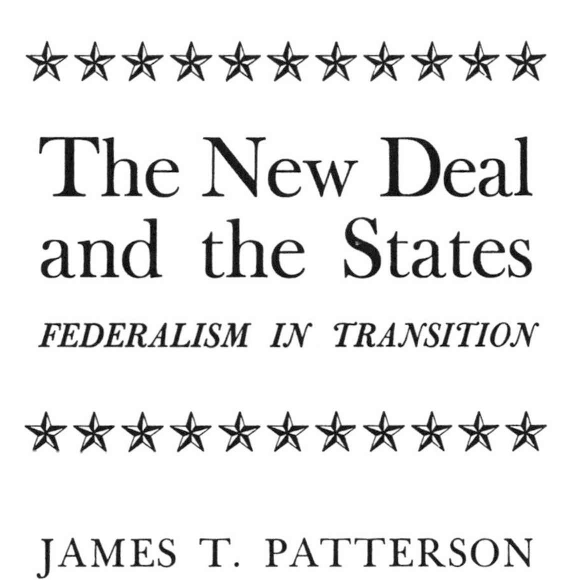

The New Deal and the States

FEDERALISM IN TRANSITION

JAMES T. PATTERSON

PRINCETON UNIVERSITY PRESS

PRINCETON, NEW JERSEY · 1969

L.C. Card: 69-17313

This book has been composed in Baskerville type.

Publication of this book has been aided by the Whitney Darrow Publication Reserve Fund of Princeton University Press

PRINTED IN THE UNITED STATES OF AMERICA BY
PRINCETON UNIVERSITY PRESS

TO MY FATHER,
who served his state well
for many years as a legislator
and speaker, and
TO MY MOTHER,
who encouraged him

Preface

THIS book covers both more and less than the title suggests. Because the New Deal years cannot be studied intelligently without some background, two chapters deal with state policy before the Roosevelt administration. The task of scanning all the state documents and newspapers, however, would take decades, and consequently this book does not even pretend to be definitive. Instead I have tried to suggest a few important trends in state affairs and in American federalism between 1920 and 1940. A more solid study of these subjects must await that distant day when scholars turn from the excitement of Pennsylvania Avenue to the more prosaic events of Albany, Atlanta, and Santa Fe.

Readers expecting dramatic new insights into national decision-making or into New Deal ideology may be disappointed. The focus here is as much on the states as it is on the federal government. How did the states act before the New Deal? How did they respond to Hoover, to the 100 days and thereafter? Did the New Deal promote forward-looking state administrations, or did it weaken state initiative? Was it discriminatory, and did it encourage cooperative federalism? In what states, or kinds of states, did it seem to have the greatest impact?

Generalizations on federal-state relations can be misleading. It may be that the most faithful way of describing them in the 1930's—or in any period—is to begin with the assumption that only a state-by-state analysis would give proper emphasis to the great dissimilarities among the states. This is a tenable view, and distinctive state traditions and institutions indeed posed formidable and at times insurmountable barriers in the way of New Deal planning.

But a state-by-state approach risks losing the forest for the trees, and it surrenders the chance of finding the generalizations which give meaning to history. Accordingly, I have tried to compromise, describing some of the countless variations in state responses, but searching always for whatever broad trends or patterns may have existed.

My thanks go to Professor Frank Freidel of Harvard University, who first suggested to me the need for studying the states during the depression years, and to Indiana University, which generously provided the financial aid necessary for travel and typing. Professors George I. Juergens and G. Cullom Davis of Indiana University offered very helpful comments on parts of the manuscript, as did Michael Webster, an Indiana graduate student. Marjorie Putney of the Princeton University Press proved a very patient and skilled editor. I am especially grateful to Professors Chase C. Mooney, John E. Wiltz, and David M. Pletcher of Indiana University and to William E. Leuchtenburg of Columbia University. Each read the entire manuscript very critically and saved me from many errors of fact and interpretation. My wife, Nancy, encouraged me every step of the way and devoted countless hours to improving the manuscript—without her, the book could not have been done.

JAMES T. PATTERSON

Bloomington, Indiana
January 1969

CONTENTS

The New Deal and the States

Federalism in Transition

1. The 48 States in the 1920's

"IT IS ONE of the happy incidents of the federal system," Supreme Court Justice Louis D. Brandeis wrote in 1932, "that a single courageous state may, if its citizens choose, serve as a laboratory, and try novel social and economic experiments without risk to the rest of the country."[1] Governor Franklin D. Roosevelt of New York shared Brandeis' faith in the states. "There is a tendency," he insisted, "and to my mind a dangerous tendency, on the part of the national government to encroach, on one excuse or another, more and more upon state supremacy. The elastic theory of interstate commerce . . . has been stretched almost to the breaking point."[2]

Brandeis, a devout Wilsonian liberal, maintained his faith in states through the vastly changed period of the depression, while Roosevelt, himself flexible almost to a breaking point, veered to a more nationalistic course. Yet Roosevelt, too, was sincere, and his remarks not only represented the views of many politicians, especially governors, in the 1920's, but were considered sound and forward-looking at the time. Few party leaders between 1919 and 1929 expected meaningful reform from the national government, and fewer still called for federal aid to the needy or legislation to benefit the laboring man. Even those who pursued the

1 New York State Ice Co. v Liebmann, 285 US 262 (1932).

2 Cited in Alfred B. Rollins, Jr., *Roosevelt and Howe* (New York, 1962), 271. The speech was delivered at the annual governors conference, and though the implied stress on state responsibility was sincere, the warning about federal intrusion was exaggerated to suit the occasion.

quest for social justice often preferred to work on the state instead of the national level.

Their faith in the states was understandable, for states and municipalities remained basic institutions with the background to indulge in progressive experiments. Though judicial decisions had discouraged some reforms, states still had managed to expand their powers considerably before 1920. They had preceded the federal government in regulating large corporations, establishing minimum labor standards, and stimulating economic development. By the 1920's state and local governments accounted for 74 percent of public spending and 67 percent of taxes.[3] They dominated the fields of education and public welfare, and their impact on American citizens was considerably more tangible than that of Washington. The activism of governors such as Roosevelt and Alfred E. Smith of New York contrasted sharply with the more relaxed pace of the United States Congress.

Indeed, the national government profoundly discouraged reformers. Theodore Roosevelt and Woodrow Wilson were gone; complacency replaced concern in the White House; and conservatives were usually able to restrain progressives on Capitol Hill. Congress gladly supported such "reforms" as prohibition, immigration restriction, and tariff revision, and it happily approved legislation for large commercial farmers and corporations. But it refused to pass welfare bills, broaden the authority of regulatory agencies, or spend surplus revenue to help low income groups.[4] The

[3] *Federal, State, and Local Fiscal Relations,* 78th Cong., 1st Sess., Sen. Doc. 69 (Washington, 1943). This excellent source contains many relevant statistics on state and local finance during the 1930's. (Hereafter cited as *Fiscal Relations*).

[4] My interpretation contrasts with that of Arthur Link, in "What Happened to the Progressive Movement in the 1920's?" *American Historical Review,* LXIV (July 1959), 833-51. He argues that progressiv-

progressive impulse had become so feeble that in 1929 Congress gave up aid for child and maternal hygiene, approved only eight years before. Other federal operations, such as grants for agricultural extension work, vocational education, and highways crept forward in the 1920's, but they ignored the low income masses in the cities.[5] Although regulatory agencies such as the Federal Trade Commission continued to function, they did so under increasingly conservative guidance.[6] The national government was hardly a fount of progressive legislation during the decade.[7]

---

ism remained strong in the 1920's, in Washington as well as in the states. His evidence for state progressivism, however, seems limited to Wisconsin, New York, and Louisiana, and he admits the need for state studies covering the 1920's. So does Herbert F. Margulies, in "Recent Opinion on the Decline of the Progressive Movement," *Mid-America,* XLV (October 1963), 250-68.

[5] Total expenditures for these programs hovered around $110 million per year during the 1920's. Approximately 80 percent of this money was for highways, distributed according to a formula favoring large and thinly populated states. In 1913, prior to the introduction of aid for roads, federal assistance to states had totaled $12 million, and in 1927 aid except for highways had even dropped a bit—to $11 million. See U.S. Dept. of Commerce, Bureau of the Census, *Historical Statistics on State and Local Government Finances, 1902 to 1953* (Washington, 1955), 17, 22; and Dept. of Commerce, Bureau of Foreign and Domestic Commerce, *Statistical Abstract of the United States, 1929* (Washington, 1929), 127, 177. Also Austin F. MacDonald, "Recent Trends in Federal Aid to the States," *American Political Science Review,* XXV (August 1931), 628-33; and Bureau of Census, *Historical Review of State and Local Finance* (Spec. Study No. 25, Washington, 1948), 19.

[6] G. Cullom Davis, "The Transformation of the Federal Trade Commission, 1914-1929," *Mississippi Valley Historical Review,* XLIX (December 1962), 437-55.

[7] It is arguable that prewar reform on the national level had never been very striking, that it had been dominated by businessmen seeking to preserve their socioeconomic position or to bring order to a distended society. See Gabriel Kolko, *The Triumph of Conservatism: A Reinterpretation of American History, 1900-1916* (New York, 1963), and Robert Wiebe, *The Search for Order, 1877-1920* (New York, 1967), for such interpretations. See also Irwin Yellowitz, *Labor and the Progres-*

With so little reform coming from Washington, the way was open for the states. The 1920's thus seemed a kind of crossroads. Governors could either seize the initiative for social progress from an indifferent Congress, or they could turn away from an opportunity to prove themselves enlightened and responsible leaders.

Some state legislation of the 1920's seemed to justify progressive hopes. Several states created deposit insurance in an effort to cope with periodic bank failures. Although the insurance was to prove woefully inadequate in 1929, it was a precedent upon which Congress would draw in establishing the Federal Deposit Insurance Corporation in 1933.[8]

A more important development was the effort of a few conscientious legislatures to introduce modern, efficient means of administration. This movement, an outgrowth of the progressive era, first succeeded in Illinois during 1917 and accelerated rapidly after the war. Between 1918 and 1928 sixteen more states enacted administrative reorganization plans. Aimed at strengthening gubernatorial powers, coordinating staff services, and eliminating waste, the move-

---

sive Movement in New York State, 1897-1916 (Ithaca, 1965), for a case study suggesting the weakness of labor unions as promoters of reform in the progressive period. Grant McConnell, in *The Decline of Agrarian Democracy* (Berkeley, 1953), shows that large commercial farmers dominated the drafting of farm legislation from the progressive period on.

From this perspective prewar reform was mild: it had never stressed social welfare, spending for lower income groups, or regulation *of* (as opposed to regulation *for*) big business. It was "business," not "social" progressivism. While such a view of the progressive period is persuasive, it does not negate the case for the weakness of social-welfare progressivism in the 1920's; on the contrary, it helps account for it. A relevant article is George Tindall, "Business Progressivism: Southern Politics in the Twenties," *South Atlantic Quarterly*, LXII (Winter 1963), 92-106. Tindall emphasizes the efficiency minded character of southern progressivism after the war.

[8] W. Brooke Graves, *American State Government* (Boston, 1941), 12-14.

ment was attractive not only to progressives but also to businessmen and economy conscious citizens. While these laws were hardly revolutionary, they indicated the persistence of the efficiency ideal of mild progressives; and a few states, notably New York and Virginia under governors Alfred E. Smith and Harry F. Byrd, became better equipped to provide positive government.[9]

Easily the most remarkable development in state government in the 1920's was the increase in spending. Increases in school attendance on the one hand and in automobile ownership on the other presented states and municipalities with rapidly rising costs for education and highways, and most politicians moved to meet the needs.[10] Total state expenditures rose from some $400 million in the prewar year of 1913 to $1.2 billion in 1921, and to nearly $2.1 billion in 1929. Using the 1926 dollar as a standard, the per capita increase in state spending between 1922 and 1929 was some

[9] Arthur E. Buck, *The Reorganization of Governments in the United States* (New York, 1938), 7-37.

[10] Automobile registrations increased from 6.7 million in 1919 to 23.1 million in 1929, and state spending for roads rose from $221 million to $1.1 billion in the same period. Bureau of Census, *Historical Statistics: Colonial Times to 1957* (Washington, 1960), 462, 459. (Hereafter cited as *Historical Statistics.*) Average elementary and secondary public school attendance rose from 16.1 million in 1920 to 21.2 million in 1930, and the average length of the school term increased during the same period from 162 to 173 days. State spending for public schools grew accordingly—from $202 million in 1922 to $398 million in 1932. *Ibid.*, 207, 228. Whether these activities should be called "progressive" is debatable, and in many states the backing for these programs was widespread. Nevertheless, such legislation did represent an increased willingness to use state government for positive purposes. Two case studies are: Elmer S. Puryear, *Democratic Party Dissension in North Carolina, 1928-1936* (Chapel Hill, 1962), 62-90; and Cullen B. Gosnell, *The Government and Politics of Georgia* (New York, 1936), 107ff. These states were leaders in the movement toward assumption of support of schools and roads. For statistics, William G. Carr, "School Finance Legislation in 1929," *State Government,* III (June 1930), 10-11.

60 percent.[11] Highway needs caused most of this increase—state expenditure per capita for roads in 1919 was 59 cents; in 1930 it was $2.06.[12] In some states the absolute sums spent for roads and schools grew remarkably. Expenditures for Missouri highways literally "lifted her out of the mud." Under Governor Smith, New York spent $80 million for schools in 1928; in 1919 the expenditure had been $9 million.[13] Total state spending in California increased from $36 million in 1919-1920 to $110 million in 1928-1929.[14] While the rate of increase in state spending during the 1920's was not quite so high as that of the 1910-1920 period, the absolute sums were a good deal larger, and except for the 1940's no subsequent decade matched the per capita rate of increase.[15]

[11] Relevant articles are Henry Black, "Taxes Will Grow Heavier," *New Republic*, LXXII (October 26, 1932), 290-91; and Mabel Newcomer, "Tendencies in State and Local Finance and their Relation to State and Local Functions," *Political Science Quarterly*, XLIII (March 1928), 1-31.

[12] See the excellent study, James A. Maxwell, *The Fiscal Impact of Federalism in the United States* (Cambridge, Mass., 1946), 25. Also his *Financing State and Local Governments* (Washington, 1965).

[13] For Missouri see Duane Meyer, *The Heritage of Missouri: A History* (St. Louis, 1965), 587-88. For New York, Bernard Bellush, *Franklin D. Roosevelt as Governor of New York* (New York, 1955), 31-2. The volume by Meyer is one of many scholarly histories of western states to appear in recent years. They fill a very large gap. Others include Edwin C. McReynolds, *Missouri: A History of the Crossroads State* (Norman, 1962); Carl Ubbelohde, *A Colorado History* (Boulder, 1965); T. A. Larson, *History of Wyoming* (Lincoln, 1965); James C. Olson, *History of Nebraska* (Lincoln, 1955); Warren A. Beck, *New Mexico: A History of Four Centuries* (Norman, 1962); Edwin C. McReynolds, *Oklahoma: A History of the Sooner State* (Norman, 1954); and Elwyn B. Robinson, *History of North Dakota* (Lincoln, 1966). See also Gilman M. Ostrander, *Nevada: The Great Rotten Borough, 1859-1964* (New York, 1966); and Seth S. McKay and Odie B. Faulk, *Texas After Spindletop* (Austin, 1965).

[14] Graves, *State Government*, 507ff.

[15] *Historical Statistics*, 22. For figures on some individual states see

State debts reflected this surge in spending. Although many new taxes appeared—total state revenue from taxes rose from $1.1 to $2.1 billion during the decade—they seldom covered the entire increase in expenditures.[16] Gross state debts per capita rose from $8.65 in 1922 to $15.38 in 1929, and annual interest charges jumped from $41 million to $94 million.[17] The rate of per capita increase in state debt was higher than that of local or federal debt (which decreased absolutely in the 1920's), and was never again so high.[18] States, it seemed, were not only anxious to spend but were willing to incur deficits to do so.

This readiness to go into debt would leave many states in desperate straits when the depression came in 1929, but there were some compensations. With little help from the federal government, states and municipalities improved schools and highways during the 1920's, and the experience of shouldering these burdens prepared states for still more onerous tasks in the years to come. If the concept

---

Howard Odum's exhaustive study of the South, *Southern Regions of the United States* (Chapel Hill, 1936).

16 See *Historical Statistics*, 727, for figures on state taxes. States varied greatly in debt accumulation in the 1920's. Seventeen states, including 11 plains and mountain states, reduced their gross per capita debt. Many others had huge relative per capita increases, topped by Arkansas ($1.50 to $54.60 per capita) and North Carolina ($13.10 to $56.50). Most other southern states also accumulated large debts in the decade. Debts in densely populated, wealthy states varied considerably, but tended to increase at a slower rate than those in the South, and faster than those in the West. The federal matching grant formula for highways enabled western and plains states to control their indebtedness, but sheer need to overcome past omissions, combined with low per capita incomes, helped account for the rise in southern state debt. For figures on debt by states see *Statistical Abstract, 1931* (Washington, 1931), 226-27.

17 *Fiscal Relations*, 359. Also "Going into the Red," *State Government*, v (April 1932), 10-11.

18 Edna Trull, "Two Decades of State Borrowing," *National Municipal Review*, xxvi (June 1937), 277-82.

of positive government existed in any strength during the 1920's, surely it was most evident in state spending for schools and roads.

There was another side to the picture. Though state governments in the 1920's improved administration and began providing more money for selected purposes, their overall record was mediocre.

One disappointment was the promising administrative reform movement itself. Except in Illinois, New York, and Virginia under strong governors Frank E. Lowden, Smith, and Byrd, the changes were modest. Civil service reform was largely ignored between 1920 and 1937. Moreover, some of the so-called reforms involved attempts by governors to strengthen their hold on the distribution of patronage or to expel rival factions from entrenched posts; others, as in Virginia, aimed primarily at cutting costs.[19] A survey of administrative reorganization laws in 1938 found that the statutes of the previous twenty years had had little effect.[20] When the depression began, outdated administrative structures and impotent governors too often prevented effective action against hard times.

More serious was the failure of states to adopt social legislation. Advances occurred only here and there: Alabama abolished her iniquitous convict labor system in 1926; Wis-

[19] Smith's motives in New York included the desire to reduce boss influence over patronage; similar aims were important in Ohio. Leslie Lipson, *American Governor from Figurehead to Leader* (Chicago, 1939), 103-10.

[20] William H. Edwards, "A Factual Summary of State Administrative Reorganization," *Southwestern Social Science Quarterly*, XIX (June 1938), 53-67. For a gloomy assessment of government in Oklahoma see Brookings Institute survey as reported in *New York Times*, July 7, 1935, II, 3. Also G. Lyle Belsley, "Trends in State Personnel Legislation and Administration," *State Government*, X (May 1937); and Arthur A. Schwartz, "Legislative Laboratories Compared," *ibid.*, III (August 1930), 3-7.

consin outlawed yellow dog contracts in 1929; North Carolina improved its workmen's compensation law in 1929; and the administrations of Gifford Pinchot in Pennsylvania, Smith and Roosevelt in New York, and George W. Hunt, governor of Arizona from 1911 to 1929, were somewhat friendly to labor.[21] Existing legislation dating from the progressive era—laws limiting working hours for women and children and providing aid to the needy blind, dependent, and disabled—also remained on the books. More often than not, however, they were poorly financed and indifferently enforced. Even the social workers continued to tap private rather than public sources for welfare money.[22]

[21] For Alabama, *Nation,* CXXVII (July 18, 1928), 55; for Wisconsin, Edwin E. Witte, "Labor's New Deal," *State Government,* VI (April 1933), 3-5; for North Carolina, Puryear, *Democratic Party Dissension,* 54; for Pinchot, M. Nelson McGeary, *Gifford Pinchot: Forester-Politician* (Princeton, 1960); for Smith, Oscar Handlin, *Al Smith and His America* (Boston, 1958), 90-111; for Roosevelt, Bellush, *Roosevelt*; and for Hunt, Mary Austin, "Americans We Like: Hunt of Arizona," *Nation,* CXXVII (November 28, 1928), 572-74. See also Rowland L. Mitchell, Jr., "Social Legislation in Connecticut, 1919-1939," Unpublished Ph.D. thesis, Yale University, 1954; Josephine C. Brown, *Public Relief, 1929-1939* (New York, 1940), 1-62; and Irving Bernstein, *The Lean Years: A History of the American Worker, 1920-1933* (Boston, 1960), 1-82 and passim.

[22] In 1918, 40 states had maximum hour laws for women workers; between 1919 and 1932 two more added laws, and 12 of the 40 improved theirs. But many exceptions to these statutes remained, and social workers were despondent. Clarke A. Chambers, *Seedtime of Reform: American Social Service and Social Action, 1918-1933* (Minneapolis, 1963), 61-66. The record in child labor reform was little better—only 6 states (Arkansas, Arizona, California, Washington, Montana, and Colorado) ratified the federal child labor amendment from 1924 to 1932; 14 would ratify it in 1933 alone. *Ibid.,* 34-45, 203. For a slightly different perspective see Jeremy P. Felt, *Hostages of Fortune: Child Labor Reform in New York State* (Syracuse, 1965), 195-224. Felt notes the political liabilities of the amendment (it set the age for child labor at a high of eighteen), and the narrow, piecemeal tactics of its New York sponsors. State minimum wage laws, rendered useless by the Supreme Court in 1922, received little subsequent attention by states in the 1920's; and

Perhaps the most publicized advance in social welfare during the decade was the gradual spread of the movement for old age pensions. Beginning with Montana in 1923, ten states enacted such laws before 1930. Seven more followed suit by 1931.[23] But the measures were hardly sweeping. In most states recipients had to be at least seventy years old and to have established a residency of fifteen years. Pensions were very small, the highest annual award amounting to $390. Most systems were optional and left administration to penurious counties. Only 75,000 elderly Americans received help annually in 1931.[24]

The laboring man also obtained little aid from states in the 1920's. By 1933 eighteen states had enacted anti-injunction statutes, but none was effective. Only three states had mediation boards of any utility. The attitude of most legislators toward unions was at best neutral, more often hostile. In southern textile communities bloody battles broke out between strikers and police, with public officials consistently aiding mill owners. The failure of the states to enact protective legislation for labor in the 1920's stemmed neither from a lack of funds nor from legislative factionalism but from a prevailing feeling that labor unions were undesirable and dangerous.[25]

---

no state passed an unemployment insurance law until Wisconsin in 1932. See Chambers, *Seedtime,* 66-76, 174-180. For other discussions of social legislation in the 1920's see Brown, *Public Relief,* 56-64; and Bernstein, *Lean Years,* 475-504.

[23] They were Nevada, Pennsylvania, Wisconsin, Kentucky, Colorado, Maryland, Minnesota, Utah, New York, Massachusetts, Delaware, Idaho, New Jersey, New Hampshire, California, and Wyoming. See Chambers, *Seedtime,* 163-68.

[24] "A Brighter Outlook for the Aged," *Review of Reviews,* LXXXI (May 1930), 126-28; Allen Moore, "De Senectute," *State Government,* V (May 1932), 10-12; and Gertrude Springer, "A New Year for the Old," *Survey,* LXV (January 15, 1931), 434-35.

[25] Bernstein, *The Lean Years,* is an almost encyclopedic study of

The record of the states in the regulation of public utility holding companies was also unencouraging. Although most states had created public utility commissions before 1920, these proved inadequate to deal with holding companies, which rapidly dominated the industry thereafter. Throughout the 1920's states amended existing legislation—in 1927 alone 35 states enacted new provisions—but until the end of the decade few states even tried to curb holding companies.[26] And then they failed: in 1929 stringent bills went down to defeat in the eight legislatures where serious efforts occurred.[27] Such a bill finally succeeded in New York in 1930, but even it did not permit officials to examine the books of out-of-state companies within holding company empires which had invaded the state.[28] One authority remarked in 1929 that "men of mediocre ability [were] filling the regulatory commissions. Under such conditions, regulation is likely to be little more than a farce."[29] Adequate control of holding companies would have to await federal action in the 1930's.

Tax policy also revealed the fundamental conservatism

---

legislation relating to labor and social welfare in the 1920's. See 20-33 for an account of textile strikes, 204-05 for court actions against strikers, and 83-143 for the "paralysis of the labor movement." A liberal's account of textile mill troubles is "The South Fights the Unions: What the State Stoops Did at Elizabethton," *New Republic*, LIX (June 10, 1929), 202-03. States were also careless of civil liberties. See O. G. Villard, "New Fight for Old Liberties," *Harpers*, CLI (September 1925), 440-47.

26 Orren C. Hormell, "State Public Utilities Legislation in 1927," *American Political Science Review*, XXIII (February 1929), 106-11.

27 H. S. Raushenbush, "The Triumph of the Power Companies," *Nation*, CXXIX (September 18, 1929), 294-96.

28 William E. Mosher, "Regulating Utilities," *State Government*, III (December 1930), 7-10.

29 Hormell, "State Public Utilities," 110. An exception was North Dakota, where state-owned projects existed. Alfred S. Dale, "Public Ownership in North Dakota," *New Republic*, LIX (July 3, 1929), 174-76.

of state government in the 1920's. For some time reformers had eagerly supported progressive personal and corporate income taxes, and between 1911 and 1921 thirteen states had enacted such legislation. Without exception the rates had been mild, yet to progressives the taxes were a promising sign. When the federal government reduced income taxes in the 1920's, states had an unusually auspicious chance to fill the gap. Progressive taxes could help reduce the gap between rich and poor as well as serve as a source of revenue for services.

Few states seized the opportunity. Only New Hampshire enacted an income tax law between 1921 and 1929, and though the total amount collected in state corporate and individual income taxes rose from $101 million in 1922 to $162 million in 1927, the increase reflected improved economic conditions, not stiffer rates—in 1934 the total would slide to $129 million.[30] In an effort to attract wealthy residents Florida went so far in 1924 as to pass a constitutional amendment forbidding income or inheritance taxes. One authority concluded that income taxes in 1930, whether personal or corporate, played a "very minor role in state and local finance."[31] Such levies accounted for more than 10 percent of state-local revenue in only Delaware, Massachusetts, New York, and Wisconsin, and the combined yield of state individual and corporate income taxes in 1927

[30] Maxwell, *Fiscal Impact*, 261-62; *Historical Statistics*, 727. State personal income taxes totaled $43 million in 1922, $70 million in 1927, $80 million in 1934; corporate taxes for the same years brought in $58 million, $92 million, and $79 million.

[31] Clarence Heer, "The Place of Personal Income Taxes in a Modern Fiscal System," *Annals of the American Academy of Political and Social Sciences*, CLXXXIII (January 1936), 78-85. For surveys of types and yields of state taxes, *State Government*, III (January 1930), and *ibid.*, VI (April 1934), 78-84.

was only 10 percent of state revenue.[32] In the 1930's more states turned to income taxes, but by then it was too late, for decreased national wealth and higher federal rates combined to prevent states from collecting much revenue from this source.[33]

Gasoline taxes, not those on income, were the chief source of new revenue. Because the main reason for increased costs was road building, the levy was a natural development, and it spread with astonishing speed. By 1929 every state had adopted such a tax. In that year gasoline taxes provided $450 million, or about 25 percent of total state tax receipts.[34] Easily collectible, the gasoline levy seemed an excellent substitute for increased income tax rates.

But the gasoline tax was progressive only in that it affected those wealthy enough to own cars. Moreover, the proceeds were ordinarily reserved for highways, and were often insufficient even for this purpose. Reliance on the gasoline tax as a major source of funds showed that states were marking time. By failing to provide enough revenue either to guard against overindebtedness or to inaugurate needed social services, they invited trouble in 1929.[35] State tax struc-

[32] The percentage had been 12 in 1922, and would be 7 in 1932. *Historical Statistics,* 727.

[33] It is interesting to speculate on the nature of New Deal and post-New Deal tax policy had states in the 1920's moved aggressively into the personal income and corporate tax fields.

[34] Emery Fact, "The Growing Gas Tax," *State Government,* III (August 1930), 8-10.

[35] That states might have harvested more revenue from taxes in the 1920's is suggested in a comparison of tax yields in the United States and various western European countries, in Harold M. Groves, "Taxation in America and England," *American Mercury,* XXXII (June 1934), 138-46. The United States (federal, state, and local) collected a considerably smaller percentage of its national income in taxes than did many other nations.

tures in the 1920's were no more progressive than they had been in the prewar years, were only moderately productive, and were not geared to the idea of a positive social state.

The atmosphere in many states was often as dreary as their legislative records. Contemporary magazines seemed to enjoy exposing—and at times exaggerating—state house ignorance. Len Small, the unimpressive Republican governor of Illinois from 1925 to 1929, was a particular target, as were some more colorful governors such as Ma Ferguson of Texas and Theodore Bilbo of Mississippi. Other articles bluntly insulted entire states. Arkansas, one writer observed, "has a civilized minority. But it is a disheartened minority. It is scattered, isolated, inarticulate, and leaderless. No man with anything worthwhile to say ever comes among us. We have to listen to scheming politicians and pulpit morons or stay at home." Another reporter asked rhetorically, "How do people live in Utah? They join the businessmen's calisthenics class at the gymnasium. Or they buy Fords on the five-dollar-a-week basis. Or they yawn. Or they die."[36]

More recent accounts have not brightened the picture. One of them described an Oklahoma governor of the period as having "but a feeble grasp of political affairs."[37] Far western states featured the "politics of fundamentalism," with the Ku Klux Klan strong in Oregon, anti-communism rampant in Washington, and conservatism entrenched in

[36] Irving Dilliard, "Len Small—'Back to Prosperity,'" *Nation*, CXXXV (October 19, 1932), 352-53; Clay Fulks, "Arkansas," *American Mercury*, VIII (July 1926), 290-94; and Bernard DeVoto, "Utah," *ibid.*, VII (March 1926), 317-23. Accounts of Bilbo's governorship are Albert Kirwan, *Revolt of the Rednecks: Mississippi Politics, 1876-1925* (Lexington, 1951), 270-71, 297-99; Adwin W. Green, *The Man Bilbo* (Baton Rouge, 1963); and Reinhard H. Luthin, *American Demagogues: Twentieth Century* (Gloucester, Mass., 1959), 44-76. For an account of the Fergusons (Ma and Pa) see *ibid.*, 153-81.

[37] McReynolds, *Oklahoma*, 352.

Utah.[38] "Crusading in Colorado," declared one writer, "abruptly ended with the close of the first World War. . . . The emphasis of the age was derived from attention to material gain, personal well-being, and a return to Republican rule."[39] And the political scene in Indiana, dominated by the Klan during part of the decade, was perhaps most depressing of all.[40]

Even those states with progressive traditions slipped into the trough of conservatism in the 1920's. In Massachusetts, long a pioneer in welfare legislation, not one major reform measure appeared on the statute books from 1920 through 1928, and in 1929 the legislature defeated an old age pension plan, a measure opposing yellow dog contracts, and a bill to regulate public utilities.[41] In California, once the bailiwick of Hiram Johnson's progressives, efforts for reform stalled, and one student has concluded that by 1922 the pro-

[38] Earl Pomeroy, *The Pacific Slope* (New York, 1965), 216-41.

[39] Ubbelohde, *Colorado*, 281.

[40] William E. Wilson, "Long Hot Summer in Indiana," *American Heritage*, XVI (August 1965), 57-64. A substantial literature on the Klan exists. See especially Charles C. Alexander, *The Ku Klux Klan in the Southwest* (Lexington, 1965), for studies of Oklahoma, Arkansas, Texas, and Louisiana; Arnold S. Rice, *The Ku Klux Klan in American Politics* (Washington, 1962); and Emerson Loucks, *The Ku Klux Klan in Pennsylvania* (Harrisburg, 1936). Among Alexander's many useful articles the most relevant is "Secrecy Bids for Power: The Ku Klux Klan in Texas Politics in the 1920's," *Mid-America*, XLVI (January 1964), 3-28. See also David Chalmers, "The Ku Klux Klan in the Sunshine State: the 1920's," *Florida Historical Quarterly*, XLII (January 1964), 209-15.

[41] J. Joseph Huthmacher, *Massachusetts People and Politics, 1919-1933* (Cambridge, 1959), 59. It is also true, however, that much of Massachusetts' progressive legislation antedated the progressive era. See Arthur Mann, *Yankee Reformers in an Industrial Age* (Cambridge, 1954); and Richard Abrams, "A Paradox of Progressivism: Massachusetts on the Eve of Insurgency," *Political Science Quarterly*, LXXV (September 1960), 379-99. Abrams shows that Massachusetts seemed conservative during the progressive era because many of its reforms came before 1900.

gressive movement had dissipated. Another authority suggests that "progressivism had not died in California; it had become shattered, disillusioned, and leaderless."[42] Even Wisconsin, home of the La Follettes, marked time before 1930. Reformers there remained numerically strong, and John J. Blaine, governor from 1921 to 1927, succeeded in increasing income and corporate taxes in the upper brackets.[43] But factionalism harmed chances for social reform. During the decade the legislature failed to pass bills for unemployment compensation, an eight-hour working day, and old age pensions on a state basis. One party chieftain commented ruefully, "our party leadership is all shot to hell since Old Bob died."[44]

Most states managed to avoid the iniquitous influence of the Klan, but few escaped the potent pressure of citizens more interested in economy than in services. Missouri gov-

[42] H. Brett Melendy and Benjamin F. Gilbert, *Governors of California* (Georgetown, Calif., 1965), 322; Ronald Chinn, "Democratic Party Politics in California, 1920-1956," unpublished doctoral dissertation, University of California at Berkeley, 1958, 26. Jackson K. Putnam, in "The Persistence of Progressivism in the 1920's: The Case of California," *Pacific Historical Review*, XXXV (November 1966), 395-413, argues that progressivism remained fairly strong except in the years 1923-1926.

[43] Robert S. Maxwell, "The Progressive Bridge: Reform Sentiment in the United States Between the New Freedom and the New Deal," *Indiana Magazine of History*, LXIII (June 1967), 83-102, stresses Blaine's role, notes the existence of progressive administrations in North Dakota, North Carolina, Alabama, and Tennessee, and emphasizes the strength of progressivism in the 1920's. His examples are well chosen, but, in my view, exceptions to the general pattern. For problems faced by Wisconsin social reformers in the 1920's, see Daniel Nelson, "The Origins of Unemployment Insurance in Wisconsin," *Wisconsin Magazine of History*, LI (Winter 1967-68), 109-21.

[44] Bennington Orth, "The Progressive Holy Land," *American Mercury*, XVIII (November 1929), 266-70. More scholarly treatments noting earlier weaknesses of Wisconsin progressivism are Herbert F. Margulies, "The Decline of Wisconsin Progressivism, 1911-1914," *Mid-America*, XXXIX (1957), 131-55; and Margulies, "Political Weaknesses in Wisconsin Progressivism, 1905-1908," *ibid.*, XLI (1959), 154-72.

ernors were perhaps more aware of contemporary needs than their constituents, who consistently voted down referenda for reforms.[45] Wyoming's moderately progressive governor from 1919 to 1923 failed in his bid for renomination when a primary opponent charged him with extravagance.[46] Similar economy movements swept through Plains states such as Nebraska which were struggling to escape a long agricultural depression.[47] And no governor was more successful during the decade than A. Victor ("Honest Vic") Donahey of Ohio, who endeared himself to voters by vetoing 74 bills in the 1923 session and 43 in 1925; many of these saved money, and they helped him win two elections.[48] State policies in the 1920's too often featured cost-conscious administration at the expense of needed public services.

The high value attached to efficient, economical government helps to explain the publicity accorded Democrats Albert C. Ritchie of Maryland and Byrd of Virginia, two of the most lavishly praised governors of the decade. Ritchie, a successful politician who served fifteen years as governor before his defeat in 1934, was an able, honest, and efficient administrator. He reorganized state government, reformed the prison labor system, and lowered taxes. Above all, he was a confirmed states righter who even proposed a House of Governors to aid Congress in safeguarding the prerogatives of states.[49]

[45] McReynolds, *Missouri*, 348. Texas voters also repudiated reforms in referenda in the 1920's. See Rupert N. Richardson, *Texas: The Lone Star State* (2nd edn., New Jersey, 1958), 311-12.

[46] Larson, *Wyoming*, 454.

[47] Olson, *Nebraska*, 292-93.

[48] Francis R. Aumann, in Harlow Lindley, ed., *Ohio in the 20th Century* (Columbus, 1942), 41-45.

[49] O. G. Villard, "Governor Albert C. Ritchie," *Nation*, CXXVI (January 1, 1928), 121-22; William Cabell Bruce, "Governor Albert C. Ritchie," *North American Review*, CCXXIV (December 1927), 606-11.

A consistent states rights advocate, Byrd was equally anxious to streamline government, and he too sponsored a successful reorganization bill during his tenure (1927-1931). He helped outlaw lynching, reduced taxes, and succeeded in enticing northern industry to Virginia. One admirer concluded that "no Virginian living in 1926 would have dared to hope that any one man in four short years could possibly accomplish as much as Harry Byrd."[50] Both men considered themselves progressive, but theirs was a rather cold, austere progressivism confined to honesty in government, care in public spending, and administrative order. They were poles removed in spirit from Robert La Follette, Sr., on the one hand, and Herbert Lehman on the other.

Many factors contributed to this rather barren record of most governors. To begin with, lawmakers were badly paid. Only eight states guaranteed them more than $1,000 per year, and the majority paid a great deal less. Connecticut legislators got along with $150 annually, and six other states paid $4 or less per day of session.[51] While generous salaries are unreliable guides to legislative competence, such sums were hardly adequate to attract able men.

Partly as a result of the poor salaries, few men remained legislators for long. Between 1925 and 1935, 25 percent of all state lawmakers were first-termers; another 35 percent were second or third-termers.[52] Only 15 percent of the legis-

[50] Virginius Dabney, "Americans We Like: Governor Byrd of Virginia," *Nation*, CXXVI (June 6, 1928), 631-33; Junius F. Fishburn, "The New Virginia," *Review of Reviews*, LXXXI (June 1930), 114-19.

[51] "What Price Lawmakers," *Book of the States, 1935*, 67. The most generous states were California, Illinois, Massachusetts, Ohio, Pennsylvania, Wisconsin, and New York.

[52] The classic study of such questions is Charles S. Hyneman, "Tenure and Turnover of Legislative Personnel," *Annals of the American Academy of Political and Social Science*, CXCV (January 1938), 21-31.

lators leaving office between 1925 and 1933 lost at the polls; the rest retired voluntarily, presumably to seek more responsible or remunerative pursuits. In states with little party competition the turnover was still greater, leaving a hardy handful to rule unchallenged.[53] Venal bossism often followed.[54]

Compounding the problem of turnover were short sessions: in 22 states legislatures convened for 60 days or less in a two-year period, a term which one authority complained was "barely long enough to enable a city dog-catcher to become familiar with the duties of his office."[55] Only five states had annual sessions, and only six allowed representatives to sit for more than one session before they had to face the electorate again. State legislators were amateurs under the guise of poorly paid professionals.

Inequitable districting added to the difficulties of progressives anxious to cope with the critical needs of growing cities. The situation in some states was absurd. "Cow-pasture majorities" ruled in Georgia under its antiquated sys-

---

See also Thomas R. Dye, "State Legislative Politics," in Herbert Jacob and Kenneth Vines, eds., *Politics in the American States: A Comparative Analysis* (Boston, 1965), 170-72.

[53] For a revealing study of one legislature (Kentucky) see J. Catron Jones, "The Makeup of a State Legislature," *American Political Science Review*, XXV (February 1931), 116-20. Also Samuel Soloman, "American Governors Since 1915," *National Municipal Review*, XX (March 1931), 152-58. James D. Barber's important behavioral study of freshman legislators in Connecticut in 1959 suggests some of the problems state legislatures have in finding and keeping able men. See *The Lawmakers: Recruitment and Adaptation to Legislative Life* (New Haven, 1965), esp. Chap. 6. For a study suggesting the decreasing importance and prestige of state legislators see Joseph A. Schlesinger, *How They Became Governor: A Study of Comparative State Politics, 1870-1950* (East Lansing, 1957), esp. 51-52.

[54] For one such boss-ridden state see Alexander Kendrick, "The End of Boss Vare," *Nation*, CXXXVII (November 29, 1933), 621-22.

[55] Henry W. Toll, "The 48: A Smiling Comparison of Some Features of Our Legislators," *State Government*, III (May 1930), 3-11.

tem favoring rural counties.[56] In Rhode Island each town received at least one senate seat, with Providence getting but four.[57] Similar systems plagued Connecticut, New York, and other populous urban states. In all but a few relatively homogeneous states districts were laid out to favor rural or small town areas. Their legislators were naturally willing to spend money for roads and schools but not for factory inspection, public housing, welfare, or the other essentially urban needs of the decade.[58]

Party factionalism also impeded progress. In Pennsylvania bitter warfare between Governor Gifford Pinchot and other Republicans destroyed party discipline and with it Pinchot's chances for constructive legislation.[59] Democratic dissension in Oklahoma caused legislators to impeach and convict two governors during the period.[60] Factions wracked potentially progressive parties in New Mexico and North Dakota.[61] Upstate-downstate rivalries divided Democrats in Illinois and New York, and dissident groups in southern states shifted about like sand in the sea. Ethnic and urban-rural divisions stymied reform in states such as Massachusetts.[62] Some of this factionalism, as in Pennsyl-

[56] Carter Brooke Jones, "The Georgia Plan," *American Mercury,* XXIII (July 1931), 311-20.

[57] *New York Times,* January 1, 1933, IV, 6.

[58] David O. Walter, "Reapportionment and Urban Representation," *Annals of the American Academy of Political and Social Science,* CXCV (January 1938), 11-20. For an article warning against overemphasizing the effects of malapportionment, see Herbert Jacob, "The Consequences of Malapportionment: A Note of Caution," *Social Forces,* XLIII (1964), 261.

[59] McGeary, *Gifford Pinchot,* passim; and Samuel J. Astorino, "The Decline of the Republican Dynasty in Pennsylvania, 1929-1934," unpublished doctoral dissertation, University of Pittsburgh, 1962, passim.

[60] Cortez A. M. Ewing, "Impeachment of Oklahoma Governors," *American Political Science Review* (August 1930), 648-52.

[61] Beck, *New Mexico,* 307ff; Robinson, *North Dakota,* 380-93.

[62] Studies stressing factionalism are V. O. Key, Jr., *Southern Politics in State and Nation* (New York, 1949); John H. Fenton, *Politics in the*

vania and Massachusetts, contained an ideological or ethnic basis capable of maintaining loyalties, but most of it was erratic and unpredictable. Either way, it hampered chances for substantial reform, especially since few governors possessed the power to coerce party blocs into line.

But none of these problems—amateur legislators, unfair districting, factionalism—was unique to the 1920's or necessarily insurmountable. New York, for instance, faced many of these disadvantages but responded well to the strong leadership of Al Smith. Moreover, most states enjoyed greater financial resources and more efficient administration in the 1920's than they had at the height of progressivism between 1900 and 1910. Institutional and political patterns were damaging but seldom fatal to the reform programs of the decade.

More serious causes lay elsewhere, and to a degree resembled those which plagued the national movement. In the absence of crisis, legislation in a democracy depends heavily upon support from leaders in the society at large. Many of these leaders were businessmen who had supported progressive programs before World War I.[63] At this time,

---

Border States: A Study of the Patterns of Organizations and Political Change (New Orleans, 1957); Puryear, *Democratic Party Dissension in North Carolina, 1928-1936*; Allan P. Sindler, *Huey Long's Louisiana: State Politics, 1920-1952* (Baltimore, 1956); and Thomas Donnelly, ed., *Rocky Mountain State Politics* (Albuquerque, 1940). For Massachusetts see Huthmacher, *Massachusetts People and Politics*, 48-76.

[63] That business is central to American culture has been stressed by Thomas C. Cochran in many writings. See especially *The Inner Revolution* (New York, 1964), 157-77, and "The History of a Business Society," *Journal of American History*, LIV (June 1967), 5-18. For a case study of the role of businessmen in progressive reform see Samuel P. Hays, "The Politics of Reform in Municipal Government in the Progressive Era," *Pacific Northwest Quarterly*, LV (October 1964), 157-69. See also Kolko, *Triumph of Conservatism*; and Alfred D. Chandler, Jr., "The Origins of Progressive Leadership," *The Letters of Theodore Roosevelt*, VIII, Elting E. Morison, ed. (Cambridge, Mass., 1954), 1462-65.

however, these leaders achieved many of their goals, and after 1920 they became less active in reform movements.[64] Some reforms, such as old age pensions, unemployment insurance, and regulation of wages and hours, had never appealed to these businessmen, and they simply remained unattractive in the 1920's.[65] While more study of state legislative sessions in the 1920's is necessary, it is arguable that one reason for the difficulties of state progressivism after 1916 was the rather limited character of progressivism itself.[66] Thus it is probable that state legislators, like congressmen, felt little pressure for social reform from opinion leaders in the 1920's.[67]

Finally, states were already being overtaken by the nationalizing of modern economic life. Though the progressive path was far from straight or simple, it seems to have begun in the towns and cities, moved to the states, and led inexorably to the national government of Theodore Roosevelt and Woodrow Wilson. Many reforms remained within the potential of states, but many more did not: only Congress could regulate railroads, establish nationwide labor standards, curb monopolies and holding companies, and

[64] Among the goals achieved by businessmen reformers before World War I were the Federal Reserve Act, Clayton Antitrust Act, Hepburn Act, and the Federal Trade Commission. For business ideas in the 1920's, see Morrell Heald, "Business Thought in the Twenties: Social Responsibility," *American Quarterly,* XIII (Summer 1961), 126-39; and James W. Prothro, *Dollar Decade: Business Ideas in the 1920's* (Baton Rouge, 1954).

[65] Andrew M. Scott, "The Progressive Era in Perspective," *Journal of Politics,* XXI (1959), 685-701, argues to the contrary that progressives were "centrally . . . concerned" with social legislation.

[66] It is perhaps relevant that many progressives opposed much or all of the New Deal from the beginning. See Otis L. Graham, Jr., *An Encore for Reform: The Old Progressives and the New Deal* (New York, 1967), 24-100 and passim.

[67] For the important role of opinion leaders see Angus Campbell, et al., *The American Voter* (New York, 1960), 271-72.

control the increasingly interstate character of commerce. Recognizing these facts of economic life, many reformers had gone beyond the states well before 1920 and campaigned for national laws.[68] Some of these reformers, disillusioned with wartime excesses, national prohibition, or the complacency of the Harding-Coolidge years, lost faith in all levels of government in the 1920's. Others, refusing to surrender entirely, awaited more auspicious years. But few returned enthusiastically to the states. Economic centralization was in some ways a boon to national reform; to state progressivism it was a stunning blow.

When Franklin Roosevelt called for broad executive power in 1933, Americans responded quickly. One reason was the economic crisis; another was the feeling that national problems required national remedies.[69] By 1940 progressive opponents of excessive federal centralization such as Brandeis seemed like voices from a bygone era.

68 See Charles Forcey, *The Crossroads of Liberalism: Croly, Weyl, Lippmann and the Progressive Era, 1900-1925* (New York, 1961), for discussion of political thought in this period. See esp. "Liberalism and Leadership," 194-98, and "Liberalism and Nationalism," 209-17.

69 This is not to say that all reformers ignored the possibility of cooperative state action. Roosevelt himself continued to stress state responsibility, as reflected in the assistance and unemployment compensation aspects of social security. Moreover, states continued to assume functions formerly handled by local governments, and they are perhaps more important in the 1960's than they have ever been. The growth of federal authority, however, has far outdistanced that of the states since 1929.

2. Confusion Reigns, 1929-1933

THE DEPRESSION staggered state and local officials, and it was years before they recovered from the blow. Already deep in debt from the deficit spending of the 1920's, they now faced sharply rising welfare costs at a time when tax revenues were falling with equal speed. The economic crisis, descending so quickly and unexpectedly, paralyzed the state governments. The resulting chaos between 1929 and 1933 exposed the limits of the states in an increasingly centralized age.

First to feel the crisis were local governments, especially the larger cities with high unemployment. During the previous decade counties and municipalities, deriving some funds from state sources, had disbursed between 55 and 60 percent of all public funds and had accumulated a gross debt of $9 billion.[1] Two-thirds of the revenue for this spending had come from property taxes, which fell off drastically—20 percent or more in some cities—between 1929 and 1932.[2] Yet by 1933 approximately 15 million people were unemployed, most of whom had no savings and received little help from bankrupt private agencies. They turned desperately to local relief boards for assistance.

These boards were all but helpless. To increase property taxes was unthinkable, and other levies—personal income, corporate, gasoline, and sales—were more easily collectible

[1] *Federal, State, and Local Fiscal Relations*, 78th Cong., 1st Sess., Sen. Doc. 69, 358-59; Philip H. Cornick, "Taxation in the New Social State: Local Finance," *Nation*, CXXXIX (November 21, 1934), 585-88.

[2] Bureau of Census, *Historical Statistics on State and Local Government Finances, 1902-1953* (Washington, 1955), 12.

at the state or federal levels. Borrowing was also out of the question. Eighteen states, afraid of extravagant local politicians, had long since imposed debt limits on counties and municipalities. But such restrictions were usually unnecessary, for new municipal issues were often unmarketable, even at high interest rates.[3] Confronted with mounting costs and dwindling revenue, local governments quickly pleaded for help from the states.[4]

The states responded in a bewildering variety of ways. In 1933 and thereafter many embraced general sales taxes, but during the first four years of the depression this new method was more often studied than implemented. Governors, unwilling to call unpredictable special sessions, contented themselves with reassuring statements, praising the virtues of self-help, diverting by executive order small amounts for relief, and urging administrative economy to bring shattered budgets into some kind of balance.

Meanwhile the Hoover administration began to move cautiously. In October 1930, the President appointed an Emergency Committee for Employment headed by Colonel Arthur Woods and composed of other presidential aides, some of whom had served under Hoover on Harding's Committee on Unemployment in 1921. The new committee's function was the same as that in 1921: "a 'booster engine' . . . hitched to a train temporarily to supplement the regular motive power in getting a train up an especially stiff grade."[5] Partly because Woods possessed no funds for re-

[3] James A. Maxwell, *Financing State and Local Governments* (Washington, 1965), 179-82, 194-204.

[4] This trend continued throughout the 1930's. See George C. Benson, *The New Centralization: A Study of Intergovernmental Relationships in the United States* (New York, 1941), 32, 104-05.

[5] *Preliminary Report of the President's Emergency Committee for Employment,* in Records of the President's Organization on Unemployment Relief (POUR), National Archives, Washington, D.C., Record Group 135.

lief, he stressed the need for state and local measures. "The Committee," an early report remarked, "is agreed upon the principle of State responsibility in the present emergency. . . . The task of prompting the Governors . . . to take necessary action demands a tactful approach and should probably be done by personal interview."[6] Another committee official added in November: "unemployment relief is a local responsibility and . . . the normal welfare work of American communities must be maintained. We should question the wisdom of any plan which interfered with a maximum effort by local initiative to discharge responsibility for . . . welfare purposes."[7] Through 1931 committee spokesmen continued to emphasize state-local action and to disavow the responsibility of the federal government.[8] When Hoover reorganized the group in August 1931, he granted it an imposing title—the President's Committee on Unemployment Relief (POUR)—but no money for its limitless task.

A few governors began to chafe at Hoover's parsimony as early as 1930. Governor Bibb Graves of Alabama was one. "It is just a bunch of red tape," he complained to Woods. "I want not only suggestions, but help before these people get to suffering. I want to do something to add to their buying power."[9] Governor Fred Green of Michigan added, "The government of the United States is about the worst thing

6 "Organizations Plans and Procedures" of POUR, October 31, 1930, Series 49, Drawer 407, POUR Records.

7 Porter R. Lee to Wilfred S. Reynolds, November 13, 1930, No. 620.1, POUR Records.

8 J. C. Lawrence Memo, March 5, 1931, Series 49, Drawer 407, POUR Records; and Woods Statement, July 6, 1931, Box 68, Harry Hopkins Papers, Franklin D. Roosevelt Library, Hyde Park, N.Y.

9 "Talks With Governors," November 6, 1930, No. 501, POUR Records.

I have heard of. . . . You have men there who cannot see anything but rules and regulations."[10] A committee aide, after a tour of the South, reported growing sentiment for federal help: "May I state again that throughout the South there is an insistent demand that Federal works already authorized be gotten under way, now."[11]

With no funds, Woods had to refuse material aid. Frustrated, one governor finally asked him, "What is your plan?" Woods replied: "Governor, we have no particular plan. We thought the way we could be more useful was in acting as a sort of clearing house and letting States know what was accomplished in other States."[12] He could not do more.

Other governors tried appealing directly to Hoover. John G. Pollard of Virginia wrote to thank the president for past aid, but added: "Notwithstanding what the Federal, state, and local governments have been doing, we have not yet relieved the situation." He suggested an advance in highway funds to states as a way of avoiding a dole.[13] Other governors echoed Pollard. But until the summer of 1932 Hoover stood firm, following instead counsel from his commissioner of roads, who insisted that an increase in federal aid for highways "would only result in the Federal Government paying more and the State Government less." The "place of the Federal Government," the commissioner added, "is

[10] *Ibid.*

[11] Frank Bane to Woods, December 5, 1930, "Mississippi State Committee," No. 620, POUR Records. See also Unemployment Folders Box 270, Hoover Papers, Hoover Library, West Branch, Iowa, esp. Mayor Frank W. Griese to National Unemployment League, April 16, 1930, for evidence of local demands for federal aid in 1930.

[12] Woods Conversation with Gov. Clem D. Sampson of Kentucky, "Talks With Governors," POUR Records.

[13] Pollard to Hoover, August 26, 1931, Box 163, Hoover Papers. See also Gov. Floyd Olson (Minn.) and four others to Hoover, June 29, 1932, *ibid.*

to stimulate and correlate road construction and not to take over the whole cost."[14]

But the complaints were scattered and mild. The remarkable thing in retrospect was the optimism of most state governors between 1929 and early 1932. Even the dissidents demanded only an acceleration of already authorized highway grants, not large new federal appropriations. Most governors, anxious to preserve states rights or underestimating the suffering, told Woods that they had matters in hand. In November 1930 Republican Governor John S. Fisher of Pennsylvania rejected Woods' offer to provide him with a federal advisory committee, and added: "Our people here think that we have struck bottom and that for some little time the tendency has been in the other direction."[15] Even Huey Long of Louisiana wrote that though his state had considerable unemployment, "we believe we will be able to handle our own conditions." He asked only for a change in federal personnel. "We do not get much from the government," he concluded, "but we do not want to be slowed up."[16]

This "do it ourselves" refrain sounded with remarkable frequency through 1931. The mayor of Hartford, Connecticut, insisted, "We believe in paying our own way. It is cheaper than to bear the cost of federal bungling."[17] And Vermont's governor concluded, "I think I am speaking for a great majority of the people of Vermont when I say . . . that the people of Vermont are for a government supported

[14] Thomas MacDonald to Hoover, June 13, 1930, Box 3, Hoover Papers.

[15] Fisher Conversation with Woods, November 6, 1930, Box 68, Hopkins Papers.

[16] Woods Conversation with Long, "Talks With Governors," POUR Records.

[17] Quoted in Rowland L. Mitchell Jr., "Social Legislation in Connecticut, 1919-1939," unpublished doctoral dissertation, Yale University, 1954, 360.

by the people rather than a people supported by the government. We have the belief that the unemployment situation is being magnified and utilized for selfish and political purposes."[18] Had state officials, especially beleaguered Republican politicians, pleaded for help in 1930-1931, it is conceivable (though hardly likely) that the Hoover administration would have responded. As it was, the stringent federal policy aroused surprisingly few protests from state house politicians.

But by 1932 even the more confirmed "do it ourselves" governors were plunged in doubt. At this time the crisis had practically exhausted local resources, and tax delinquencies for 150 of the nation's largest cities had increased from 10 to 26 percent. One POUR man reported that 100 of New Jersey's 532 communities were bankrupt. State and local tax collections had fallen from $6.8 billion in 1930 to $5.7 billion, and the proportion of state and local bond issues carrying interest rates in excess of 5 percent had leaped during the same period from 7 percent of total sales to 38 percent. Worse, South Carolina, Arkansas, and Louisiana were beginning to default on their debt.[19] Pinchot, Roosevelt, and a handful of other progressives called for action, and Governor Julius Meier of Oregon wired, "We must have help from the federal government if we are to avert suffering . . . and possible uprisings."[20] After vetoing one

[18] Stanley G. Wilson to Hoover, September 17, 1931, Box 69, Hopkins Papers. For an equally strong statement in the same vein see Gov. Wilbur M. Brucker to Hoover, August 21, 1931, Box 68, Hopkins Papers; and Gov. George Hunt to Gov. George Dern, June 11, 1931, Dern Papers, Box 43-3, Utah State Archives, Salt Lake City.

[19] Rowland Haynes to Fred Croxton, March 21, 1932, No. 620, POUR Records; Alvin H. Hansen and Harvey S. Perloff, *State and Local Finance in the National Economy* (New York, 1944), 51-58. See also Box 68, Hopkins Papers, for evidence of increasing concern—even despair—among state officials in 1932.

[20] Meier to Hoover, June 28, 1932, Box 275, Hoover Papers.

plan, Hoover finally signed a relief bill in July 1932. It offered states $300 million in federal funds, to be distributed through the Reconstruction Finance Corporation. The money was to be lent, not given, and deducted from future highway grants.[21] Thanks to these loans the amount of federal aid to states jumped considerably—from the $100 million annually in the 1920's to $240 million in 1932-1933.[22] But the money was far from enough to relieve distress and tended to antagonize rather than pacify state officials.

The method of distribution infuriated governors. The bill required states to swear the "necessity for such funds" and to certify the inadequacy of state resources "then available and which can be made available." Congress had intended these passages to obviate flagrant freeloading, but the RFC chose to interpret them strictly. Hotheaded state and local officials, many of whom had earlier claimed they could solve their problems alone, now fumed over red tape in Washington. Mayor Anton J. Cermak of Chicago had to plead for relief four times, each time getting less than he wanted and much less than he needed; on one occasion only a potential riot by the unemployed sufficed to press the RFC into action. Pinchot, whose harsh criticisms of Hoover had already offended the administration, had even greater difficulty. The RFC required him to provide detailed reports about local relief boards, and not until late Septem-

[21] For the reaction of POUR officials see Haynes to Croxton, May 12, 1932, No. 004, POUR Records. For attitudes at the time of passage see Josephine Brown, *Public Relief, 1929-1939* (New York, 1940), 109-27.

[22] Council of State Governments, *State-Local Relations* (Chicago, 1946), 70. Other information concerning federal aid during the Hoover years is in H. J. Bitterman, *State and Federal Grants-in-Aid* (New York, 1938), 145ff; and Austin F. MacDonald, "Recent Trends in Federal Aid to the States," *American Political Science Review*, XXV (August 1931), 628-33.

ber did Pennsylvania receive its first grant.[23] RFC policies, Pinchot complained, caused a "senseless embargo on feeding the starving in this state."[24] Although thirteen states had applied for a total of $175 million within ten days after the bill's passage on July 21, only $35 million had been disbursed by October.[25] One reporter commented that state officials were developing the "sad and growing feeling that the finance corporation is not Santa Claus, Inc., but a business organization not much more liberal than a farsighted bank."[26]

Other governors, refusing to acknowledge their empty treasuries, still hesitated to bid for help, and six states never applied for money.[27] Aubrey Williams, later a high ranking New Deal relief official who was then working for the American Public Welfare Association, sadly recalled the devious means which he used to persuade state politicians to apply. The governor of North Dakota had to be dragged on a guided tour of poverty before he called for assistance. In Alabama, Williams secured the governor's ear only by claiming falsely to be a relative of former Senator John Sharp Williams of Mississippi, an idol of the governor. In Texas he overplayed his hand, and the state legislature, afraid that he would uncover corruption, passed a resolution demanding his departure from the state.[28]

[23] Irving Bernstein, *The Lean Years: A History of the American Worker, 1920-1933* (Boston, 1960), 470-72.

[24] Pinchot to Hoover, Sept. 20, 1932, RFC Files, Box 934, Hoover Library.

[25] Edith Abbott, "The Fallacy of Local Relief," *New Republic*, LXXII (November 9, 1932), 348-50.

[26] *New York Times*, September 11, 1932, II, 6.

[27] For remarks on attitudes of different states, Bitterman, *State and Federal Grants*, 293-94.

[28] Williams, "The New Deal—A Dead Battery," unpublished MS, Williams Papers, Roosevelt Library, 9. For the reminiscences of another knowledgeable welfare official see Frank Bane, "Public Administration

The financial aid of the Hoover administration awakened state officials to the potential harvest in Washington. But it came too late to be of much service during 1932. Before 1933 states had to combat the pressing crisis largely by themselves.

To some governors the chance to act on their own meant the freedom to do nothing. Governor Harry G. Leslie of Indiana stubbornly refused to borrow for unemployment relief. "The wisdom of our Fathers," he proclaimed, "was never more strikingly demonstrated than in the sound constitutional provision which prevents the state from assuming bonded indebtedness in order to meet the financial demands of modern government."[29] Indiana's relief commission echoed the governor's attitude. The "important point to be gained by experience," it argued, "is to beware of exaggerations. Some people comprise a certain type who will be known as a sub-normal person. . . . The only thought they have in mind is how much they can get for nothing. . . . Any director of any relief program must expect the receivers to exaggerate greatly their needs. . . . We have learned to disregard information of this type."[30]

This attitude was unusually reactionary—most governors tried to do something. Governor John G. Winant of New Hampshire, a liberal Republican and later chairman of the Social Security Board, proclaimed the virtues of his "New Hampshire Plan." Emphasizing job sharing, the cost

---

and Public Welfare: An Interview Conducted by James R. W. Libby," Berkeley, Calif., 1965. Copy among files of Council of State Governments, University of Chicago, Chicago, Ill. Bane notes that relief experts themselves were sharply divided in 1932 on the advisability of federal relief. See 122.

[29] Quoted in *National Municipal Review*, xx (July 1931), 393.

[30] "Report of Indiana Commission for the Relief of Distress Due to Unemployment," March 19, 1932, No. 620, POUR Records.

was to be distributed between management and workers. "It can be as progressive as scientific management, as conservative as an arithmetic formula, and as humane as the Golden Rule," he contended.[31] In Oklahoma homespun William (Alfalfa Bill) Murray prevented policemen from arresting the unemployed as vagrants, set up relief stations to alleviate suffering, and secured a new, moderately progressive tax law.[32] And in Connecticut Democratic Governor Wilbur Cross, a former English professor at Yale, managed to obtain approval of a public works bill and of additional expenditures for state institutions.[33]

Others were very progressive for the time. One was Pinchot. A staunch foe of reactionary industrial interests, he sought unsuccessfully to curb them, and in November 1931, he called the first of many special sessions to provide state grants for unemployment relief. The session ended in sharp intraparty disagreement and enacted only a dole which Pinchot scorned as "stage money." An uncooperative legisla-

[31] John G. Winant, "The New Hampshire Plan," *Review of Reviews,* LXXXV (November 1932), 24. See also Ethel M. Johnson, "The Mr. Winant I Knew," *South Atlantic Quarterly,* XLVIII (January 1949), 24-41.

[32] Keith L. Bryant, Jr., *Alfalfa Bill Murray* (Norman, 1968), 191-209; Karl Pretshold, "How We Solved It At Oklahoma City," *Nation,* CXXXIII (October 7, 1931), 359-61; Edwin McReynolds, *Oklahoma: A History of the Sooner State* (Norman, 1954), 366-67.

[33] Mitchell, "Social Legislation," 350. North Carolina and Georgia approved administrative reforms in 1931 giving themselves more control over schools and highways. *New York Times,* October 25, 1931, III, 6; Gov. O. Max Gardner, "North Carolina Curbs Spending," *Review of Reviews,* LXXXVI (January 1933), 59ff; Paul W. Wager, "State Centralization in North Carolina," *American Political Science Review,* XXV (November 1931), 996-1003; and Cullen B. Gosnell, *Government and People of Georgia* (New York, 1936), 107-08. For other state centralization acts see *New York Times,* April 19, 1931, III, 5 (Maine); and *ibid.,* March 13, 1932, III, 6 (Virginia).

ture spiked most of Pinchot's proposals through 1934, but his appeals were among the most advanced in the nation during the period.[34]

Another activist governor was Philip La Follette of Wisconsin. Young and fiery, he worked tirelessly to combat the crisis. Aided by legislators more helpful than Pinchot's, he had some success, securing an $8 million appropriation for unemployment relief, a surtax on personal incomes, a corporate dividend tax, and a voluntary unemployment compensation plan. La Follette also regulated public utilities more stringently and appointed David E. Lilienthal, later a TVA director, as head of the state utility commission. In 1932 La Follette was defeated in a primary, but his reforms, though incomplete, were impressive.[35]

Minnesota under Governor Floyd Olson also enjoyed forceful leadership after 1930. Charismatic and intelligent, Olson was also impatient with his opponents, and his programs seemed radical to many. Confronted with a hostile legislature, he accomplished less than he wanted before 1933, but even in 1931 he succeeded in pushing through a $15 million highway bond issue and in regulating hours and wages for highway workers. He also demanded, without applying too much pressure, an old age pension plan, reduction of taxes on farm land, and exemption of labor unions from state anti-trust laws. A shrewd politician who had greater success with later legislatures, Olson was regarded by many

[34] For Pinchot, McGeary, *Gifford Pinchot*, 355-74. See also *New York Times*, June 7, 1931, III, 6; and December 31, 1931, 6, for results of acrimonious legislative sessions.

[35] *New York Times*, February 7, 1932, III, 5; "The Wisconsin Earthquake," *New Republic*, LXXII (October 5, 1932), 194-95; and Mauritz A. Hallgren, "Governor La Follette," *Nation*, CXXXII (April 29, 1931), 473-75; Daniel Nelson, "The Origins of Unemployment Insurance in Wisconsin," *Wisconsin Magazine of History*, LI (Winter 1967-68), 109-21.

advanced progressives in 1935 as a possible left-wing alternative to President Roosevelt.[36]

Of all the governors in 1930-1932 Roosevelt made the greatest impression. Less radical than Olson, less contemptuous of states rights than Pinchot, he compiled a creditable record before assuming the presidency in 1933. Among his accomplishments were an extension of workmens compensation, prohibition of temporary injunctions against unions without notice of hearing, a 48-hour week for women, and increased public works and highway spending. He also pressed unsuccessfully for a compulsory old age pension law and for tighter regulation of holding companies and banks.

Roosevelt also popularized various plans adopted by states later in the decade. One was state unemployment compensation, which he supported strongly at the national governors' conference of 1930. Realizing that state competition for industry often prevented such legislation, he called a meeting of northeastern governors in January 1931 in an effort to stimulate collective action. Except for Pinchot, however, his proposals received little support.[37]

Roosevelt also took the lead in requesting state money for unemployment relief, which until then had been the province of private agencies or of penurious county and township trustees. Undaunted by partisan opposition, he called a special session in August 1931—at a time when most governors were happy to be free from legislative wrangling—and called for passage of $20 million for unem-

[36] George H. Mayer, *The Political Career of Floyd B. Olson* (Minneapolis, 1951), 67-96; J. O. Meyers, "Governor Olson of Minnesota," *Nation*, CXXXIII (November 18, 1931), 539-40.

[37] See *Proceedings of the Governors Conference of 1930*, 152-55, for Roosevelt and unemployment compensation, and 156-74, for reactions of other governors. See also "Seven Governors and Unemployment," *Survey*, LXV (January 15, 1931), 546, for comments about his conference of northeastern governors.

ployment relief, an increase in personal income taxes, and creation of a state relief agency. After prolonged controversy, the lawmakers acquiesced, creating a Temporary Emergency Relief Administration which served as a model relief organization throughout the depression. Always conscious of political realities, Roosevelt worked no miracles. But with Olson, La Follette, and Pinchot, he showed that state government under aggressive leadership could respond positively to the depression.[38]

But none of these states, whether reactionary or progressive, was typical between 1930 and 1933. Shocked by the crisis, hopeful that conditions would improve by themselves, most governors temporized. One lamented frankly to a friend, "I picked a bad year to be governor."[39] Legislators, not to be outdone, often compounded problems with factionalism, mindless criticism, and deadly doses of partisan politics. The result before 1933 was a sadly unproductive record.

Labor legislation suffered during these years. Governors and lawmakers, fighting financial chaos, ignored the arguments of social workers and union officials, and resisted any attempts to increase the expenses of state labor departments. Very few governors in 1930 called for labor laws, and even in Massachusetts one despairing liberal lamented, "in no state is there greater pretense of progressive labor administration and less reality."[40] Olson, Roosevelt, and Pinchot

[38] Bernard Bellush, *Franklin D. Roosevelt as Governor of New York* (New York, 1955), passim.

[39] Gov. George White to Andrew T. Peters, March 23, 1931, White Papers, Personal Correspondence "P" (Ohio Historical Society, Columbus).

[40] Harvey Walker, "Governors' Messages, 1930," *American Political Science Review*, XXIV (May 1930), 380-92. Also Gardner Jackson, "Women Workers in Massachusetts," *Nation*, CXXXI (December 3, 1930), 609-11.

made some headway in 1931, but deficits preoccupied most other governors, and labor departments almost always lost out.[41] Although child labor spread, no legislature acted to ratify the proposed constitutional amendment against child labor or to tighten existing state regulations.[42]

Advocates of public utility regulation were a little more successful, mainly because the depression helped to expose the irresponsibility of some holding company executives. South Carolina and Oklahoma provided funds to investigate holding companies, and Ohio and Vermont strengthened their regulatory agencies. Kansas, North Carolina, and Oregon passed laws to regulate holding companies, while Wisconsin and New York tightened theirs. Overall, 39 states acted positively in 1931, and though regulation in most states remained ineffective, the trend encouraged reformers.[43]

But finance, not labor or utility law, worried most states between 1930 and 1933. As tax revenues dwindled and unemployment increased, economy in government became a magic word. Governor Harry Woodring of Kansas, later Roosevelt's Secretary of War, proposed the answer: "There is only one way to reduce taxes and that is to reduce expenditures."[44] Most other governors agreed emphatically, and retrenchment dominated the governors' messages of 1931 and thereafter.[45]

The drive for economy sometimes created comic situations. When Governor Roland H. Hartley of Washing-

41 Harvey Walker, "The Results of Governors' Messages in 1931," *American Political Science Review*, XXVI (February 1932), 77-83.

42 "Child Labor Comes Back," *New Republic*, LXXIII (January 18, 1933), 257.

43 Orren Hormell, "State Legislation on Public Utilities in 1931," *American Political Science Review*, XXVI (February 1932), 84-95.

44 *Proceedings of the Governors' Conference of 1931*, 18.

45 "Our Governors Recommend," *Review of Reviews*, LXXXIII (March 1931), 86-87.

ton refused to provide money for a bicentenary celebration of the birth of George Washington, the Daughters of the American Revolution protested vigorously, blaming the governor's Canadian birth for his unpatriotic position. Unruffled, the governor retorted that the state lacked "even money to carry letters about it."[46] In Alabama even political hangers-on suffered from a rigid economy campaign, and one reporter observed that "unemployed politicians are beginning to strew the state from Sheffield to the sea."[47] The movement for economy did indeed push governors, who reluctantly discharged veteran state employees and lowered the salaries of political allies.

More serious were cuts in appropriations for public works. In 1928 the states had spent $1.35 billion for this purpose. In 1930 the figure dropped slightly to $1.27 billion. In 1932 the total fell to $630 million, and the sum for the first eight months of 1933 plummeted to $290 million.[48] Though the RFC took up some of the slack, the sharp reductions in state spending merely compounded the unemployment crisis.

While states cancelled proposed works projects for lack of funds, it was less easy to reduce the fixed costs comprising the bulk of budgets. Thus, states were able to reduce per capita spending for highways from $15 in 1927 to $14 in 1932, and for education from $19 to $18.50, but total outlays for these most expensive items stayed the same because of population increases. And since local governments were unable to bear the burden after 1931, state spending for relief and welfare rose dramatically, from $1 per capita in 1927 to $3.50 in 1932. Total per capita state expenditures thus *rose* slightly during this five-year period, from

[46] *New York Times,* March 29, 1931, III, 8.
[47] *Ibid.,* February 1, 1931, III, 5.
[48] *State Government,* VI (December 1933), 11.

$60.50 to $62.[49] That governors managed to stem the rapid increase in state spending of the 1920's vouched for their tenacity. That they failed to reverse it testified to the inescapable duties imposed on them in the depression. When economic conditions improved after 1935, state appropriations resumed a rate of increase close to that of the 1920's.

Some governors promoted economy merely to balance budgets. To others, however, administrative economy was a way of salvaging more money for unemployment relief. Indeed, from 1931 until the injection of substantial federal funds in 1933, relief was easily the most time-consuming and troublesome question of the day.

Relief administration as it existed in 1931 appalled progressives. Although 45 states had boards of charity to aid the needy, blind, insane, and disabled, these bodies were neither adequately staffed nor disposed to handle unemployment relief. Many states also had employment offices to help the jobless, but these too were weak and were often "operated by low-paid and dispirited political hacks."[50] No state in early 1931 had a centralized unemployment relief commission, and none provided state funds for relief. The needy had to turn to private agencies or to local boards who distributed so-called outdoor relief in the belief that joblessness was equivalent to laziness.[51]

A few states began to move forward early in 1931. Okla-

[49] Bureau of Census, *Historical Statistics on State and Local Finances,* 22.

[50] Paul H. Douglas, "Connecting Men and Jobs," *Survey,* LXV (December 1, 1930), 253-56.

[51] For examples of the ways governors tried to handle the problem before 1931 see Harvey Walker, *Constructive Government in Ohio: The Administration of Governor Myers Y. Cooper* (Columbus, 1948), 224ff; and Gov. Albert Ritchie (Md.) to Col. Arthur Woods, Dec. 21, 1930, No. 620.1, POUR Records. See also Series 49, Drawer 408, POUR Records for state-by-state survey in March 1931.

homa doled out the token sum of $300,000 for relief, to be financed through gasoline taxes and distributed by existing county agencies. Maryland set aside $24,000 for unemployment assistance, and California dipped gently into its contingent fund. West Virginia and Ohio expanded the financial freedom of counties by permitting them to issue relief bonds. These limited, halting ventures toward state responsibility were as far as legislators were willing to go in the spring of 1931.

More fruitful measures followed creation of New York's relief fund in September. New Jersey acted a month later, appropriating $10 million, and by March 1932 Pennsylvania, Wisconsin, Rhode Island, Illinois, and Ohio had also provided state money, either by diverting gasoline taxes, issuing bonds, or extending credit to municipalities. Special sessions of the legislatures later in 1932 added to the amounts granted by these states. In mid-1931 all states had provided a total of less than $500,000; by the end of 1932 they had spent close to $100 million.[52]

After the spring of 1932, however, no more states followed the path of these pioneers, and when the New Deal began, only eight states were offering money for relief. The reasons for this negligence were many: the RFC bailed out some; other states lacked—or claimed to lack—the money; many others preferred to drift rather than to call special sessions before election time in 1932.[53]

[52] An authoritative brief survey is Rowland Haynes, *State Legislation for Unemployment Relief from January 1, 1931 to May 31, 1932* (POUR, 1932). See also Brown, *Public Relief*, 72-96; and Bitterman, *State and Federal Grants*, 153ff, 286ff. Two useful articles are Joanna C. Colcord and Russell H. Kurtz (eds.), "Unemployment and Community Action," *Survey*, LXVIII (November 15, 1932), 612-15; and Marietta Stevenson, "The Out of Work," *State Government*, V (February 1932), 3-5.

[53] For state relief activities in 1932 and early 1933 see L. Laszlo Ecker-R, "Revenues for Relief," *State Government*, VII (November

Even when legislatures met, they were often unwilling to cooperate with indecisive and cost-conscious governors. Massachusetts Governor Joseph B. Ely, later a staunch anti-New Deal Democrat, proposed a relief program in 1931 which included a $20 million highway bond issue. Legislators passed a much reduced version, but popular cries against mounting debt led Ely to reverse his field. In 1932 he demanded drastic economy, calling for a 10 percent tax increase, a 10 percent salary cut, and a $3 million reduction in spending for the next biennium. These proposals enraged Democrats loyal to Mayor James M. Curley of Boston. For the rest of 1932 party dissension stymied Ely's program, and the state provided no substantial relief for the jobless.[54]

The unemployed in other states fared no better. California Governor James Rolph, friendly and easy-going, told his legislature in 1931 to make its own decisions. Freed from leadership, lawmakers proceeded to do nothing, while "matters most vital to the welfare of the public . . . were ignored."[55] The question of reapportionment, compounded by politics, tied up sessions in other states.[56] The impending elections in 1932 also tended to intensify partisanship, and Democratic senators in Rhode Island even refused to attend the traditional bipartisan banquet after Repub-

---

1934), 235-46. Alex Gottfried, *Boss Cermak of Chicago: A Study of Political Leadership* (Seattle, 1962), 253-63, deals with the especially complex legislative picture concerning relief spending in Illinois during this period.

54 Huthmacher, *Massachusetts People and Politics,* 222-63; James H. Powers, "Massachusetts Drifts to Hoover," *Nation,* CXXXV (October 12, 1932), 329-30.

55 *New York Times,* May 24, 1931, III, 7.

56 *Ibid.,* March 29, 1931, III, 6. Reapportionment became a key issue in 1931 because Congress, having failed to reapportion in 1920, finally did so after the 1930 census.

licans jammed through a bill giving themselves control of Providence fire and police administration.[57]

Dissension among Democrats in southern and border states was particularly disruptive. One reporter observed that the work of the Missouri legislature was "nil. . . . Not within the past quarter century has so much turmoil been in evidence, and paradoxical as it may seem, the fighting has been intra-party."[58] Florida's heavily Democratic legislature met for three sessions at a cost to taxpayers of $300,000, but was unable to agree on a tax relief and economy program. Finally it managed to raise the gasoline tax to 7 cents a gallon.[59] Factionalism also paralyzed the Tennessee legislature, which eventually adjourned leaving a $9 million deficit, $3 million in unpaid state warrants, and many rural schools closed for lack of funds.[60] And Mississippi almost defaulted on $500,000 of obligations because Governor Theodore Bilbo refused to call a special session until lawmakers promised not to impeach some of his cronies who were under suspicion of corruption. Bilbo eventually had his way, but not before he had callously announced that the state, for all he cared, could "go to the damnation bow-wows."[61]

Interstate cooperation was even less productive than these weak individual efforts. Since the first governors' conference in 1908, annual meetings had become a custom. State legislators also had met irregularly since the mid-1920's, and a magazine, *State Government,* began to appear in 1930. Gov-

[57] *Ibid.,* May 3, 1931, III, 5.

[58] *Ibid.,* Feb. 8, 1931, III, 5.

[59] *Ibid.,* Aug. 23, 1931, III, 6.

[60] *Ibid.,* July 19, 1931, III, 5; Oct. 25, 1931, III, 6

[61] *Ibid.,* April 19, 1931, III, 5; May 3, 1931, III, 6. For a survey of state action in 1932 see Harvey Walker, "Governors' Messages and the Legislative Product in 1932," *American Political Science Review,* XXVI (December 1932), 1058-74.

ernors and legislators, however, had tended to concern themselves with intrastate matters and had not even promoted the various federal aid bills beginning in the Wilson administration.[62]

The depression failed to change old habits. At the 1930 conference in Salt Lake City the governors managed to squeeze in a discussion on the causes of the crash but avoided the problem of remedies. Host governor George H. Dern, later Roosevelt's Secretary of War, proclaimed that states should "resist the tide of Federal encroachment which threatens to engulf them and to hinder them in the proper discharge of their legislative functions."[63] The legislators were no more enlightened. Topics for discussion at the American Legislators Association conference that year included, "the essentials of a model state constitution," "the need of constitutional revision," "constitutional vs legislative home rule for cities," and "the extent of legislative control of city governments." Hardly a word about the depression.[64]

The 1931 governors conference was slightly more newsworthy, mainly because a few activists insisted on dragging the depression into discussion. Pinchot, assigned the safe subject of "Timber Needs of the Future" by the program committee, spoke instead on the iniquity of the power trust, and Roosevelt managed to turn his topic of "Land Utilization and State Planning" into an eloquent plea for social insurance.[65] Otherwise, the conference was hardly a forum

[62] For trends in governors conferences see Glenn E. Brooks, *When Governors Convene: The Governors' Conference and National Politics* (Baltimore, 1961), 14-30.

[63] "When Governors Confer," *State Government,* III (July 1930), 15-16.

[64] "All Roads Lead to Cleveland," *State Government,* III (September 1930), 15.

[65] "Roosevelt, Ritchie, and Pinchot," *Nation,* CXXXII (June 17, 1931), 650. Also *Proceedings of the Governors Conference of 1931,* passim.

for serious discussion. The *New York Times* headline was accurate: "THE GOVERNORS MEET—AND DODGE REAL ISSUES."[66] The host governor summed up the gathering: "I think at this time we have in our country too many politicians and too few statesmen. . . . I think we are long on pleasantries and short on intestinal fortitude."[67] His remarks applied equally to the 1932 conference.[68]

The last chance for meaningful state action before the New Deal had to take place during the 1933 legislative sessions. Most state legislatures met in January, two months before Roosevelt took office, and recessed in May, before federal laws concerning states had taken effect. At this time unemployment was increasing, and banks were teetering on the brink of a catastrophe which would force many closings between January and March.

These sessions were little more productive than those of 1931 and 1932. The legislatures contained an unusually large number of new members as a result of the Democratic sweep in November, and most of them were inexperienced and baffled by the crisis.[69] Many Democrats shunned bold new programs, preferring to await the wonders of Roosevelt and the new Congress.

Lack of funds continued to plague the lawmakers, for neither state parsimony nor federal aid had prevented deficits in 1931-1932. Some states began to turn to the general sales tax, popularized as an excellent revenue producer by Mississippi in 1932.[70] Others tried still one more round of

[66] June 7, 1931, III, 5.

[67] *Proceedings of Governors Conference, 1931*, 93.

[68] *Ibid., 1932*, passim.

[69] Two articles stressing legislative inexperience in 1933 are in *Des Moines Register*, January 8, 1933, 1; and *Charleston* (S.C.) *News and Courier*, January 8, 1933, 2A.

[70] Gov. Sennett Conner, "Mississippi Tries the Sales Tax," *Review of Reviews*, LXXXV (October 1932), 28-9. Also *New York Times*, June 8, 1932, III, 5.

gasoline, tobacco, and excise taxes. But economy was the byword. "For the first time since the early days," a reporter commented, "the cry of economy has been something more than a campaign catchword. It has amounted to an obsession with the average legislator."[71] The ensuing budget slashing was little short of phenomenal. Arizona cut hers 35 percent; Illinois, 25 percent; Texas, 25 percent; Vermont, 25 percent. Many states even reduced legislative and gubernatorial salaries, and prior to the New Deal none responded to RFC pleas for unemployment relief appropriations.[72]

The cuts tended to be as indiscriminate as they were drastic, and schools and universities suffered. The South Carolina legislature, after sitting a record 128 days (many states were to break such records in 1933) finally reduced the budget by 33 percent, including a reduction of 19 percent in state aid to schools and universities.[73] Kansas legislators approved all kinds of draconian measures to root out educational "frills."[74] One observer calculated that state educational institutions in 1933 suffered cuts of 40 percent in Maryland, 53 percent in Wyoming, 42 percent in North Carolina, 40 percent in Mississippi, 32 percent in New

[71] *New York Times*, April 9, 1933, IV, 6.

[72] Dorothy Schaffter, "Governors' Messages and the Legislative Output in 1933," *American Political Science Review*, XXVII (October 1933), 784-99. For details in a few individual states see also *New York Times*, April 2, 1933, IV, 6 (Vermont); *Des Moines Register*, April 23, 1933, 1; *Detroit News*, January 13, 1933, 1; *Charleston* (S.C.) *News and Courier*, January 8, 1933, 3A (South in general); Gov. Joseph B. Ely, "How Massachusetts Has Kept Her Costs Low," *National Municipal Review*, XXII (July 1933), 320-22; and Gov. Albert C. Ritchie, "The Crisis in Government Economy," *ibid.*, 323-28. The poorer (and more desperate) the state, the more severe the cuts; Hansen and Perloff, *State and Local Finance*, 54-82.

[73] *Charleston* (S.C.) *News and Courier*, May 5, 1933, 1.

[74] W. G. Klugston, "Kansas Begins to Doubt the Public School," *American Mercury*, XXVIII (March 1933), 454-56.

Hampshire, and 34 percent in Washington.[75] It was some time before state universities recovered.

If state economizing was sometimes careless, the factionalism of the 1933 sessions was often disgraceful. To some new administrations the possession of power was an opportunity to play politics with relief, while in other states the problems of patronage were the most time-consuming and disruptive—job-seekers in Missouri were so insistent that the governor had to post armed guards around his office.[76] In others, as in Georgia, intraparty strife led one observer to report that no legislature in forty years could "compare in stupidity, selfishness, and lack of purpose with the body which twiddled its thumbs while the fires of hope died to ashes in the hearts of citizens."[77] Another assessment of the state scene in 1933 was harsh, but not greatly exaggerated. Lawmakers, it said, were "ignorant, confused, and frightened, with hardly more than a handful in each legislature capable of transacting the legislative business. . . . Around the splendid domes of the State capitols they themselves simply play tag."[78]

Just as frightened as their legislative cohorts, the various governors struggled to keep a semblance of order while slashing budgets wherever they had the chance. Indeed, few governors offered clear programs. Isador Lubin, a knowledgeable economist later to serve the New Deal, approached the governors in February with a progressive nine-point program. But after checking their speeches, he gave up in despair. "When I asked one of the liberal leaders

[75] William B. Thomas, "The Educator and the Depression: The College Instructor," *Nation*, CXXXVII (August 23, 1933), 213-15.

[76] *New York Times*, April 23, 1933, IV, 6.

[77] *Ibid.*, March 26, 1933, IV, 7.

[78] William Seagle, "The Clown as Lawmaker," *American Mercury*, XXVIII (March 1933), 330-37; "Recent State Legislation," *Survey*, LXIX (May 1933), 200.

for the names of six progressive governors," he told Pinchot, "I was met with the reply, 'there aren't that many.' "[79] Far from bringing a youthful crew of activists to state houses in 1933, the 1932 elections had substituted a group of inexperienced Democrats for the old Republican stalwarts. Few emerged in 1933 or later as prominent liberal leaders.

Two weeks before assuming the presidency Roosevelt informed Pinchot of his plan to assemble the governors in Washington early in his administration. But the president-elect, a veteran of many such meetings, was pessimistic. "I hope we can get some definite results," he said, "but you know what Governors' conferences are."[80] Perhaps an unwonted modesty prevented him from adding that only his state and a few others had enjoyed the caliber of leadership that enabled them to escape the confusion which plagued state houses and legislatures between 1929 and 1933.

Political squabbling, intraparty factionalism, and empty treasuries all contributed to this unhealthy condition. But these were less causes than symptoms, and they had not killed reform in the progressive era. The truth was that state remedies could not alone heal the national sickness. Even Roosevelt, working as a governor during the period, was a little slow to recognize the changing times; besides, like other governors, he was happy to exalt power at his own level.[81] State fumbling before 1933 was unfortunate, but it did teach a lesson. It exposed for all to see the fact that national solutions had to be devised to cure the complex and centralized economy of 1933.

[79] Lubin to Pinchot, February 24, 1933, Box 1939, Pinchot Papers, Library of Congress.

[80] Roosevelt to Pinchot, February 25, 1933, Box 1939, Pinchot Papers.

[81] Frank Freidel, *Franklin D. Roosevelt: The Triumph* (Boston, 1956), 71-74.

3. Battles over Relief, 1933-1935

NOT everyone liked Harry Hopkins. Lean and drawn, he was intense, offhand, sometimes brusque. But he was dedicated and humane, a veteran social worker who became Roosevelt's relief administrator in New York. When Congress approved an appropriation for federal relief in early 1933, President Roosevelt turned to his friend and associate for help. Unhesitatingly, Hopkins accepted his new mission, and hurried to Washington to take charge of the newly created Federal Emergency Relief Administration. From that day until the end of FERA in late 1935, federal-state relations passed through a dramatically changed if not always happy era.

The new agency stemmed from Roosevelt's conviction that only federal help could save the unemployed. It received $500 million to distribute to states, of which $250 million was for matching grants, with states contributing $3 for every $1 of federal funds. The remaining $250 million was to be expended at Hopkins' discretion to states facing emergencies.[1] The money would come as a gift, not a loan, and was to be given as a dole to the jobless.

Hopkins acted decisively. Contemptuous of organization charts and anxious to speed the flow of money, he presided over the most rapid extension of federal welfare in American history. By the end of June, 45 states had already received $51 million in matching funds, and on June 27 Texas collected the first of many discretionary grants. By the end of 1933, the FERA had given out $324 million, and

[1] Brown, *Public Relief*, 146ff; Maxwell, *The Fiscal Impact*, 136-48.

by 1936 the grants, augmented by several additional appropriations, exceeded $3 billion.[2] The states added $450 million and the localities $600 million during the same period, making a total of more than $4 billion in three years. This sum represented an enormous increase over the amounts spent from 1930 through 1932.[3]

The FERA introduced other features. To receive federal grants the states had to provide adequate administrative supervision. Anxious for funds, most states acted quickly to create centralized relief agencies and to appropriate at least token sums to operate them. While most of these new agencies were destined to be temporary, the duration of the crisis turned some of them into permanent adjuncts of state government. The FERA helped force the eventual removal of relief administration from archaic local bodies.[4]

The FERA was especially beneficial where politicians cooperated in pushing for adequate state contributions. Indeed, Hopkins' field agents in these states lauded the progress made in public relief. Aubrey Williams, a difficult man to please, wrote that "the leadership in Texas, including Governor Miriam Ferguson . . . has accepted the general position that social work is a public responsibility and should be handled by legally constituted public agencies."[5]

[2] Theodore E. Whiting, *Final Statistical Report of the F.E.R.A.* (Washington, 1942), 103.

[3] "Amount of Obligations Incurred for Emergency Relief By Sources of Funds, By States, Jan. 1933—Sept., 1935," in General Correspondence, Box 97, National Emergency Council Records, Record Group 44, National Archives, Washington, D.C.

[4] Brown, *Public Relief*, 183-87. For an example of the FERA's quick administrative and financial impact in one state, see Wilbur Cross, *Connecticut Yankee: An Autobiography* (New Haven, 1943), 282-85.

[5] Aubrey Williams to Hopkins, undated [July 1933], No. 401.2-410 Box 285, FERA Records, Record Group 69, National Archives. See also M. J. Miller to Williams, October 1, 1934, *ibid.* Seth S. McKay and Odie B. Faulk, *Texas After Spindletop* (Austin, 1965), 132-34, also comment favorably on the Ferguson administration.

Another agent wrote about Governor Henry Blood of Utah: "It was a great pleasure to finally fall into a state where there was no bitterness, no quarrelling and all that goes with it. In addition—to add to this picture of paradise—the governor . . . is by all odds one of the finest state executives that I have met. I told him he must be an accident."[6]

Hopkins' hardboiled aides praised a few other states as well. In Minnesota Olson and his advisors, one agent reported, were "doing more real thinking in a big way about this problem, than any men that I have met in this territory."[7] Another field man wrote of Indiana: "if you know the history of local politics in this state, you might agree with me that relatively this state has made some great progress in its administration of relief."[8] And a happy social worker wrote: "Social consciousness in Alabama has been lifted by the bootstraps since the inauguration of FERA."[9] In these states federal money brought relief to the jobless, persuaded state officials of the need for public welfare, and encouraged harmonious federal-state relations.

Though the record of the FERA was remarkably good—almost revolutionary—in these respects, it was inevitable, given the financial requirements imposed on deficit-ridden states, that friction would develop between governors and federal officials. This conflict typified the problems which would sadden advocates of a cooperative and mutually beneficial federalism under the New Deal.

Personality clashes especially pained social workers. Hop-

[6] Benjamin Glassberg to Hopkins, March 27, 1934, No. 401.1-440 (Utah), Box 293, FERA Records.

[7] T. J. Edmonds to Hopkins, December 16, 1933, No. 406-20 (Minn.), Box 144, FERA Records.

[8] Howard O. Hunter to Hopkins, December 1933, No. 401.1-420, Box 91, FERA Records.

[9] Quoted in Maxwell, *Fiscal Impact,* 150. Similar remarks are fairly numerous in the FERA Records. See Boxes 81, 102, 151.

kins and his aides, hurrying to relieve distress, often bluntly criticized state administrators. They in turn tended to resent what they called the arrogance or impetuosity of federal agents. Connecticut officials, hoping to impress Hopkins with a careful, town-by-town description of unemployment, took offence when Hopkins, lacking time to examine mountains of data, brusquely replied, "I'm too busy to look at all that."[10]

Personal rancor in Arkansas was sharper. Aubrey Williams, visiting the state in August 1933, clashed with Governor J. Marion Futrell, whom he was later to remember for splattering the walls with tobacco juice as well as for his hostility to the New Deal.[11] The "situation in the state," Williams wrote in 1933, "is desperately bad and political from state organization on through to the county unit."[12] Incensed, Futrell shot a letter to Hopkins. "I do not like the ideas of Mr. Aubrey Williams. . . . He says he cares nothing about politics. . . . He has an idea of employing largely social welfare workers. . . . I don't think he has any practical ideas."[13] Hopkins backed his man, and the controversy subsided, but the spat had not established a happy precedent for federal-state relations.

Arkansas was not Williams' only trying experience. Arriving in Oklahoma, he called on Governor "Alfalfa Bill" Murray. An unkempt but colorful agrarian, Murray's populistic

[10] Rowland Mitchell, Jr., "Social Legislation in Connecticut, 1919-1939," unpublished doctoral dissertation, Yale University, 1954, 377.

[11] "The New Deal—A Dead Battery," unpublished MS, Williams Papers, Roosevelt Library, Hyde Park, N.Y., 37.

[12] Williams to Hopkins, July 2, 1933, No. 401.1-406.2, Box 16, FERA Records.

[13] Gov. Futrell to Sen. Joseph Robinson (Ark.), July 1, 1933, Official File (OF) 444, July 1933, Roosevelt Library. Also F. H. Crozier to Corrington Gill, September 6, 1933, No. 406.2-420, Box 17, FERA Records; and Williams to Hopkins, August 9, 1933, and September 13, 1933, No. 401.1-406.2 Box 16, *ibid.*

forays against the rich seemed to stamp him as a champion of the common man. But the governor quickly offended Williams by wearing dirty socks and no shoes, by using his handkerchief as a strainer to make his guest a cup of tea, and finally, by cursing Roosevelt. With the last, Williams stalked out. Williams also uncovered "thieving and favoritism on all sides. I found that every Tom, Dick, and Harry in the state was getting relief whether they were unemployed or not."[14] Murray finally discharged some inefficient county officials, but as soon as Williams left the state, the governor named a new group of cronies, blaming Williams for the removals and taking credit for the new appointments. Relations deteriorated until Murray, tired of what he termed interference, snapped at a federal agent, "if you don't like it, why don't you run it yourself!" The agent agreed, and early in 1934 Hopkins federalized relief in Oklahoma for the following year.[15] The only people who had suffered from Murray's crotchety attitude were Oklahoma's unemployed.

State rivalry for the $250 million (and later much more) of discretionary funds also plagued the FERA. While Hopkins' generosity at first satisfied most states, charges of favoritism soon proliferated. The FERA, critics claimed, favored certain states (or political allies in these states) at the expense of others. In later years disgruntled state officials advanced all kinds of statistical evidence of FERA discrimination.

Some of these statistics appeared convincing. The average monthly relief payment per family varied considerably over

[14] Williams, "The New Deal . . . ," 36ff. For Murray's administration, see Keith L. Bryant, Jr., *Alfalfa Bill Murray* (Norman, 1968), 238-55.

[15] Report by William J. Plunkert, December 15, 1933, No. 401.2-406.2, Box 237, FERA Records. For a sketch of Murray see Reinhard Luthin, *American Demagogues: Twentieth Century* (Gloucester, Mass. 1959), 111-16.

the nation: in May 1934 it was $23.90 per month, but a Kentucky family received only $6.78 while New Yorkers received $45.12. City families averaged $30.80, others, $18.53.[16] Most middle Atlantic, Middle Western, and mountain states received higher amounts per capita than southern and New England states. Nevada got $56 per capita per year, South Dakota $46, and Montana $41, compared to less than $15 for twelve other states, including Connecticut, Rhode Island, Texas, and Virginia.[17] Variations even existed within regions, and one authority partial to the FERA admitted that grants, because of the necessity of speed, were sometimes "impulsive."[18]

Such figures told only part of the story. The differences in payments to southern rural and northern urban areas stemmed partly from varying living costs. Southern farmers had to pay a little less for food than northern urbanites, and much less for clothing. More significant, southern states, much poorer than those in other regions, were often unable to meet the $3 for $1 requirement for nondiscretionary funds. Indeed, the federal government paid 90 percent or more of all public relief money in each of nine southern states between 1933 and 1935. By contrast it gave less than 70 percent in eleven states, including Massachusetts, New York, California, and Indiana.[19] One simple reason for the disparity in per capita payments to states was the wide difference in amounts contributed for matching money.

16 Brown, *Public Relief,* 233-34.

17 H. J. Bitterman, *State and Federal Grants-in-Aid* (New York, 1938), 168.

18 Brown, *Public Relief,* 204, 464-65; see also Larry Whatley, "The Works Progress Administration in Mississippi," *Journal of Mississippi History,* XXX (Feb. 1968), 35-50.

19 "Amount of Obligations Incurred . . . ," NEC Records. George B. Tindall, in *The Emergence of the New South, 1913-1945* (Baton Rouge, 1967), 480-82, notes that low southern contributions, plus a low standard of living, combined to depress relief payments in the South.

Lack of sound data on unemployment also confused matters. Hopkins' avowed purpose was to send money where it was most needed. But given the unreliable figures on unemployment available to him, how was he to judge precisely that one state or area was more desperate than another? He could not, and grants tended to go where his roving field agents reported emergencies. Because such a method involved human judgment, it probably resulted in injustices here and there.

Other federal agencies pumping in money at the same time compounded the problem of citing meaningful statistics. The Public Works Administration sent millions to localities. So did the Agricultural Adjustment Administration, especially to rural regions in the southern and plains states. Both organizations generally bypassed state administration, granting or lending money directly to contractors, municipalities, or agricultural districts, and neither agency aimed specifically at providing relief for the unemployed. Yet each decisively altered statewide economic conditions and in so doing affected the level of unemployment.[20] In complaining that their tax dollars vanished in the form of relief money into other states, critics sometimes overlooked the many ways in which the New Deal distributed its favors.

Above all, conditions differed—and not only in the eyes of the field agents. The New England states seemed to profit least from the FERA, receiving from Washington the lowest percentages of total funds for relief as well as the smallest per capita grants. The Rocky Mountain states, by contrast, tended to get high per capita grants while spending little from state sources. The reason was simple: the New

[20] See Donald A. Laird, "The Tail That Wags the Nation," *Review of Reviews and World Week,* XCI (November 1935), 45, for an attempt to show the amount of aid received by states from the FERA and AAA.

England states were wealthier per capita, unaffected by drought, and better able to handle part of the burden themselves, while the plains and mountain states were practically prostrate.[21] More than anything else, variations in conditions confounded critics anxious to demonstrate the discriminatory practices of the New Deal. That the FERA enriched some states at the expense of others is doubtful.[22] Moreover, no evidence suggests that Hopkins deliberately discriminated or that he conceived of the FERA as a means of redistributing national income.

While charges of favoritism bothered Hopkins occasionally, state politics annoyed him all the time. No political amateur, he anticipated political difficulties and ordinarily handled them smoothly. But because Congress handed relief administration to state agencies, he inevitably had to deal with squabbles among ambitious state politicians hoping to use federal funds for their own advancement.[23]

One of Hopkins' most persistent headaches was caused by frustrated Republicans who clung tenaciously to local posts under Democratic state administrations. To these forlorn figures, money from Washington gleamed as a way of maintaining influence. "The real trouble in Arizona," a

[21] "Per Cent of Total Population in Each State Receiving Unemployment Relief from Public Funds, July 1934," *State Government*, VII (November 1934), 236.

[22] For a breakdown by regions of relief received, taxes paid, and percent of population receiving relief see Howard Odum, *Southern Regions of the United States* (Chapel Hill, 1936), 180.

[23] This problem was especially acute during the lifetime of the Civil Works Administration, a short-lived work relief program during the winter of 1933-1934 which operated under Hopkins' guidance. As one agent reported, "The politicians did not especially mind turning relief over to a group of citizens, for they felt there was nothing but grief in that job. However, it drove the politicians wild to find themselves without anything to say about who was going to get a job on public work." Pierce Williams to Hopkins, February 6, 1934, Box 73, John Carmody Papers, Roosevelt Library.

field man reported, "is that there is a gang . . . the remnants of the old Republican machine, who endeavor in every way to embarrass the Governor and the relief administration."[24] Another agent grumbled that Republicans controlled 70 of Iowa's 99 counties, and the governor of Ohio complained that "as the smoke clears the Republicans get the major share of the jobs."[25]

The most outspoken critic of Republican obstructionism was Lorena Hickok, a sensitive yet salty social worker who served as Hopkins' chief roving field agent. Her reports brimmed with indignation about abuses in the states. Visiting traditionally Republican South Dakota, she angrily protested the misuse of federal money. Relief spending, she fumed, "is being run by a bunch of Republicans. . . . I can't see that leaving it all in the hands of the gang that handled it under Hoover—and who are about as popular out here as grasshoppers—was exactly smart. It hasn't 'taken' well, I can assure you. Yours for a REAL DICTATORSHIP!"[26]

States with Republican administrations were sometimes worse. Complaints about relief spending in Pinchot's Penn-

[24] Pierce Williams to Hopkins, August 4, 1933, No. 400-406.2, Box 10, FERA Records. Fiscal difficulties also complicated the picture in Arizona. *New York Times*, April 9, 1933, IV, 6, and May 14, 1933, IV, 7.

[25] T. J. Edmonds to Hopkins, February 2, 1934, No. 406-420, Box 97, FERA Records; Gov. George White to Cong. A. P. Lamneck, December 16, 1933, White Papers, Personal Correspondence, Ohio Historical Society, Columbus, Ohio.

[26] Hickok to Hopkins, November 9, 1933, Box 89 (FERA-WPA Reports), Hopkins Papers, Roosevelt Library. Her reports, while perhaps overcritical on many occasions, also received Roosevelt's attention, as he acknowledged to top administrators in December 1933. "I think Lorena Hickox's [sic] reports have been perfectly grand. She is trained to follow a trail; she is after quail and she won't flush a rabbit." Quoted in Lester G. Seligman and Elmer E. Cornwell, Jr., *New Deal Mosaic: Roosevelt Confers with his National Emergency Council* (Eugene, Ore., 1965), 17.

sylvania were especially bitter. Miss Hickok, while absolving Pinchot personally, reported that "our chief trouble in Pennsylvania is due to politics. From the township to Harrisburg, the state is honeycombed with politicians all fighting for the privilege of distributing patronage, and the professional relief staffs who have gone in to reorganize the distribution have put up a superb fight against terrific odds."[27]

Democratic congressmen from Pennsylvania were less charitable. One told Hopkins in 1934 that Pinchot was "playing politics to the 'nth' degree with the relief money that you so generously awarded him."[28] Another added that relief "was administered so unfairly in my district last winter, I am very much interested in having a federal administrator appointed."[29] Although Hopkins' field agents were unable to substantiate these claims, such grievances from Democratic congressmen bothered Hopkins and his administration.[30]

If Republican meddling was predictable, Democratic obstructionism proved both frustrating and time-consuming. In some states, factionalism was the culprit. An agent in Illinois charged that the state relief administration had "done a pretty lousy job . . . the whole Illinois Commission set-up is largely political, and I am honestly considerably

[27] Hickok Report, August 13, 1933, Box 89, Hopkins Papers, Roosevelt Library.

[28] Cong. Pat Boland (D-Pa.) to Hopkins, September 1, 1934, Pennsylvania General Minutes, Box 257, FERA Records.

[29] Cong. Charles N. Crosby (D-Pa.), August 25, 1934, *ibid.*

[30] See Report of Arch Mandel to Aubrey Williams, March 19, 1934, No. 401.1-406.2, Box 250, FERA Records. Perhaps the most flagrant use of relief for political purposes was in North Dakota, where Gov. William Langer, an aggressive Republican, was found guilty of collecting relief money for political reasons and removed from office. Cleared in 1935, he was reelected in 1936. See Elwyn B. Robinson, *History of North Dakota* (Lincoln, 1966), 410-12.

disturbed about the whole business there."[31] Miss Hickok called Texas "a Godawful mess . . . they're having a big political fight in Austin. . . . And in the meantime—God help the unemployed. . . . If I were twenty years younger, and weighed 75 pounds less, I think I'd start out to be the Joan of Arc of the Fascist movement in the United States."[32]

One special annoyance arose through the desire of Democratic governors to consolidate their power through the use of federal money. Murray of Oklahoma was not the only one. Of Florida's governor one reporter wrote, "The Governor has a bad reputation around the state, and it's getting worse. . . . It's generally assumed on the part of the public . . . that he is playing politics."[33] Governor C. Ben Ross of Idaho, an ambitious, independent Democrat, was "quite obviously manipulating the Emergency Relief Commission for his own interests."[34] And Governor Charles E. Bryan of Nebraska, brother of the peerless orator, received the most unflattering portrait of all. Bryan, an agent wrote, "seemed just as politically minded as ever. . . . His idea of social work is that performed in cleaning up a political situation, with possibly some value done in work by ladies of the W.C.T.U. or the Elks in distributing Christmas baskets."[35] It is probable that many of Hopkins' field agents, recognizing the activism of their chief, underestimated the governors—Bryan, for one, was not so incompetent as he was portrayed. It is certain also that the agents exaggerated the ability of states to pay a full share. Yet their

[31] Howard O. Hunter to Hopkins, March 20, 1934, No. 402-420, Box 81, FERA Records.

[32] Hickok Report, April 11, 1934, Box 89, Hopkins Papers.

[33] Hickok Report, January 28, 1934, *ibid.*

[34] Eva Nance to Hopkins, October 4, 1934, No. 401-420, Box 74, FERA Records.

[35] Report by Sherrard Ewing, June 23, 1933, No. 401-406.2, Box 173, FERA Records. For Bryan see also Hickok Report, November 18, 1933, Box 89, Hopkins Papers; and *New York Times,* March 25, 1934, IV, 7.

reports do reveal clearly the difference between the slow-moving, politically conscious governors and the impatient federal officials.[36]

Of all the uncooperative Democrats, none outdid Martin Davey, Ohio's governor from 1935 to 1939. A small-town tree surgeon with little conception of the economic crisis, Davey quickly annoyed Hopkins by refusing to press the legislature for adequate relief contributions and by using FERA funds to advance his party faction. Denouncing the wastefulness of federal welfare, he tried to decentralize it, abolishing the state relief commission and turning control over to political allies in the counties.[37]

When Davey publicly criticized federal procedures in March 1935, the controversy flared openly. Claiming that Ohio was too poor to appropriate more matching funds, he also grumbled about Hopkins' appointments. "You will find bitter complaint among Democrats all over Ohio that they have been discriminated against. They have been almost completely barred from participation." Unimpressed, Hopkins answered politely but firmly: "I cannot believe that this represents the desires of the people of Ohio, and I am sure they wish to contribute their reasonable part to-

[36] Evaluating the fairness of these reports is made doubly difficult because of the relative paucity of state records which give the governors' point of view. The historian is easily tempted to use the bountiful federal records uncritically.

[37] Francis R. Aumann, "From White to Bricker," in Lindley, *Ohio in the 20th Century*, 78ff. See also Richard L. Mahler, "Ohio, Oxcart Government," in Robert S. Allen, ed., *Our Sovereign State* (New York 1949), 166-77, for an unfavorable view of Davey. For Ohio's relief policy in the depression years, David Maurer, "Public Relief Programs and Policies in Ohio, 1929-1939," unpublished doctoral dissertation, Ohio State University, 1962. Hopkins also had problems with the Ohio legislature during the term of Gov. George White (D.), 1931-1935. White prided himself on his economy, reducing the budget from $84 million to $46 million in four years. White to S. W. Burlingame, February 28, 1933, Legislature 1933, A-B, White Papers.

ward the costs of the needs of the unemployed."[38] Davey's allies fought back, and the Democratic state chairman denounced Hopkins for naming Republicans to relief posts—"especially Republicans of the uplift type, the long haired men and the short haired women. They have betrayed the President."[39] This was enough for Hopkins. Aroused by persistent reports of corruption, he ordered an investigation which found that Davey was staffing field operations with political allies. Hopkins then federalized Ohio relief. It was but the beginning of a four-year war of nerves between the New Deal and the Democratic Ohio gangs of the 1930's.

When men such as Davey, Murray, or Huey Long of Louisiana openly challenged New Dealers, Roosevelt moved vigorously to shut off all assistance. Thus Long, whose defiance had antagonized the administration by 1935, was the subject of the following high-level discussion among federal officials.

> ROOSEVELT: "Don't put anybody in and don't keep anyone that is working for Huey Long or his crowd! That is a hundred percent!"
>
> VICE-PRESIDENT JOHN GARNER: "That goes for everybody!"
>
> ROOSEVELT: "Everybody and every agency. Anybody working for Huey Long is not working for us."[40]

Roosevelt and Hopkins also warned their own men against playing politics, advising them to deal firmly with

38 Correspondence, March 1935, in OF444, Roosevelt Papers.

39 *New York Times*, March 21, 1935, 14; and March 24, 1935, IV, 6.

40 Seligman and Cornwell, *New Deal Mosaic*, 437 (February 5, 1935 meeting). One governor to lose federal patronage was James Michael Curley of Massachusetts. See Harold Gorvine, "The New Deal in Massachusetts," unpublished doctoral dissertation, Harvard University, 1962, 127-61, 457-65.

uncooperative state machines. "We want you to be absolutely hard-boiled if you find any local person within your states who is trying to get political advancement out of human needs," the president told field men. "You will have the backing of this administration even if you hit the biggest political boss in the United States on the head in carrying out this general program."[41]

Unhappily, politics in relief continued to harass New Dealers long after the demise of the FERA. For one thing, it was impossible to please all parties and factions, and nothing prevented dissident politicians from making capital out of exaggerated charges. As the astute Garner phrased it, "The Democrats say we appoint too many Republicans and the Republicans say we appoint too many Democrats."[42] Most important, Hopkins lacked the trumps to outplay ambitious state politicians. Miss Hickok sadly expressed this fact: "There are of course states that openly chisel. Ohio, for instance. Vastly irritating. But don't ever forget that the people who REALLY suffer in these rows are the relief clients. And even if one chooses to ignore the social consequences, these people have votes."[43] If a governor misused federal money, Hopkins sometimes named his own men to administer relief, as in Oklahoma and Ohio. But he was very reluctant to stop the outflow of money, for the social and political costs were too high. The result was that though FERA was an essential relief operation, it became vulnerable for unavoidable political reasons.

Political meddling was not the FERA's only worry. A

[41] *New York Times,* July 3, IV, 3. It is doubtful that Roosevelt practiced what he preached. See Lyle W. Dorsett, *The Pendergast Machine* (New York, 1968), 109-115 for evidence that Roosevelt catered to the state machine in Missouri.

[42] Seligman and Cornwell, *New Deal Mosaic,* 68 (January 23, 1934 meeting).

[43] Hickok Report, October 31, 1935, Box 89, Hopkins Papers.

more fundamental difficulty was the loyalty of state relief employees to time-honored American principles of self-reliance. As one agent said of welfare officials in Arizona, "there is a well defined belief that people can endure hardships and that life need not necessarily be very easy." And Miss Hickok said of Maine: "To be a 'deserving case,' a family has got to measure up to the most rigid Nineteenth Century standards of cleanliness, physical and moral. . . . As a result, a woman who isn't a good housekeeper is apt to have a pretty rough time of it. And Heaven help the family in which there is any 'moral problem.' "[44]

Such attitudes produced sloppy, impersonal, and unfeeling administration. Hopkins insisted on a minimum of order, but he could not change attitudes ingrained through many decades of American history. The cost-conscious "progressivism" which had given birth to state reorganization laws in the 1920's was as harmful to welfare in the 1930's as all the self-seeking politicians of the decade.

Above all, financial controversies burdened the FERA. Hopkins faced perennial appeals for more money from governors. Pinchot, one of the more demanding, complained as early as July 1933, "Hoover did his best to prevent R.F.C. from giving help to Pennsylvania, and the whole state knows it. I am extremely anxious that no such impression should be made by your administration." Adroitly, he cited Pennsylvania's constitutional prohibition against borrowing to explain the small state contributions: "We ought not to be penalized for a constitutional provision with which we had nothing to do."[45] Other governors, less subtle, demanded rather than appealed for help, as if the claim to federal aid, so recently denounced as blasphemy, were a di-

[44] *Ibid.*, September 30, 1933.

[45] Pinchot to FDR, July 25, 1933, President's Personal File (PPF) 289, Roosevelt Papers.

vine right. By January 1934 such pleas caused Stephen Early, Roosevelt's press secretary, to comment: "If the Federal Government appropriated funds in the grand totals asked by the various Governors, it would make a joke of the budget, wreck the Treasury, and bankrupt the nation."[46] Early exaggerated only slightly; the governors sensibly assumed that asking for too much was better politics than requesting too little. Besides, some charitable bureaucrat might be moved to comply.

Had these same governors limited their claims of poverty to half-hearted efforts at satisfying home consumption, Hopkins could have listened calmly. But from the start many governors sincerely believed that they could not begin to pay $3 of state money for every $1 from the FERA. Searching desperately for revenue, these states barely possessed the resources to prevent starvation, let alone carry three-fourths of the load. Indeed, most states of low per capita wealth were already taxing their residents more heavily than wealthy states. These cases too were so clear that the FERA usually responded by paying most of the bill.[47]

But some states seemed to exaggerate their inability to pay, infuriating impatient FERA agents and leading to constant federal-state friction. Observing West Virginia's

[46] Early to Samuel Rosenman, January 25, 1933, OF91, Roosevelt Papers. Few governors were more frank about their intentions to milk the federal treasury than C. Ben Ross of Idaho. He told legislators that Idaho had not contributed much for relief because "we had a Scotch governor that talked them out of it. We got by for two years and Uncle Sam paid the bill." Cited in Michael P. Malone, "C. Ben Ross and the New Deal in Idaho," unpublished doctoral dissertation, Washington State University, 1964, 125.

[47] Alvin H. Hansen and Harvey S. Perloff, *State and Local Finance in the National Economy* (New York 1944), 29-32. For one such destitute state see correspondence concerning New Mexico in Gov. A. E. Hockenhull Papers, Relief File, New Mexico State Archives, Santa Fe.

good credit rating and low taxes, Hopkins himself accused Democratic Governor Herman G. Kump of political cowardice. "The governor simply does not wish to face the music," he complained to Roosevelt.[48] He followed by threatening to reduce federal funds.

Kump, who was fighting factional opponents, was unmoved. Disgusted, a field agent wrote that "the Governor whined and cried and beat his chest vigorously explaining how hard it would be to get the West Virginia legislature to do much about this situation and told us his sob story about the present tax jam they are in."[49] Hopkins then ordered Kump to call a special session of his legislature or face federal takeover of relief—and with it the replacement of many of his political allies. The governor still procrastinated, and the state supreme court compounded his difficulties by ruling against various tax plans. Not until April 1934, six months after Hopkins' "final" threat, did the legislature pass a $3 million relief appropriation.

The same round of delays and recriminations occurred in many other states. "Utah is the prize 'gimme' state of the Union," an agent insisted, and he quoted a Mormon sign: "Pay your Tithes before you pay your taxes."[50] Another field man was even angrier at Michigan's Democratic administration: "Michigan really gives me a pain in the neck because we do not get a damn thing out of these communities in the way of money . . . the state and local officials, I

[48] Hopkins to Roosevelt, August 16, 1933, OF444-Misc., Box 6, Roosevelt Papers. See also "Status of Relief and School Aid Legislation," March 15, 1935, FERA Records, 100, for evidence of the close touch kept by federal officials on state relief activities.

[49] Howard O. Hunter to Mr. Bookman, October 27, 1933, No. 401.1-406.2, Box 313, FERA Records. Also Charles H. Ambler and Festus P. Summers, *West Virginia: The Mountain State* (New Jersey, 1958), 481-82.

[50] Pierce Williams to Hopkins, June 27, 1933, No. 401.1-440, Box 293, FERA Records.

am confident, believe that Santa Claus will keep on coming down the chimney no matter how bad they are."[51]

The most celebrated cases, again involving Democratic administrations, were Kentucky and Colorado. The poverty of Kentucky's mountain counties was especially severe. After visiting this area, Miss Hickok submitted a report which she admitted sounded "sobby" but which was "all true and not a bit exaggerated." An agent had seen men and boys averting their eyes as they passed a certain roadside shack. When he asked why, they replied, "Well, you see the women folks in that thar place hain't got no clothes at all. Even their rags is clean wore out and gone."[52]

Even before this report, Hopkins had aimed a sharp press release at Kentucky officials. "There are a few recalcitrant states," he warned in July, "that want to sit down and let the federal government pay 100 percent of the cost of unemployment relief within their borders. . . . Some states are in for a rude shock in the very near future, if they do not come through with action. . . . The FERA means business, and we are not going to string along with these situations." The next day he threatened to cut Kentucky off unless its legislature acted by August.[53]

No one listened. Governor Ruby Laffoon, facing serious intraparty dissension, was afraid to call a special session, and finally told Hopkins to federalize the system.[54] He did so, and Laffoon relaxed. But Hopkins still insisted that

[51] Howard Hunter to Hopkins, February 7, 1934, No. 401.3-420, Box 137, FERA Records. Similar complaints amount to a refrain in FERA records. For hassling in Missouri see papers of Gov. Guy Park (D.), 1933-1937, Folders 1804, 1819, University of Missouri Library, Columbia, Mo.

[52] Hickok Report, September 6, 1933, Box 89, Hopkins Papers.

[53] See Russell H. Kurtz, "Two Months of the New Deal in Federal Relief," *Survey*, LXIX (August 1933), 284-90.

[54] Howard Hunter to Hopkins, November 13, 1933, No. 401-406.2, Box 107, FERA Records.

the state pay its share, and directed his agents to press state officials. Complying gladly, one field man reported that "I will meet with the legislative boys this week, and unless you tell me otherwise, I am going to put some tight screws on them and take my coat off to get them to pass some legislation which will actually produce some relief money."[55]

The field man described the meeting in his next report: "We had a two-hour discussion, which probably got nowhere. These birds insisted on telling about their own local troubles . . . frankly most of them . . . think we are kidding and if they hold out long enough, we will never stop paying the bills." Kentucky, he observed, "is in as good financial condition as any state in the Union. However, these fellows were elected on the usual Kentucky platform of saving money, and having just gotten to Frankfort, they apparently were scared to even talk about spending money for relief."[56] The agent told the politicians that the FERA was "not kidding," but he feared that his remarks had again been in vain.

He was right. Except for turning over the pittance of $280,000 in beer and whiskey taxes to the state relief commission, lawmakers did nothing. After more threats, they finally responded in June 1934, passing a regressive sales tax and appropriating $2.4 million for relief. But Laffoon, according to federal agents, then proceeded to hoard the money, spending it with political aims in mind. Still more ineffectual warnings followed until the end of FERA in 1935.[57] The losers were Hopkins; Laffoon, who was defeated in a primary anyway in 1935; and the unemployed of Kentucky, who received less assistance than any of the unemployed in the nation.

[55] Hunter to Hopkins, January 10, 1934, *ibid.*

[56] Hunter to Hopkins, January 19, 1934, *ibid.*

[57] See Hunter to Hopkins, January 26, 1934, June 21, 1934, August 6, 1934, *ibid.*

The controversy in Colorado was unusually complicated. In the first place, personality clashes created a great deal of bad feeling. Democratic Governor Edwin Johnson, who was sharply at odds with a more liberal party faction headed by Senator Edward Costigan, believed that FERA agents were trying to destroy him. Federal officers on the scene were just as sure that Johnson, a tenacious and independent opponent, wanted to use the FERA to bury liberalism in the state. During squabbling over appointments between 1933 and 1935 federal agents managed to fire two of Johnson's administrators, but the governor fought back and eventually forced Hopkins to replace his Rocky Mountain regional director.[58] The bickering wrecked the state's already politically divided relief apparatus.

Skimpy state appropriations for relief intensified these disputes. Colorado legislators, convinced that the federal government would never cut off funds, earmarked only $60,000 for relief in their 1933 session—an amount intended to last until mid-1935.[59] They guessed correctly, for Hopkins, aware of urgent needs in the Dust Bowl of eastern Colorado, granted the state $330,000 per month plus additional sums for surplus commodities, care of transients, and aid to cooperatives.[60] At the same time he threatened to stop federal aid unless the state increased its contribution.

Johnson's position was unenviable. For one thing, retail interests hotly opposed a sales tax, arguing that it would destroy business near the borders. Johnson asked one protestor: "Do I understand that your position is to refuse to comply with Washington's request and stop the flow of this

[58] This most complex story receives detailed treatment in James F. Wickens, "Colorado in the Great Depression: A Study of New Deal Policies at the State Level," unpublished doctoral dissertation, University of Denver, 1964, 43-114.

[59] *Ibid.*, 43.

[60] *Ibid.*, 59-61.

huge sum into our state?"[61] But when retailers persisted, Johnson procrastinated, weighing the alternatives of higher taxes, a costly bond issue, or no action at all. Disgusted, the field agent grumbled that the governor was "not capable of providing any real leadership in this matter."[62] Finally, Johnson gave in to federal pressure and called a special session of the state legislature for August. Even this concession failed to placate the field man, however, for he reported that Johnson wanted FERA to draft a letter which he could use as a club. "Governor Johnson," he complained, "expects us to make up his program of state legislation for him so he can say to the State Legislature that 'this is what the Federal Administration requires.' Of course we cannot go that far."[63]

To the agent's surprise, the legislature responded, approving an auto license tax expected to net $3 million, most of which was reserved for relief. The state supreme court, however, invalidated the law, intoning that it imposed double taxation on car owners. The state was again without matching funds.[64] Johnson then called another special session for December, but in vain. "You can lead a horse to water but you cannot make him drink," Johnson complained. "I begged, threatened, and prayed with the legislature to courageously face the problem and enact a sensible remedy, but without results."[65]

This was enough for Hopkins. Angrily, he cut off relief in mid-January of the coldest, most desperate winter of the

[61] Johnson to Carl O. Nelson, May [?], 1933, Johnson Papers, Correspondence, 1933, Taxes 83A, Colorado State Archives, Denver.

[62] Pierce Williams to Hopkins, July 11, 1933, No. 406-420, Box 39, FERA Records.

[63] Williams to Hopkins, July 25, 1933, *ibid.*

[64] Wickens, "Colorado . . . ," 66-69. See also *New York Times*, October 29, 1933, IV, 6.

[65] Johnson to J. S. Elowar, December 22, 1933, Correspondence, 1933, 73B, Johnson Papers.

century. The unemployed protested strongly, and pressure mounted on legislators. "Word is beginning to come back to Denver," a federal officer wrote, "that members of the legislature are having an uncomfortable time at home."[66] Moving quickly, Johnson called another special legislative session which relief marchers quickly, though briefly, dispersed. Unable to procrastinate any longer, lawmakers increased the gasoline tax and diverted highway funds for relief.[67]

Threatened by anarchy, Colorado had finally contributed a share to the relief fund, and while friction over appointments continued, the struggle was less newsworthy throughout the rest of 1934 and 1935.[68] The unemployed suffered more than either Johnson (whom voters shortly elevated to the Senate) or the FERA.[69] No controversy more clearly revealed the inherent federal-state problems under the agency.

The FERA was efficient, remarkably free of scandal, and indispensably humane. Without it, deprivation would have been a great deal more serious. But primarily because of its $3 for $1 matching provision, federal-state relations suffered. It antagonized politicians and forced Hopkins reluctantly to adopt the role of Simon Legree. As he admitted

[66] Pierce Williams to Frank Bane, December 1933, No. 406-420, Box 39, FERA Records.

[67] Wickens, "Colorado," 70-74.

[68] See Benjamin Glassberg to Hopkins, January 30, 1934, No. 406-420, Box 39, FERA Records. Also Glassberg to Hopkins, March 1, 1934, *ibid.*; and *New York Times*, November 18, 1934, IV, 6.

[69] Like most other Democrats anxious for high office, Johnson always protested his loyalty to Roosevelt and the New Deal. For an example, see Johnson to Roosevelt, May 9, 1936, in which he objected to an article in the *Nation* (April 29, 1936) calling him a "reactionary who has fought the New Deal at every turn." Roosevelt replied on May 14, soothing the senatorial candidate and adding that writers for the *Nation* represented what Theodore Roosevelt had called a "lunatic fringe." Exchange in Johnson Papers, Correspondence, 1936, No. 43.

early in 1934, "Whether we have been right or wrong in going after the states I don't know. I tell you it isn't any fun, but what can you do? Here's the State of Kentucky. It would not put up money and you say, 'You put up some money or we won't give you any.' They do not put it up. Who gets licked? The unemployed. They always get licked. . . . Believe me, that is a tough order to give. It is going to be a long time before I give another one. There will have to be somebody else to cut off this food from the unemployed."[70]

Hopkins also deplored a still more unfortunate result of the matching requirement. When states did contribute money, he complained, "they would take out public funds for relief with their right hand while cutting their budgets with their left. It licked them."[71] Edith Abbott, an experienced social worker, agreed. Observing that the FERA caused states to cut appropriations for education and welfare, she demanded a strongly centralized federal plan. "The New Deal," she charged, "has been persuaded to keep alive a thoroughly antiquated pauper-relief system that belongs to the days of the oxcart and the stagecoach."[72]

These complaints rang true. Given the sad condition of most state budgets in 1933, the federal government would have been wiser to avoid conflict over state contribu-

[70] Hopkins Remarks to National Emergency Council Conference of State Directors, January 31, 1934, in Case 19, Frank Walker Papers, Notre Dame University Library, South Bend, Ind. Hopkins' reluctance to stop the flow of money did result in dramatically higher amounts of federal aid to states. Between 1932 and 1934 the percentage of state spending from federal sources rose from 8 to 28. It decreased after the end of FERA to 15 percent in 1940. See Frederick C. Mosher and Orville F. Poland, *The Costs of American Governments: Fact, Trends, Myths* (New York, 1964), 162.

[71] Hopkins Remarks.

[72] Edith Abbott, "The Crisis in Relief," *Nation*, CXXXVII (October 11, 1933), 400-02.

tions by replacing the matching fund principle with a system of minimum federal grants plus bonuses to generous states. Yet in 1933-1934, relief was the most pressing need of all, and in requiring state as well as federal funds the FERA merely bowed to a concept of federalism—strong in Canada as well as in the United States—which continued to affirm an ideal of shared responsibilities.[73] To have let the states off scot-free in 1933 might have been as perilous politically as it seemed undesirable economically.

From this perspective the deficiencies of the FERA seem not only predictable but relatively transitory compared to the effect of the agency on the development of state welfare programs. For it forced the states to devote time and money to welfare if they wanted precious dollars from Uncle Sam. Having coped with welfare problems however reluctantly between 1933 and 1935, most of the states found it politically difficult to return in subsequent decades to the poor-law philosophy of the 1920's. Economic crisis and federal response had combined to push the states into a new role which neither prosperity nor conservatism could destroy completely.[74]

[73] The problems of Canadian federalism are excellently portrayed in the *Report of the Royal Canadian Commission on Dominion-Provincial Relations. Book I: Canada, 1867-1939* (Ottawa, 1940). For pertinent remarks on the 1930's see 160-77.

[74] See Tindall, *Emergence of the New South*, 490, for remarks on the effect of federal relief on southern welfare policies. He speaks of a "welfare revolution." For the nation as a whole, change was considerable but somewhat short of revolutionary.

4. State Relief & Welfare, 1935-1940

THE DOLE pleased no one. Chafing at the cost, conservatives attacked it as early as 1934, and even Hopkins yearned for a law which would provide the jobless with useful work. And Roosevelt himself, while also regretting mounting federal deficits, began searching for a more systematic plan of welfare. Prodded into action, Congress finally responded with two key measures in 1935: a work relief law, and social security. Together they would alter permanently the nature of American federalism.

The first to run the congressional gauntlet was the work relief bill which provided the record sum of $4.8 billion. Roosevelt then created the Works Progress Administration to disburse the money and named Hopkins as its head. The WPA's peak years, 1935-1938, occurred under Hopkins' tenure. During this period it gave work to as many as three million jobless annually and spent most of the $10.7 billion distributed from 1935 through 1942.[1] Without it, states could not have begun to handle the task which confronted them.

Like FERA, WPA was a relief program. But it differed in many respects. It provided work relief rather than a dole, was run by federal instead of state officials, and required no specific amount of matching state money. Instead, WPA

[1] U.S. Works Projects Administration, *Final Report on the W.P.A. Program, 1935-43* (Washington, 1946), 110-20, contains useful and convenient statistical data on WPA. The FERA was the New Deal's chief relief agency from 1933 to 1936, aided by the Civil Works Administration, a short-term work relief program, in the winter of 1933-34. The WPA operated from 1935 to 1943.

required states to bear the entire cost of aiding unemployables—"general relief," as it was called. This provision supposedly distinguished between relief for the able—federal jobs—and general relief for the others—doles from states and localities.[2] By creating the two distinct relief categories the government hoped to reduce the federal-state bickering over money which had plagued the FERA.

A few governors objected even before Congress voted the money in May 1935. Most vociferous of these was Eugene Talmadge of Georgia, a rural reactionary who as early as 1933 had told a federal agent, "I don't want to see them [the unemployed], don't let me see them . . . we must steel our hearts against them all as we did against wounds and death in the war."[3] Opposing national control of relief, the governor insisted that states be given money to distribute themselves. Talmadge said he could "make a Garden of Eden out of Georgia," an agent reported. "He stated that the way to handle a relief program was like Mussolini was handling it in Italy, namely 'to line these people up and take the troops and make them work.' "[4] When the WPA began in Georgia, Talmadge did his best to manipulate the money for his own political ends.[5]

Johnson of Colorado, still feuding with Senator Costigan, also grumbled. "Do you not know that you cannot purchase people like so many cattle, and that the respectable people of Colorado will not tolerate the Tammany Hall that you

[2] *Ibid.*, 12ff. See also Maxwell, *Fiscal Impact*, 151ff; and Arthur H. Benedict, "Federal Centralization Through Congressional Legislation," unpublished doctoral dissertation, Ohio State University, 1948, 55ff.

[3] Allen Johnston to Hopkins, September 18, 1933, No. 401.2-420, Box 66, FERA Records, Record Group 69, National Archives, Washington, D.C.

[4] Johnston to Hopkins, March 6, 1935, *ibid.*

[5] Erle Cocke (Georgia State NEC Director) to Major Noce, August 12, 1935, Division of Field Operations, Box 174 (G., 1935), National Emergency Council Records, Record Group 44, National Archives.

are building with Federal funds in the interest of Senator Costigan?" he snapped at the regional WPA administrator.[6] He added that he wanted "no piddling around with leaf-raking projects."[7] Never so callous toward suffering as Talmadge, Johnson continued to prevent smooth administration of relief in Colorado.

Contrary to expectations, the WPA also failed to stop squabbling over money. Conflict stemmed from demands of the states for more money than Hopkins could possibly afford or from federal reprimands to states suspected of parsimony in relief to unemployables.[8] But because the two categories—work relief for the able and state doles for the others—were fairly distinct under the new system, these disagreements amounted to little more than the predictable differences which naturally surround any large distribution of money.

Misunderstandings about the meaning of "unemployable" created further bickering. Both Johnson and Ross of Idaho complained that Hopkins should assume the burden of caring for itinerant farm workers after harvest time. Hopkins disagreed, and the governors sulked.[9] Even Governor Herbert Lehman of New York, Roosevelt's friend, periodically protested WPA rulings. Roosevelt, Lehman contend-

[6] Johnson to Paul D. Shriver, November 18, 1935, Johnson Papers, Correspondence, 1936, No. 181, Colorado State Archives, Denver.

[7] James F. Wickens, "Colorado in the Great Depression: A Study of New Deal Policies at the State Level," unpublished doctoral dissertation, University of Denver, 1964, 287-89.

[8] Governors also constantly demanded speedier action on approval of state-sponsored projects. See WPA records, Boxes 132.1-132.5, August 1935, Record Group 69, National Archives, Washington, D.C.

[9] Ross to FDR, December 23, 1935 and Johnson to FDR, January 27, 1936, Official File (OF) 444-c, Box 24, Roosevelt Papers, Hyde Park, N.Y., for these and many other complaints and suggestions from governors. For an able treatment of Ross see Michael P. Malone, "C. Ben Ross and the New Deal in Idaho," unpublished doctoral dissertation, Washington State University, 1966, esp. 83-120.

ed, had promised that federal money would provide for 396,000 jobless in 1935, leaving only 165,000 for the state to handle. Instead, the WPA included in its quota men previously employed by the Civilian Conservation Corps, thereby dumping some 70,000 new clients on Lehman.[10] Arguing that New York's relatively liberal aid to unemployables was no reason to saddle the state with an extra burden, Lehman continued to protest without success through 1937.[11]

Other governors complained of discrimination. Southern politicians insisted that their states received less per capita than northern and Middle Western states. Governor Kump of West Virginia, furious at the WPA's "deliberate and studied affront . . . expressed in billingsgate and profanity," argued vigorously and persistently along these lines.[12] Urban states countered that they paid much more in federal taxes than they received in benefits. And many states contributing what they considered to be generous amounts for relief of unemployables protested that they received little WPA help in contrast to states which were stingy.

Some of these points were justified. Recalling the squabbling of 1933-1935, Hopkins did not pry too closely into the amount of state aid to unemployables and tended instead to distribute WPA money according to his evaluation of need.[13] One liberal critic, perhaps harshly, termed this method "a kind of super guesswork process," and an economist has argued that "often the well-to-do governmental

10 Lehman to FDR, November 13, 1935, OF 444-c, Box 24, Roosevelt Papers. See also Johnson to FDR, January 22, 1936, Johnson Papers, Correspondence 1936, No. 43, Colorado State Archives.

11 Lehman to FDR, January 18, 1937, Box 29, Roosevelt Papers.

12 Letter, November 7, 1935, Box 23, Kump Papers, University of West Virginia Library, Morgantown. Also Kump to C. L. Allen, November 15, 1935, Box 22, *ibid.*

13 For relevant remarks, Donald S. Howard, *The WPA and Federal Relief Policy* (New York, 1943), 68-69, 110-20, 675ff.

units were more successful at evading their responsibilities than were the poor."[14] It is probable that some states could have appropriated more for general relief, and that the WPA could have penalized parsimony by granting less for work relief.

But Hopkins' primary aim continued to be to provide aid where it was most needed. If urban industrial states received more per capita than southern states, it was because of their higher unemployment per capita and because their higher cost of living made relief more expensive; if southern states received more than they paid in taxes, it was because they were too poor to be important sources of federal revenue. The correlation between relief received and state need seems to have been fairly close during the lifetime of the WPA.[15]

The handling of relief to unemployables distressed liberals most of all. Left alone with this burden, the states too often proved unwilling or unable to shoulder it. Social workers and field men, perceiving acute suffering as early as the summer of 1935, dispatched memos of increasing dismay and disgust. A South Carolina agent observed: "The real problem in this, as well as most of the other states in this Area, is concerned with the fact that there is no functioning Public Welfare agency which can give care to certain groups who will need it after the liquidation of the relief program." An Arizona social worker added, "the public feels the emergency is over and it is a good move to discontinue this agency and issue a 'work or starve' edict." In November, when FERA assistance had already stopped in many states, a federal survey reported that 23 states were unprepared to pick up the burden, and that only two of the others had satisfactory programs in operation. Total

[14] Maxwell, *Fiscal Impact*, 154.

[15] See similar conclusion by Howard, *WPA*, 683-85.

state-local expenditures for relief dropped from $42 to $28 million per month between June and November 1935 and "utter confusion" reigned in many states.[16]

While some states filled this gap by 1937, suffering remained desperate through the decade. Thirteen states turned over general assistance to the local units which had so frugally dispensed relief before the FERA, and conditions in many other states were shocking. The Illinois system, one observer reported, was "truly medieval."[17] Ohio simply "seemed to tire of the relief problem." The do-nothing policy of the New Jersey legislature in 1936 provoked an angry but orderly invasion by relief clients who occupied the legislative chamber for nine days. And Vermont, despite some improvements over the township system which had ruled since colonial times, remained in the "poorhouse stage of development" at the end of the decade.[18]

[16] Report by Loula Dunn on South Carolina, September 16, 1935, No. 132.2, WPA Records, National Archives, Washington, D.C.; for attitudes in Arizona see Eugene Leggett to Frank Walker, November 27, 1935, Case 18, Box 64 (D), 12-13, Frank Walker Papers, Notre Dame University, South Bend, Ind.; and for remarks concerning confusion see Josephine Brown, *Public Relief*, 321. The social security law, passed in September 1935, provided federal matching grants in aid to various types of unemployables.

[17] Samuel Lubell and Walter Everett, "The Breakdown of Relief," *Nation*, CXLVII (August 20, 1938), 171-74. For comments about Illinois relief see also *New York Times*, May 22, 1938, IV, 7; and esp. Arthur P. Miles, "Relief in Illinois Without Federal Aid," *Social Service Review*, XIV (June 1940), 283-300. For more general information see "Direct Relief: State and Local," *State Government*, XIII (January 1940), 12-13; and Brown, *Public Relief*, 350ff.

[18] For Ohio, see David Maurer, "Public Relief Programs and Policies in Ohio, 1929-1939," unpublished doctoral dissertation, Ohio State University, 1962, 3, 134-44; *New York Times*, May 18, 1938, IV, 7; and Clayton Fritchey, "Relief in Ohio," *American Mercury*, L (May 1940), 74-81. For New Jersey see Allan Johnson, "New Jersey Tries Starvation," *New Republic*, LXXXVII (May 13, 1936), 14-15. For Vermont consult the excellent study by Richard M. Judd, "A History of the

A federal report in May 1936 was especially critical. It found general relief "inadequate" in Arizona and Arkansas and "barely adequate" in Idaho. In Colorado it was "very inadequate," in Illinois "critical" and "chaotic," in Nevada "inadequate to maintain health standards." Nine other states were rated "critical" and in nine more, appropriations were "so low it will be impossible to maintain health standards."[19] As social worker Edith Abbott complained justly, "the truth is, of course, that some states are UNABLE—and others are UNWILLING—to carry the load."[20]

The framers of federal policy in 1935 were partly responsible for this situation: the WPA system, unlike the FERA, neither required any minimum state contribution nor provided any means to force stingy states to cooperate. Hopkins, who did not relish punishing the unemployed in order to battle governors, shrank from cutting off federal funds and contented himself with relieving as much suffering as possible through WPA. The jobless would have fared better had the law provided a minimum federal grant for general assistance and given a bonus to those states who exceeded it.

The most debated aspect of the WPA was not its financial but its political effect. Remembering the charges and countercharges under the FERA, New Dealers expected

---

New Deal in Vermont," unpublished doctoral dissertation, Harvard University, 1959, 270.

[19] Report by Lyle Alverson to Hopkins, May 1, 1936, Gen. Correspondence, Box 97, NEC Records. See Papers of Gov. Guy Park (D. Mo., 1933-1937), Folder 1853, for chilling minutes of the state relief commission, January 7, 1936 (University of Missouri Library, Columbia).

[20] Quoted in Maxwell, *Fiscal Impact*, 154. Other careful studies are E. P. Witte, "Social Security Legislation in Nebraska," *Social Service Review*, X (March 1936), 79-108; and William Haber and Herman M. Somers, "The Administration of Public Assistance in Massachusetts," *ibid.*, XII (September 1938), 397-416

such complaints. But because many WPA administrators, unlike their FERA counterparts, were federal appointees, it was difficult to blame state officials for injecting politics in the setup. Instead, Hopkins himself became the target of most of the critics.

Many of these protests came from Republicans or conservatives hostile to continued deficit spending. Regarding WPA grants as pre-election handouts, they pointed to the remarkable success of Democratic bosses such as Senator Joseph Guffey of Pennsylvania and maintained that WPA money was creating "statewide Tammany Halls."[21] And many Democrats, such as Johnson of Colorado, saw the WPA as Roosevelt's way of populating states with New Dealers. These critics insisted that the WPA was little more than a sophisticated and centralized vote buying machine.

Republicans and conservative Democrats were not alone in grumbling. Partisan Democrats protested Hopkins' refusal to reserve key appointments for the party faithful. Hopkins, one wrote in 1935, "seems to entertain the opinion that anyone engaged in political activity must necessarily be totally lacking in brains and ability. His is the silly, effete, and totally mistaken notion that engaging in political life is 'not quite nice.' "[22] Another congressman insisted: "I do not want relief in politics and I know the President doesn't, but when it gets to the point that the Republicans are in charge of it and Democrats are discriminated against both in respect to securing local jobs and in securing food and clothing, it is no wonder that our folks are wondering how such a thing could happen."[23]

[21] Ray Sprigle, "Lord Guffey of Pennsylvania," *American Mercury*, XXXIX (November 1936), 273-84.

[22] Henry Glass, Jr., to Marguerite Le Hand, July 7, 1935, OF 444-Misc, Box 7, Roosevelt Papers.

[23] Rep. Fred Vinson (D. Ky.) to James A. Farley, August 10, 1936, Box 4, Farley Correspondence, Democratic National Committee Rec-

Democrats in New Mexico, where politics were raw and open, were especially demanding. From the start Democratic Governor Arthur Seligman requested—and got—lists noting the political preference of all relief and CCC workers in the state.[24] While no evidence exists to show that he made improper use of the lists, they revealed concern for his alliance with progressive Republicans under the leadership of Senator Bronson Cutting. But this partiality to Cutting infuriated Democrats, one of whom insisted that "the most important thing to be done is to wean the nondescript Cutting adherents from the relief tit which they have been and are now sucking and at the same time biting the hand that feeds them."[25] Seligman's death in 1933, Cutting's in 1935, and hardheaded organization by partisan Democrats pushed the progressive Republicans from prominence by 1936 and opened the way for new feuding within the dominant Democratic party. In the meantime, repeated warnings from the WPA testified to the precarious position of relief administration in politically conscious New Mexico.

Most of these feuds were restrained before 1937, but when the tide began to turn against the Democrats, local politicians spoke more frankly, demanding that WPA be a purely Democratic operation. One critic wrote, "What I think will help is to change the WPA management from top to bottom. Put men in there who are . . . in favor of using these Democratic projects to make votes for the Democratic

---

ords, Roosevelt Library. These records, especially Boxes 4 and 6, contain many complaints along this line.

[24] Seligman Papers, New Deal Agencies, February-September, 1933 Folder, State Archives, Santa Fe.

[25] Claude T. Smith to Gov. Clyde Tingley, January 7, 1935, Tingley Papers, Political File, New Mexico State Archives. Tingley, an anti-Cutting Democrat, replied, "The situation may be improved in the near future." (January 10, 1935, *ibid.*) It was.

Party."[26] A distraught New Hampshire Democrat complained after the 1938 elections, "it is my personal belief that to the victor belongs the spoils and that Democrats should be holding most of these positions so that we might strengthen our fences for the 1940 election."[27] These politicians were not simply greedy; they understandably resented the "holier than thou" attitude of nonpartisan administrators.

The most troublesome cases occurred in states where Democratic factions warred with one another. One such state was West Virginia, where Governor Kump's friends were locked in battle against a group headed by Senator Matthew Neely. Miss Hickok, surveying the situation, was dismayed. "It is just one awful political mess," she wrote. "A Kump controlled relief administration out to wreck a Neeley [sic] -Holt controlled works progress administration. I declare I don't know who is worse."[28] Another was Indiana, where a federal agent warned: "The Democratic Party . . . is seriously split at the present time. . . . WPA is being used to aid and abet the state house faction. If this is allowed to continue, the Federal Administration will fall heir to all of the opprobrium that is now visited upon the state administration."[29] Similar expressions of concern came from agents in Davey's Ohio, Guffey's Pennsylvania, Laffoon's Kentucky, and other states.

Serious enough in 1935-1936, these accusations could no

[26] V. G. Coplen (Democratic County Chairman, Ind.) to Farley, December 12, 1938, OF 300, Box 104, Roosevelt Papers.

[27] James W. Doherty to Farley, December 23, 1938, *ibid.*, Box 105. This is a most useful collection of letters concerning state attitudes on the WPA after the 1938 election.

[28] Hickok Report, November 3, 1935, Box 89, Hopkins Papers. Also Helene Gifford Report, September 16, 1935, No. 132.2, WPA Records.

[29] Clarence Manion to executive assistant of NEC, August 26, 1935, Box 404, NEC Records.

longer be ignored in 1938, when a particularly unsavory senatorial primary in Kentucky led to well-substantiated charges that both Democratic protagonists, Governor Albert B. (Happy) Chandler and Senator Alben W. Barkley, were using relief money to build political machines. Concerned, the Senate established an investigating committee whose report in January 1939 revealed "unjustifiable political activity" in Kentucky, Tennessee, and Pennsylvania.[30] From then on the WPA had to fight constant congressional criticism, more investigations, and repeated cuts in appropriations. Well before Pearl Harbor, its future was bleak.

Because of these controversies, many came to regard WPA as a gigantic giveaway to loafers who became lifelong Democrats in the process. In fact, not Hopkins but congressmen and state politicians were to blame for most of the political favoritism which did exist. Had the WPA been unable to name most of its key personnel, the relief program might well have spawned feuds, maladministration, and political preference on a scale undreamed of by Hopkins' most persistent critics.

A primarily national operation, the WPA was for that reason more successful than the FERA in avoiding federal-state controversy over money and appointments. Moreover WPA funds saved the jobless in practically every state. But its political impartiality infuriated all partisans in faction-ridden states, and its division of responsibility for welfare into work and direct relief was disastrous to unemployables. It is even arguable that the bickering engendered by the FERA's matching grant principle, however distressing, was preferable to the separation of duties under the

[30] For substance of report see *New York Times*, January 4, 1939, 1. A report emphasizing the *lack* of political use of WPA is "WPA Scandals of 1938," *New Republic*, XCVII (January 18, 1939), 300-01.

WPA. At any rate, neither agency succeeded in perfecting cooperative federalism in relief policy.

But the weaknesses of both operations were more the fault of lingering laissez-faire ideology than of organization. The *sine qua non* of successful relief policy was abundant appropriations. But sources of revenue were scarce. More important, most congressmen and state legislators were unfamiliar with Keynesian ideas of deficit spending in times of depression, and they carefully watched every penny. And any system of federal bonuses for generous states—while preferable from the humanitarian point of view—was politically unrealistic because of objections by fiscal conservatives to its expense. A wholly satisfactory relief program depended on the creation of new attitudes toward public spending for those unable to help themselves. But such changes in thinking rarely occur quickly, and the 1930's were no exception. That states and counties continued to bear the major responsibility for general relief in the 1960's reveals the persistence of the notion that they, together with private charity, could or should do the job themselves.

The WPA was but half of a double-barrelled federal plan to attack social deprivation after 1935. The other was social security. Where WPA was an emergency relief measure, the social security law sought to provide permanent government assistance to the blind, dependent children, and elderly.

The necessity for such a program, long accepted in many other Western nations, had been obvious to social workers for decades. But few politicians had answered the call. In 1934, 24 states supplied money for the needy blind and 28 for the indigent over 65. Aid to dependent children was available in 45 states. But these laws generally provided tiny sums to insignificant numbers. Old age assistance in

1934 offered an average of $16.21 per month per recipient to but 400,000 people.[31] By 1933 only Wisconsin had an unemployment compensation system—and even it had yet to pay benefits.

Anticipating federal action, some legislatures in 1935 moved tentatively toward remedies.[32] Seven states approved old age assistance plans by August 1935, leaving only 13 (9 of them southern) without such legislation when Congress acted in September.[33] Fifteen others liberalized existing laws.[34] And 7 states passed unemployment compensation programs.[35] But because none provided the necessary funds, these acts offered little meaningful assistance. All states awaited magic from Washington.

The package they received was extremely complex, for the social security law featured many formulas for the needs to be serviced. Perhaps the simplest provision was for old age insurance. It imposed a federal tax on employers and employees to be deposited into a reserve fund. Contributors would receive pensions from this fund at age 65. Because this part of the bill involved a direct federal-employer and federal-employee relationship, it had only an indirect effect on state politics or finance.

Not so with the other two key clauses. One, unemployment compensation, was a compromise plan calling for a mandatory 3 percent federal tax on payrolls. Those em-

[31] Richard E. Dawson and James A. Robinson, "The Politics of Welfare," in Herbert Jacob and Kenneth Vines, eds., *Politics in the American States: A Comparative Analysis* (Boston, 1965), 371-410. Also Abraham Epstein, "Killing Old Age Security with Kindness," *Harpers*, CLXXV (July 1937), 182-92.

[32] "State Legislation Proposed," Boxes 66-75, Committee on Economic Security, Social Security Records, Record Group 47, National Archives.

[33] *Labor Information Bulletin*, II (August 1935), 4.

[34] *Monthly Labor Review*, XLI (November 1935), 1178-83.

[35] Joseph P. Harris, "State Responsibility," *State Government*, VIII (October 1935), 191-96.

ployers who contributed specified amounts to state-sponsored unemployment compensation funds would be relieved of 90 percent of this tax. Because no state dared to encumber its corporations with the entire burden, this requirement forced states to pass legislation implementing the federal plan. The act also forbade states to divert these funds for other purposes and necessitated disbursement of the money through federally approved public agencies on the state level. An amendment in 1939 also required hiring of state unemployment compensation personnel on a merit basis.[36] Otherwise, states enjoyed a free hand.

Provisions to help the indigent aged, dependent children, and blind were just as complicated. Most previous federal grants—for highways, agricultural extension work, and vocational education—had apportioned specific annual amounts according to population and such other physical factors as road mileage or area.[37] The new assistance grants featured percentages. The federal government promised to pay $1 for every $2 contributed by states for assistance to the blind and aged and $1 for every $3 appropriated for dependent children.[38] The act also set maximum federal grants—$15 per month per recipient to the aged or blind and $6 per recipient to dependent children. Other sections demanded federally approved state agencies, cash payments, and more liberal eligibility requirements than existed in most state laws.[39]

The states responded quickly. Before 1935 many had feared that unemployment compensation plans (which called for employer contributions) would drive marginal corporations to states without such laws, resulting in unem-

[36] Benedict, "Federal Centralization," 65ff.

[37] V. O. Key, Jr., *The Administration of Federal Grants to States* (Chicago, 1937), 320-31.

[38] Benedict, "Federal Centralization," 67ff.

[39] Harris, "State Responsibility," 191-96.

ployment and loss of tax revenue. The new federal tax relieved this fear by requiring all businesses with eight or more employees to participate. Anxious to provide employers with rebates for the 1935 tax year, states hurriedly called special sessions to pass the necessary cooperative laws. A few recalcitrant states, unwilling to be pushed, waited until 1936. But by 1937 all states had enacted approved systems, and by mid-1939 all plans were operating.[40]

States were almost as fast in taking advantage of matching funds for the aged, the blind, and dependent children. By 1939 all had passed acceptable old age assistance plans, and benefits for all three types of aid had increased. The new atmosphere in many states resembled that of Texas, where "federal money not only encouraged the legislature to take action, but made the state financially able to make the transition from a complete laissez-faire attitude toward social welfare functions to a more positive approach toward solving the many problems in that area."[41]

The act also modernized administrative procedures. Many states had already centralized relief operations to receive FERA funds. The new stipulations against local supervision encouraged still more centralization and reorganization. Many states passed social welfare acts creating departments of public welfare, and practically all made some improvements.[42] "Several years ago," one authority remarked

[40] Harry Malisoff, "The Emergence of Unemployment Compensation," *Political Science Quarterly*, LIV (June, September, December 1939), 237-58, 391-420, 577-99; and R. Gordon Wagenet, "Job Insurance Looks Toward a New Year," *State Government*, XII (January 1939), 5-6, 15ff.

[41] William M. Griffin, "The Impact of Federal Grants-in-Aid on Certain Aspects of Texas State Government," unpublished doctoral dissertation, University of Texas, 1959, 102. A brief general survey is in *State Government*, XI (May 1938), 86.

[42] For changes in Connecticut see Rowland Mitchell, Jr., "Social Legislation in Connecticut, 1919-1939," unpublished doctoral dissertation, Yale University, 1954, 431-44.

in 1935, "the discussion of welfare in a governor's inaugural address was the exception; today it has become the rule."[43]

All these developments liberalized benefits by the late 1930's. A few states provided more than the $30 per month necessary to receive the maximum $15 federal grant for old age assistance, and ten states quickly approved unemployment compensation systems which covered businesses with fewer than eight employees—the number required by law.[44] State expenditures for the three kinds of assistance rose from some $9 million in 1930 to $479 million in 1940.[45] And unemployment compensation benefits for 700,000 people totaled $480 million in June 1940, compared to nothing in 1935. "During the years between 1929 and 1939," one knowledgeable social worker concluded in 1940, "more progress was made in public welfare and relief than in the three hundred years after this country was first settled."[46]

Federal-state friction inevitably accompanied these advances. Some governors resented the "blackmail" of the unemployment compensation provision offering tax credits to cooperating states.[47] A few disliked having to call spe-

43 L. Laszlo Ecker-R, "Centripetal Force," *State Government*, VIII (May 1935), 113-15. Also R. Clyde White, "Recent Public Welfare and Social Security Legislation in Indiana," *Social Service Review*, X (June 1936), 206-26; and Wilfred S. Reynolds, "Public Welfare Administration a Patchwork in Illinois," *ibid.*, XI (March 1937), 1-8. Congressmen, however, continued to resent the staffing of state welfare posts by civil service personnel. See especially Arthur Altmeyer, *Formative Years of Social Security* (Madison, 1966), 49, for an extreme example of congressional hostility.

44 Daniel L. Goldy, "Unemployment Compensation Laws Surveyed," *State Government*, X (May 1937), 93-97.

45 Council on State Governments, *State-Local Relations* (Chicago, 1946), 3.

46 Brown, *Public Relief*, ix. For statistics see Social Security Board, *5th Annual Report* (Washington, 1941), 57; and Maxwell, *Fiscal Impact*, 131-34.

47 *Proceedings of the 1936 Governors Conference*, 7-52, 78.

cial sessions to receive these credits in 1935 and 1936. Others rebelled against administrative requirements, leading one federal worker to complain about the "constant evasion of realities which we meet on the part of those who should be leaders."[48] Still others, including some liberals, objected to federal bureaucracy. "If you don't believe us to be budget-wise," one state official wrote the social security board, "why not save thousands of dollars and get some good will, *which your Board does not have in any Unemployment Compensation Administration*, by sending someone you do trust to make up the budget. Am I mad? No. Am I personal? No. I'm just disgusted."[49]

A few ultraconservative governors stormed against federal interference on principle and even threatened to refuse the tainted money from Washington. "We claim no super-intelligence," Michigan's Frank D. Fitzgerald told fellow governors in 1935, "Yet we DO believe we know more about the conditions and requirements of our neighbors at home than do the learned theorists sitting at desks in Washington."[50] His Republican colleague in Maryland, Harry W. Nice, agreed: "People were deceived by these Hans Andersen fairy tales, only to find that at the end of the rainbow, there was no pot of gold. . . . No possible emergency can justify the philosophy which has been injected into our national government of scrapping the states and filling the land with federal agents."[51]

Considering the newness of the scheme and its intricate administrative requirements, such complaints were remarkably rare. For one reason, the social security law reflected

[48] Elsa Feuerbach to Mrs. Ben Franklin, September 26, 1936, No. 062.2/85, Box 68, Region 6, Central File, Social Security Records.

[49] C. A. Jackson to Arthur Altmeyer, January 15, 1938, Box 108, Indiana 500, Social Security Records.

[50] *Proceedings of the Governors Conference of 1935*, 103.

[51] *Ibid.*, 57-58.

Roosevelt's approval of state experimentation. While the unemployment compensation plan was certainly blackmail of a sort, states were free to adopt their own systems and were not even forced to contribute funds. Matching grant formulas for assistance offered $1 for every $2 of state money and permitted legislatures to appropriate as little as they wanted. Governors were also free to finance the plans as they wished and until 1939 to staff the new agencies with political cronies. Most governors found it easy to comply with congressional standards, and only Davey of Ohio lost benefits for failure to follow regulations.[52]

The overwhelming need for assistance explained this cooperation. Governor Wilbur Cross of Connecticut, a moderate Democrat sometimes at odds with New Dealers, described the feeling of most of his peers. "Am I to understand," he asked partisan opponents, "that if you Republicans come into power you intend to dam up the flow of Federal funds and to start a flow of your own by an enormous increase in state and local taxation to care for the unemployable and to provide work for the able bodied unemployed? . . . In the emergency I am ready to lay aside the unsubstantial ghost of state sovereignty. I am ready to accept funds for the aged, the crippled, for humane and educational institutions, for the extension of highways, and even for the extermination of mosquitos in the marshes along the shore."[53] It was an unanswerable argument which no humane and politically astute governor could afford to ignore.

Most attacks on the social security system came not from governors waving the banner of states' rights but from liberal authorities on social insurance who cried for a more strictly

[52] Maxwell, *Fiscal Impact*, 121. Able federal advisers helped states avoid pitfalls; Arthur Altmeyer, *Formative Years*, 54.

[53] Wilbur Cross, *Connecticut Yankee*, 344.

national system. These experts argued that the kind of federalism which gave ample leeway to states was impractical in the realm of social security.

One target of their criticism was unemployment compensation. To begin with, they argued, it called for an awkward administrative structure which could never accommodate the masses of mobile workers crossing state lines. It also failed to eliminate competition for industry, and most states, afraid of driving marginal businesses elsewhere, refused to approve anything more than the bare minimum. These critics demanded administration by the national government which could set its own minimum standards and then give subsidies to generous states. Or they insisted that states contribute a minimum percentage of total payrolls to the fund.[54]

The matching grants for the various kinds of assistance especially upset these critics, who observed that percentage formulas caused wide variations in benefits. Several wealthy states appropriated the full $30 to receive the maximum federal grant of $15. The indigent aged in these states thus received at least $45 per month. But because Congress had set a limit of $15 for the federal contribution, even the wealthier states were reluctant to appropriate more than $30. Rather than rewarding generosity with bonuses, the formula tended to limit state appropriations, and the average monthly payment per recipient of old age assistance in

[54] For descriptions of trends in the various states see Maxwell, *Fiscal Impact*, 225-27; and *State Government*, X (May 1937), 95, and XI (September 1938), 169. See Arthur Schlesinger, Jr., *The Coming of the New Deal* (Boston, 1958), 296-97, for the Roosevelt administration's decision to press for a state plan. See especially Altmeyer, *Formative Years*, 85ff, for wise retrospective criticism; and Hansen and Perloff, *State and Local Finance*, 157-62. Hansen noted that benefits in 1941 ranged from $5.90 per week to $14.57—hardly an end to interstate rivalry.

1942 was a lordly $21.83.[55] In the poorer states conditions were frightful. Because the formula did not specify any minimum, some states, either cautious or callous, offered as little as $4 per month per recipient—or a total of $6 including the federal grant. Even in the deflated dollar of the 1930's, this sum was below subsistence level. Although later amendments would increase the federal contribution to 50 percent, the system continued to widen rather than narrow the gap between rich and poor states. The extent of need was unfortunately the least important part of the formula.[56]

Aware of these weaknesses, liberals struggled to amend the system in 1939. They suggested a new formula by which federal assistance grants would vary inversely with state ability to pay. Congress quickly sidetracked the proposal. Rebuffed, they proposed that the federal government offer a minimum grant of $7.50 per month per recipient—a change which would have substantially increased benefits in the poorer states. But here Roosevelt himself intervened. "Not one nickel more," he snapped, "Not one solitary nickel. Once you get off the . . . matching basis the sky's the limit, and before you know it, we'll be paying the whole bill."[57] Roosevelt's fiscal conservatism served to perpetuate an awkward and badly financed relief system.

The percentage formula also helped to distort state budgets. Tempted by the assistance grants and scared by pressure groups seeking higher old age benefits, some states

55 Hansen and Perloff, *State and Local Finance,* 24-26.

56 For critical comments see Maxwell, *Fiscal Impact,* 123-30; Abraham Epstein, "The Future of Social Security," *New Republic,* LXXXIX (January 27, 1937), 373-76; *New York Times,* November 6, 1938, IV, 7; Key, *Administration of Federal Grants,* 334-36; and Brown, *Public Relief,* 421. Roy Lubove, in *The Struggle for Social Security, 1900-1935* (Cambridge, Mass., 1968), 175-78, notes Epstein's disgust with the social security law.

57 Quoted in Altmeyer, *Formative Years,* 112.

enacted unrealistically generous old age assistance laws in an effort to curry favor with the aged. Colorado adopted a constitutional amendment in 1936 legalizing extra support for the aged and lowering the age limit from 65 to 60. Governor Johnson then approved a plan giving $12 weekly per inhabitant for old age assistance—or some $4 more per resident than the next most generous state. Despite diversion of excise, license, and liquor taxes, the hard-pressed state was unable to pay the promised amounts to the aged and had to scrimp indefensibly in its payments for general assistance.[58] Combined with pressure group politics, the federal formula sometimes worked to the advantage of the aged; its effect upon others was not so fortunate.

These were considerable disadvantages. A better formula would have based the federal subsidy on need and rewarded generous states with bonuses. Such a system would have been no more difficult to administer. More important, it would have been less likely to distort state budgets, and it would have established a minimum for welfare payments. The social security law, as its critics pointed out, needed more, not less, federal control over the states.

The post-1935 welfare system had one more especially unhappy if unavoidable by-product. In asking for more welfare spending at a time when money was hard to find, social security induced states to seek new sources of revenue. The result was the creation of state tax structures more regressive than those of the 1920's.

Trends in state spending during the 1930's reflected the great impact of outlays for welfare. In 1930 states spent approximately $2 billion, more than half of which went for highways and education. The economy campaign arrested

[58] For Colorado see Wickens, "Colorado," 345ff. Joseph P. Harris, "The Future of Federal Grants-in-Aid," *Annals of the American Academy of Political and Social Science*, CCVII (January 1940), 14-26, gives a general treatment of this problem.

spending in the early depression years, but by 1934 it crept upward once again. The emergency, combined with Hopkins' insistence on state contributions under the FERA, caused a two-fold per capita increase in state welfare spending. New taxes plus somewhat improved economic conditions then netted more revenue after 1935, and state expenditures rose steadily throughout the peacetime years before 1942. Thus state spending in 1940 (exclusive of money received from federal grants) totaled $3.8 billion, almost double that of 1930.[59] Though highways and schools continued to be the most expensive items, their costs increased only slightly during the decade, while the amount spent for welfare practically tripled. States spent 1 percent of total expenditures on welfare in 1922, 5 percent in 1932, and 13 percent in 1942.[60]

Forced into such expenditure, states had to find a way to pay the bills. This was not easy, for traditional sources of revenue were drying up. Bankrupt localities, hard hit by continued decreases in revenue from property taxes, turned to states, forcing them to pay an increasing share of the state-local bill. But states, remembering the evil days of 1930-1934, dared not issue bonds. Even gasoline, liquor, and chain store taxes were far from enough to balance budgets.[61]

[59] For a careful and convincing study of changes in state spending see Solomon Fabricant, *The Trend of Governmental Activity in the United States Since 1900* (New York, 1952), 122-30, 258-59.

[60] Bureau of Census, *Historical Statistics on State and Local Government Finances, 1902-1953* (Washington, 1955), 16-17, 22.

[61] For new taxes in the depression years see Simeon E. Leland, "12 and ½ Bills," *State Government*, XI (January 1938), 9-11; James Maxwell, *Financing State and Local Governments* (Washington, 1965), 88ff; Dayton D. McKean, "The Spread of Chain Store Taxes," *New Republic*, LXXXVII (May 27, 1936), 67-69; Clarence Heer, "Taxation in the New Social State: Coordination of American Finance," *Nation*, CXXXIX (December 19, 1934), 705-07; and James W. Martin, "Depression's Taxes," *State Government*, VII (April 1934), 73-76.

Some states turned to personal and corporate income taxes, and considering the neglect into which these had fallen since the progressive era, the new trend heartened New Dealers. Whereas only one state had enacted a new personal income levy between 1921 and 1928, 15 more did so between 1929 and 1940, for a total of 29.[62] Most of these states also added corporate levies. Since income and corporate taxes were potentially the most progressive, it seemed as if either the depression or the social security system had induced states to tax the wealthy to aid the needy.

The fact was otherwise. Federal income taxes after the revenue laws of 1932 and 1935 were higher than before, and little federal-state cooperation in tax collection existed.[63] For these reasons, it was very difficult to raise state levies as well, and the amounts available from these sources were rather small. Other obstacles to such taxes were state constitutions, competition to attract industry, and a lack of legal and administrative talent in the states. New York and Wisconsin obtained substantial revenue from income levies, but in states with low per capita incomes the yield was disappointing.[64] Despite the rash of new laws, state revenue from individual income taxes rose only slightly during the 1930's.

[62] Maxwell, *Fiscal Impact*, 261-62; Clarence Heer, "The Place of Personal Income Taxes in a Modern Fiscal System," *Annals of the American Academy of Political and Social Science*, CLXXXIII (January 1936), 78-85; Roy G. Blakey and Violet Johnson, "State Income Taxation," *Taxes*, XIX (March-June 1941), 131-36, 222-33, 280-86, 353-61; and Clara Penniman and Walter Heller, *State Income Tax Administration* (Chicago, 1959), 7-9.

[63] The lack of fiscal coordination between states and the national government has worried many students of taxation and of federalism. Even Morton Grodzins, who called the 1930's the "triumph of cooperative federalism," admitted an "extreme lack of coordination between national and state fiscal policies." Ed., Daniel Elazar, *The American System: A New View of Government in the United States* (Chicago, 1966), 55.

[64] Hansen and Perloff, *State and Local Finance*, 63-64, 264.

The total income obtained from such taxes had amounted to 10.1 percent of state revenue in 1927; in 1940 it had crept upward to 10.9 percent.[65] Corporate taxes were even less productive, yielding only 4 percent of state funds.[66] While good times in the 1940's and 1950's increased income tax yields considerably—they amounted to 17 percent of state revenue in 1956—the depression years were by no means progressive in the history of state finance.

Blocked in attempts to raise revenue by traditional means, many states looked elsewhere. The result was a mushrooming of regressive sales taxes. Before 1932 a few had enacted merchants' or manufacturers' license taxes which had passed along higher prices to consumers. But revenue from these was small, and not until 1932 did Mississippi hit upon the newer, more profitable general retail sales tax on consumers' goods.[67]

Other states quickly imitated Mississippi—20 more during the dark years between 1933 and 1935. By the end of 1937, 28 states were gathering revenue from such taxes, and in 5 other cases they had been repealed, or struck down by state courts.[68] By 1938, general sales taxes brought in some $470 million, by 1940, $500 million. Other consumer taxes —on gasoline, tobacco, liquor, soft drinks, and oleomargarine—harvested an additional $1.1 billion. Together, these taxes accounted for 53 percent of state funds in 1940, as

65 Penniman and Heller, *State Income Tax*, 8. See also *Federal State and Local Fiscal Relations*, 78th Cong., 1st Sess., Sen. Doc. 69, 431-32.

66 Hansen and Perloff, *State and Local Finance*, 38.

67 Neil Jacoby, *Retail Sales Taxation: An Analysis of Economic and Administrative Problems* (Chicago, 1938), 23-72, describes the spread of sales taxes.

68 *Ibid.*, 71. For the legislative battles surrounding adoption of these taxes see Dayton D. McKean, *Pressures on the Legislature of New Jersey* (New York, 1938), 154-64; Puryear, *Democratic Party Dissension*, 156-76; and Francis R. Aumann, "From White to Bricker," in Harlow Lindley, ed., *Ohio in the Twentieth Century*, 66-76.

opposed to 43 percent in 1931.[69] States had indeed discovered a windfall.[70]

Primarily because of these taxes, most states were able to retire old bond issues, decrease property levies, and pay the increasing welfare bill while at the same time arresting the rate of increase in their debts. Some even showed surpluses. While gross federal debt increased between 1930 and 1940 from $16.4 billion to $43.4 billion, local debt inched up only from $15.6 to $16.7 billion and state debt from $2.4 to $3.5 billion.[71] The greater portion of this increase in state debt occurred during the revenue-scarce years before 1934, when indebtedness had reached $3.2 billion. While Washington was paying the bills after 1934, states were turning strongly against the deficit financing of the 1920's, adhering conservatively to pay-as-you-go, and emerging by 1940 in considerably stronger financial positions than they had enjoyed ten years earlier.

The price paid for this financial stability was higher taxes. Despite poor economic conditions, states almost doubled their revenues, collecting $2.1 billion from all sources in 1930 and $4.1 billion in 1940.[72] This remarkable change was as great as the absolute rise in federal revenue at the same time and even greater than the relative federal increase. Most of it came from essentially nonprogressive levies, especially the sales tax. As economists pointed out later, higher state taxes more than offset the mildly expansionary federal fiscal policy after 1934 and depressed

[69] Hansen and Perloff, *State and Local Finance*, 37-38. These taxes accounted for 61 percent of state revenue in 1936.

[70] Jacoby, *Retail Sales*, 351; Maxwell, *Financing*, 44-45.

[71] An excellent article which includes estimates of state debt capacities is Edna Trull, "Resources and Debts of the 48 States," *National Municipal Review*, XXVII (June 1938), 293-98. For historical trends, *Federal State and Local Fiscal Relations*, 78th Cong., Sen. Doc. 69, 358.

[72] "U.S. Taxes," *Fortune*, XVI (December 1937), 107-09, 188ff; and Mosher and Poland, *Costs of American Government*, 97-99.

purchasing power at a time when it most needed to be stimulated.[73]

The legacy of federal welfare policy after 1935 was thus somewhat uneven. WPA, while providing work for millions of people, abandoned unemployables to overly frugal states. Social security, though a milestone in the history of American social legislation, tended to magnify variations in state welfare spending and to induce distortions in state budgets. And both programs, while educating states to the need of spending for social well-being, encouraged them to adopt regressive taxes in paying their bills.[74]

Had states been assigned a lesser role, conditions probably would have been better. Unemployables could have received higher benefits. And the needy aged, blind, and dependent would have fared better under a formula which demanded minimum state expenditures and which recognized interstate differences in the extent of need.

Whether such legislation was politically possible in 1935 is debatable. While some politicians had long since despaired of state government, many congressmen disagreed —conservatives because they cherished states rights and economy, liberals because they insisted on state responsibility, and moderates because they wanted to pull states into the welfare apparatus of modern government. Led by Sena-

[73] Authoritative accounts of the regressive character of state-local finance in the 1930's are E. Cary Brown, "Fiscal Policy in the 'Thirties: A Reappraisal," *American Economic Review*, XLVI (December 1956), 857-79; and Hansen and Perloff, *State and Local Finance*, esp. 48-51.

[74] That many of these same problems occurred in Canada—and for some of the same reasons—suggests the wisdom of a gentle retrospective judgment of the welfare experts of the 1930's. The similar Canadian experience also underscores the limitations imposed by the federal system on national officials in both countries. See *Report of the Royal Commission on Dominion-Provincial Relations*, I, 160-77, and II, 125; and Robert MacGregor Dawson, *The Government of Canada*, 4th edn. rev. by Norman Ward (Toronto, 1963), 108-24.

tor Harry F. Byrd of Virginia, the Senate insisted on giving states a major role for fiscal and racial reasons, and succeeded in striking a clause which would have provided a minimum standard of assistance "compatible with decency and health."[75] Other congressmen, afraid of the conservative Supreme Court, favored state participation for practical reasons. And Roosevelt himself opposed nationalistic programs aimed at minimizing state responsibility. While experience has suggested that a national program would have been desirable, this judgment was by no means so clear in the 1930's.[76]

If a more strictly national operation was unattainable in the 1930's, an essentially state system certainly would have been disastrous. To have asked states to carry more of the load was unthinkable. If federal officials had insisted on generous state contributions, the result would have been even more regressive taxation and unlimited federal-state controversy. If they had not, few states would have had the funds and fewer yet the will to improve substantially the sorry standards of 1929.

Imperfect though it was, the mixed system of 1935 provided desperately needed dollars while carrying on the ideal of federal-state responsibility for welfare. The governor of 1929 had safely ignored unemployment; after all, were not private and local agencies relieving suffering? But the governor of 1939 enjoyed no such luxury. He might —and too often did—slight the task of general relief, but he risked political extinction if he defied the social security

[75] Altmeyer, *Formative Years*, 39.

[76] Schlesinger, *Coming of the New Deal*, 299-305; Altmeyer, *Formative Years*, 22. It is also relevant to note that the opposition to a largely national welfare program did not include many liberals; not until the 1960's would liberals steadily assail the cumbersome, bureaucratic nature of relief policy as it developed and centralized itself in the years since the New Deal.

system, with all the federal money it promised to pour into his state. It is said of some conservatives that they have had to be dragged kicking and screaming into the twentieth century. State governors were hardly so reactionary as that, but it is almost certainly true that state welfare programs in the 1930's and subsequent decades would have been less generous without the prodding, indeed the extortion, of New Deal legislation.

5. Groping for Coordination, 1933-1940

"A VERY long experience convinces me of two things," Roosevelt wrote in 1935, "If forty states go along with adequate legislation and eight do not . . . we get nowhere."[1]

Had relief and welfare presented the only battles at that time between the federal government and the states, Roosevelt might not have been so concerned. Unfortunately, however, for the advocates of limited and tidy government, the New Deal hatched a flock of additional new and controversial agencies between 1933 and 1937. To coordinate these programs in the states in a time of such rapid change proved a formidable business indeed.

Not all of these new operations directly affected governors and legislatures. The Securities and Exchange Commission and the Civilian Conservation Corps were federal organizations requiring no state administration. The National Labor Relations Board, Agricultural Adjustment Administration, and Farm Security Administration tended to bypass state government,[2] and a few other agencies, such as

[1] Roosevelt to David Grey, June 17, 1935, PPF 454, Roosevelt Papers, Hyde Park.

[2] Arthur Benedict, "Federal Centralization Through Congressional Legislation, 1924-1939," unpublished doctoral dissertation, Ohio State University, 1948, 541-42. Also Sidney Baldwin, "The Farm Security Administration: A Study in Politics and Administration," unpublished doctoral dissertation, Syracuse University, 1956, 293-347. This is not to say that these agencies ran smoothly. On the contrary, sharp conflict abounded at the *national* level. See Richard S. Kirkendall, *Social Scientists and Farm Policies in the Age of Roosevelt* (Columbia, Mo., 1966), 70-74, 109-12, for examples of friction in the Department of Agriculture.

the Rural Electrification Administration and the Federal Housing Administration, demanded only minimum state action. And in at least one case, that of the United States Housing Administration created in 1937, liberal congressmen deliberately enacted a federal-local instead of a federal-state operation in order to escape rurally based state legislatures. All these creations involved at most token state appropriations and little change in administrative structure. Most legislatures gladly complied.[3]

Of these essentially national agencies, only the Public Works Administration, headed by Interior Secretary Harold L. Ickes, managed to infuriate state officials. Most states quickly passed the enabling legislation to facilitate PWA grants and loans.[4] But Ickes, an irascible liberal suspicious of local politicians, outraged impatient governors by delaying approval of projects.[5] Other state officials resented Ickes' indifference to local politics.[6] Still others heatedly

[3] V. O. Key, Jr., "State Legislation Facilitative of Federal Action," *Annals of the American Academy of Political and Social Science*, CCVII (January 1940), 7-13. The irony of the USHA was that the federal-local relationship set up a head-to-head struggle between the housing authority and local real estate people. See Robert M. Fisher, *Twenty Years of Public Housing: Economic Aspects of the Federal Program* (New York, 1959), 109.

[4] Key, "State Legislation." Also "Report to the President of December 18, 1936, on Status of Legislation Cleared by the National Emergency Council," Entry 126, Box 1559, NEC Records, Record Group 44, National Archives, Washington, D.C. It reveals the outcome of 166 bills cleared between March 1935 and December 15, 1936. For evidence of Roosevelt's own considerable part in prodding governors to pass enabling legislation for PWA see OF 52 (Governors Conferences), 1934, Roosevelt Papers.

[5] James Wickens, "Colorado in the Great Depression: A Study of New Deal Politics at the State Level," unpublished doctoral dissertation, University of Denver, 1964, 182-92.

[6] For an example see Elmo R. Richardson, "Western Politics and New Deal Policies: A Study of T. A. Walters of Idaho," *Pacific Northwest Quarterly* (January 1963), 9-18.

opposed his efforts to create recreation areas out of land valuable in mineral content.[7] Though these conflicts were often acrimonious, states were too anxious to get PWA funds to resist effectively, and Ickes usually had his way. And because PWA was primarily a federal-local rather than a federal-state operation, states needed to make no important administrative or financial changes. Despite occasional clashes, PWA proved a financial boon to states unwilling or unable to appropriate substantially for public works.

But other programs required more active state participation.[8] Federal labor and resource planning officials tried constantly to persuade states to contribute funds or to vote more liberal standards, and other agencies deluged legislators with suggestions, appeals for cooperative laws, and gratuitous advice.[9] State officials, bewildered by the number of lobbyists crowding legislative corridors, had to consider a host of federally proposed bills with little time to study them and even less knowledge of their ultimate effect. Only a few months after the start of the New Deal, state and federal personnel were beginning to recognize the need for more efficient coordination of the many new agencies which had proliferated by the end of 1933.

Roosevelt began to move as soon as Congress adjourned in 1933. In June he created the Executive Council composed of cabinet officers plus 13 other top agency administrators, and in July he named Frank Walker, a trusted aide, as

[7] Richardson, "Federal Park Policy in Utah: The Escalante National Monument Controversy," *Utah Historical Quarterly* (Spring 1965), 110-32.

[8] Jane Perry Clark, *The Rise of a New Federalism* (New York, 1938), passim, provides a readable contemporary survey.

[9] "Status of Legislation Cleared by National Emergency Council for Regular and Special Sessions of State Legislatures, as of July 6, 1937" (and similar reports for other years), Entry 126, Boxes 30 and 155a, NEC Records. These reports reveal the scope of NEC activities.

executive secretary. This unwieldy body held almost regular weekly meetings from July until December, many of which Roosevelt attended. The president then established the smaller National Emergency Council, also headed by Walker, which was to make "more efficient and productive the work of the numerous field agencies of the government."[10] Completing the structure for state activities, the NEC appointed state directors in January. Until 1936 these directors served as one important source of federal-state coordination and cooperation.[11]

The NEC's role was essentially threefold. To cabinet members it was to supply information about federal activity in the states. To governors and state legislators it was to channel advice. And to Roosevelt, ever concerned with politics, the NEC was to help gauge public opinion.[12] Roosevelt also hoped that the council would alleviate federal-state friction, avoid unnecessary duplication of effort, and serve as a sounding board for conflicts between agencies.

An able and conciliatory administrator, Walker set to work during the summer and fall of 1933 trying to "coordinate the uncoordinatable and unscrew the inscrutable," as he was to recall in his memoirs.[13] Appalled to discover that for years only the Navy had updated its organization charts, he supervised the creation of new charts and distributed them in loose-leaf binders, an open recog-

[10] Walker Reminiscences, I, 20 (unpublished MS, Walker Papers, Notre Dame University, South Bend, Ind.) The Executive Council continued to exist in an advisory role until October 1934, when it was abolished and consolidated with the NEC.

[11] "The National Emergency Council: A Chronological Review of Its Activities, 1933-1937," Case 19, Box A, Walker Papers.

[12] Minutes of Meetings, Box B, Case 18, Walker Papers. Also Box 68, NEC Proceedings, 1933-1935, *ibid.*

[13] Walker Reminiscences, I, 6. For a study of Walker, see Paul L. Simon, "Frank Walker: New Dealer," unpublished doctoral dissertation, Notre Dame University, 1965.

nition of the rapid changes which were to occur in the federal bureaucracy. Acting on presidential orders, he also requested weekly summaries in activities from cabinet officials. These he showed to Roosevelt before the weekly Tuesday afternoon meetings, and they formed the basis for the agenda. Walker also provided executive council members with press clippings and radio reports on the popularity of federal activities in the field.

With the appointment of state agents in January 1934, Walker concerned himself more with field activities, until then largely ignored. These agents received large assignments. Besides reporting weekly on works activities, they submitted biweekly analyses of all federal programs. They also aided in compiling the United States Government Manual, clarified federal intentions, tried to improve radio and press relations, and assisted states in completing directories of federal field men. During legislative sessions they explained national proposals to lawmakers, pacified restless state officials, and informed Walker of progress or obstruction.

Like most bureaucracies, the NEC grew rapidly, and at its peak early in 1935 it was a fairly important operation. It employed 175 people in Washington and another 500 in the states, spending $670,000 in fiscal 1935.[14] Its correspondence was heavy, and its many printed reports of special meetings often ran to more than 100 pages.[15]

It was also effective at times. Beginning in late 1934 NEC directors presided over statewide "coordination meetings" attended by field men of all the various agencies. These gatherings brought together, often for the first time, the

[14] Case 19, White House Confidential, III, 1935, Walker Papers.

[15] See for example the *Directory of Federal and State Departments and Agencies* published for Colorado in 1939. It identifies 511 federal agents in the state—a list running 28 pages, exclusive of tables of contents and index. In Box 343, NEC Reports, NEC Records.

multitude of field officials, encouraged exchanges of information, and prevented some interdepartmental friction.[16] The regular reports sent to Washington also enabled Walker's staff to warn agents of problems already encountered in other states. Walker himself, pleased with progress, took a ten-month leave of absence in June 1934, having brought "some order out of the chaos attendant upon the creation of so many diversified branches of a new venture in government."[17] An impartial observer remarked in 1936 that federal agencies were "better organized, know better what they want, and are more insistent upon getting it than in any previous year in which the majority of the state legislatures were in session."[18]

Otherwise, the NEC was a disappointing experiment which Roosevelt ignored after 1935 and which looked far better on paper than in practice.[19] One weakness was its frankly emergency—and therefore temporary—nature: an executive order could abolish it as quickly as it had been created. Forced to scramble for funds from the National Recovery Administration, it was unable to attract top-level personnel. Donald Richberg, who took Walker's place during a leave of absence, informed Roosevelt that state directors were "spotty; some are very good and helpful, while others are mediocre; and some have a vague idea of what they are supposed to do."[20] Lack of funds also prevented agents from filing reports which revealed more than surface impressions culled from scattered newspaper editorials. Ob-

[16] See report by Eugene S. Leggett to Walker, October 1, 1935, Case 19, Office of Field Operations File, 1935, Walker Papers. Also Walker to New Hampshire State Director, July 31, 1935, *ibid.*

[17] Walker Reminiscences, I, 20.

[18] W. Brooke Graves, "The Future of the American States," *American Political Science Review*, XXX (February 1936), 24-50.

[19] Seligman and Cornwell, *New Deal Mosaic.* The editors' judicious comments reveal NEC weaknesses.

[20] *Ibid.*, 335 (Meeting October 30, 1934).

serving the rather flimsy foundations of the NEC, one observer concluded that it was little more than an apparatus which "assisted the President in gauging political winds."[21]

The indifference of cabinet officials also hampered the agency. Even in the fall of 1933 absenteeism from meetings was chronic for many members who perhaps wanted to avoid direct confrontations with Roosevelt or other agency heads, and they sent subordinates to the meetings.[22] Others were too busy to participate in meetings which they knew to be windy and unproductive.

Roosevelt himself was hardly an enthusiast. Relying on informal means of administration, he regarded NEC primarily as a means of preventing excessive confusion. Although he attended meetings as often as his schedule permitted, he usually came late or left early, and he seldom arrived prepared for serious discussion. Richberg, who was critical of NEC, recalled his conferences with Roosevelt immediately before the meetings: "And I sometimes had as much as five or ten minutes with the President before a meeting to go over the agenda with him. You can see what profound consideration was given to the preparation of agenda."[23] The NEC had to stagger along without the sustained interest of top Washington leaders—a considerable deficiency considering the size of its prescribed task.

Weaknesses on the state level were more harmful than those in Washington. One was confusion over the exact function of state directors. Some NEC men, anxious to

[21] Ernest Engelbert and Kenneth Wernimont, "Administrative Aspects of the Federal-State Legislative Relationship," *Public Administration Review*, II (Spring 1942), 126-41.

[22] Seligman and Cornwell, *New Deal Mosaic*, xxii.

[23] *Ibid.*, xxv. A recent favorable account of New Deal administration is A. J. Wann, *The President as Chief Administrator: A Study of Franklin D. Roosevelt* (Washington, 1968). Wann shows that Roosevelt never really expected wonders from the NEC, preferring instead to hold the administrative reins himself. See 50-71.

establish order, considered themselves the top federal men in their states, but most others were all too aware that their positions were uncertain and their support from Washington nebulous. Lacking clear authority, they were reluctant to play dominant roles.

Lorena Hickok, continuing her travels in 1935, stressed this problem in a perceptive letter to Hopkins. Surprised to discover that very few people had even heard of the NEC, she added that "NEC hasn't even begun to live up to its possibilities. . . . And I think that one trouble is that the coordinating end of it has been 'nobody's baby.' Just a grand idea that nobody ever really did much about." NEC directors, she said, should have authority to " 'crack down' on the heads of the other government agencies in the state, or to interfere with policies laid down by the heads of those agencies in Washington." She concluded with an appeal for more informal gatherings of federal officials: "There's nothing else in the world quite so effective as personal contact—hours of conversation over a highball—to break down this sort of thing."[24]

Richberg was just as perturbed. He complained in March 1935 that federal proposals often baffled state legislators. Many requests for state action, he remarked, came directly from cabinet departments, bypassing the NEC entirely. When West Virginia's Governor Kump asked the state NEC director which of 14 PWA bills he should recommend, the NEC man, ignorant of them all, had to answer he did not know.[25] On another occasion Kump protested in writing. "I have not been consulted relative to any of the activities under your direction," he snapped. "Such suggestions as I

[24] Hickok Report to Hopkins, May 27, 1935, Box 89, Hopkins Papers, Roosevelt Library.

[25] Seligman and Cornwell, *New Deal Mosaic*, 454-55 (Meeting March 12, 1935).

have made have been ignored."[26] This lack of federal-state coordination was far too common.

Roosevelt finally intervened. Recalling a recent personal experience, he told an NEC gathering in August 1935 that he had visited "a certain post office in a fairly good-sized city which also houses practically all the other functions. There is not even a director's tablet in that post office, and you cannot find out where Triple A is, or where is Farm Credit or the Home Owners' Loan, and yet in that particular city there are probably fifteen or twenty government agents and not a signboard to say where they are in this brand new post office building! You can run all around and inquire where the Home Owners Loan fellow is, and nine times out of ten they won't know. There is no coordination."[27] The president then dictated a letter to all department and agency heads. It identified state NEC men and commanded agency personnel to cooperate with them.[28]

What encouragement the letter may have given NEC directors is doubtful, for the next day Walker reminded them of their limited authority. "Your jurisdiction," he told them, "is in the field of coordination and exchange of information. *You do not have and should not attempt to exercise executive control with regard to any of the Federal activities.*"[29] Similar letters and memos warned state directors that they might advise but not rule. Like other federal administrators, Walker was anxious that his agents ap-

[26] To F. W. McCullough, December 17, 1935, Box 21, Kump Papers, West Virginia University Library, Morgantown.

[27] Seligman and Cornwell, *New Deal Mosaic*, 477 (Meeting August 6, 1935).

[28] *Ibid.*, 476. For letter see Original Reports, "Report on Activities on State Directors of the Council," December 17, 1935, Box 8, NEC Records.

[29] Walker to State Directors, August 7, 1935, Case 19, Box B, President's File-1935, Walker Papers.

pear as friends, not as superiors.[30] NEC directors remained as powerless as they had been before Roosevelt's belated effort to give them a little prestige.

Thus the field agents of the individual federal agencies continued to dominate. More secure in their jobs, strongly backed by such potentates as Hopkins or Ickes, and possessing the power to recommend cuts in funds, they completely overshadowed their coordinators. They wrote their own reports, did their own lobbying, and remained answerable to their superiors only. The degree of federal coordination in the states depended on the good sense and restraint of the agency men, not on a carefully rationalized system.

Already demoralized, the NEC faded further when Walker, again pleading personal business, resigned in December 1935. Roosevelt, busy with the politics of the 1936 election, never sat with the group again and gave it practically no attention. Neglected as a potential coordinator, the NEC contented itself after 1935 primarily with compiling reports on state and federal activities, some of which proved helpful to other government departments.[31] In 1937 it was transferred to the Bureau of the Budget and two years later was replaced by the Office of Government Reports. So ended Roosevelt's weak and unsustained attempt to ride herd on the multiplying federal bureaucracy as it raced through the 48 states.[32]

[30] See esp. Executive Assistant to Executive Director, December 3, 1935, Entry 126, Box 1559, NEC Records. He remarked that state directors could handle many problems but that "these problems must be settled, not through the use of authority assumed or granted *but by force of logic and personality*." (Italics his.)

[31] See progress reports on WPA in General Correspondence, WPA Box 123, NEC Records; and also reports on state legislation in Entry 126, Boxes 35-41, 1937-1939, *ibid.*

[32] Engelbert and Wernimont, "Administrative Aspects," present an able and authoritative critical review of NEC. In his second term the president tried again, and finally succeeded in 1939 in getting Congress

The decline of the NEC left the fate of particular pieces of federal legislation in the states up to the agencies themselves. Most were glad to forward their own aims without outside interference, but the results were mixed.

The experience of the National Recovery Administration was particularly revealing. Created in 1933, the NRA fought to improve labor standards and eliminate cutthroat competition in interstate commerce. Under the flamboyant leadership of General Hugh S. Johnson it succeeded in drawing up codes for hundreds of different types of industry, each one setting up minimum labor standards. By the summer of 1933 NRA had apparently achieved remarkable progress.

Because NRA covered only interstate business, federal officials argued that states should pass "Little NRA's" to guard against cheating by the many intrastate companies which had so often and flagrantly abused labor. Encouraging the idea, Johnson created a special division of state relations, with a permanent staff in Washington and a small but active group of field agents. Drawing up a model law, this division instructed field men to explain the bill's many advantages, especially its "principal benefit, the utilization of State Courts in prosecutions. We have found that this acts as a threat to 'chisellers' and as a deterrent against other violations. At the same time it [the bill] does not inflict any additional expense or duplication of organization upon the State."[33] Johnson himself also bom-

---

to approve reorganization bills to streamline the federal bureaucracy. The bills did not eliminate conflicting efforts on the state level, however. See Barry Karl, *Executive Reorganization and Reform in the New Deal: The Genesis of Administrative Management, 1900-1939* (Cambridge, Mass., 1963), 198-200; and Richard Polenberg, *Reorganizing Roosevelt's Government: The Controversy over Executive Reorganization, 1936-1939* (Cambridge, Mass., 1966).

[33] R. S. Beach to Evon Ford, March 28, 1935, Series 101 (Mississippi

barded governors with letters extolling the virtues of federal-state cooperation. "Decentralization," he said, "is if possible very desirable."[34]

Had this effort been made early in 1933 at the height of NRA popularity, state NRA's might have proliferated. Ten states did indeed cooperate by 1934. But as so often in the 1930's, state political calendars presented problems. Most legislatures had already completed regular sessions when Johnson began work in the summer of 1933, and when they reconvened in January 1935, the atmosphere had darkened. While the New Deal, judging from the Democratic successes in November 1934, still enjoyed great popularity, NRA did not. Handicapped by trying to enforce so many different codes and lost in a maze of litigation, its compliance machinery was already ineffective, its constitutional future uncertain.

NRA field men, dismayed but undeterred, pressed ahead for little NRA's and enjoyed occasional successes. In the state of Washington, an agent reported, anti-NRA lobbyists moved right onto the floor of the legislature to "spread their poison and propaganda to each member thereof, but we licked them."[35] The model bill also passed in Indiana, New Mexico, and Wyoming and succeeded in reaching the floor of twenty other legislatures.[36] Prospects looked fairly promising in March 1935.

File), NRA Records, Record Group 9, National Archives, Washington, D.C.

[34] To Gov. Henry Blood (Utah), June 6, 1933, NRA Folder, Blood Papers, Utah State Archives, Salt Lake City. See also Johnson to Gov. Edwin Johnson, September 2, 1933, Correspondence 1933, 202 File, Johnson Papers, Colorado State Archives, Denver.

[35] James E. Bradford to R. S. Beach, March 21, 1935, Series 101 (Washington File), NRA Records.

[36] R. S. Beach report, March 5, 1935, Series 101 (Rhode Island File), NRA Records.

From then on the trail became rougher, and events in Washington were at least partly to blame. Congressional hesitation to extend NRA beyond June 1935 convinced many state legislatures that it would die a natural death.[37] Why ask for unnecessary trouble, governors asked with good reason? A series of last-minute amendments proposed by federal agents delayed progress in other states, forcing legislatures to consider them in the hectic last days of sessions; in Montana, a field man reported unhappily, such amendments caused the bill to fail.[38]

In at least two states field men seem to have worked against their superiors in Washington. The antimonopolistic counsel for the NRA in Texas was open about it, denouncing the model bill as a "rather poor attempt to legalize the trade association racket. . . . I cannot believe that it will receive serious consideration by the Texas legislature."[39] In Missouri the NRA's regional attorney reported that "certain other Code Authority members supposed to pilot this Bill through the legislature I feel sure are secretly, if not openly, endeavoring to scuttle it."[40] Deploring such instances, a federal report complained that cooperation was being "blocked by the very people who were supposed to put it over" and recommended a "weeding out" of unsympathetic agents.[41]

[37] Lawrence M. Pinckney to R. S. Beach, May 20, 1935, Series 101 (South Carolina File), NRA Records. Also Abner E. Larned to Beach, May 17, 1935, Series 101, Box 7939, NRA Records.

[38] Miles Romney to R. S. Beach, March 26, 1935, Series 101 (Montana File), NRA Records.

[39] Howard E. Wahrenbrook to R. S. Beach, Jan. 4, 1935, Series 101 (Texas File), NRA Records.

[40] Keith Carlin to R. S. Beach, March 2, 1935, Series 101 (Missouri File), NRA Records.

[41] Report of Federal Recovery Agencies Publicity Committee, December 12, 1934, in Federal Recovery Agencies folder, Paul McNutt Papers, Indiana State Library, Indianapolis.

Federal lobbyists battled other obstacles as well. As Hopkins had warned as early as August 1933, there were "a few large industrialists who are definitely opposed to the N.R.A. principle" and there was also a "tendency, which is growing, to discharge Negroes and replace them with white labor."[42] A few state officials demanded a voice in the appointment of officials. And many, especially in the South, feared that state NRA's would wreck their plans to attract industry. "People with whom I have discussed this matter," one agent reported, "feel that if any act were passed in this state and the adjoining states failed to enact such legislation, they would be at a disadvantage in meeting competition for many articles which are manufactured here."[43]

Hostility to growing federal bureaucracy also stymied NRA bills. "There is a natural antagonism toward Federal legislation in general and NRA legislation in particular existing in the minds of a great majority of the legislators," one agent remarked. "Too many requests for legislation are coming from the various branches of the Federal Government."[44] New Jersey abolished an existing state NRA on the ground that its personnel were "leeches who are growing fat at the public's expense."[45] And Governor Alfred M. Landon of Kansas, according to an NRA official at the state capitol, claimed to cooperate with NRA proposals while secretly applying pressure on legislators to vote against them. Landon and his friends, the agent complained, "bitterly criticize the National Administration . . .

[42] Hopkins to FDR, August 29, 1933, OF444, Roosevelt Papers. See also Murray E. King, "Utah and the N.R.A.," *New Republic*, LXXVI (October 18, 1933), 276-77.

[43] Alfred A. Kinney to R. S. Beach, December 12, 1934, Series 101 (Utah File), NRA Records; John Fetree to A.N.D. Attaya, July 11, 1935, Series 101, Box 7942, *ibid.*

[44] Charles Ausley to Walter Hawkins, May 13, 1935, Series 101, Box 7939, *ibid.*

[45] *New York Times*, January 13, 1935, IV, 6.

stating that the National Government is unbusinesslike and spending money unwisely which will eventually lead to the wreck of the nation."[46] Because the NRA already looked vulnerable, some state leaders gladly opposed it as a way of demonstrating their grievances against red tape and federal interference.

Rural opposition, strengthened by inequitable legislative districting, was the most common complaint of federal agents. "We find NRA and Codes decidedly unpopular in the rural regions and it is these regions that dominate our Legislature," one reported.[47] Similar blocs defeated a state NRA act in South Dakota and caused the Texas NRA man to suggest that the bill be introduced by a "rural legislator . . . to prevent the accusation of its being a purely urban measure."[48]

This rural opposition, especially strong in the South, was partly economic. Objecting to the higher labor standards in federal codes, these spokesmen argued that they enticed workers into the cities, leaving farmers without help. But many complaints were primarily emotional. A Vermont farmer cited by a federal agent in 1935 was typical: "The farmer admitted that he had received more for his farm products in the last two years than in any periods since 1929. and also admitted that . . . his net profit was more. . . . He further admitted that the New Deal without question had been the approximate cause of his receiving more money for his products, yet hunched his shoulders and very determinedly said that he would not vote for a State Recov-

[46] Jonas W. Graber to R. S. Beach, Sept. 10, 1934, Series 101, Box 7933, NRA Records.

[47] E. J. Brennan to R. S. Beach, March 16, 1935, Series 101 (Missouri File), *ibid.*

[48] R. S. Beach to Ernest R. Tutt, February 19, 1935, Series 101 (Texas File), *ibid.* Also Eugene Mahoney to Beach, March 4, 1935, Series 101 (South Dakota), *ibid.*

ery Act."[49] Farmers and small-town residents, often conservative and individualistic, perceived in NRA a kind of blueprint which threatened their freedom.

A rapid round of setbacks followed in 1935 state legislatures. Some states either declined to renew existing statutes or refused to help prosecute even the most flagrant violators of national codes.[50] Most other states merely pigeonholed the model bills and waited for the NRA to die.[51] When the Supreme Court found NRA unconstitutional in May, few states had enacted model bills and fewer still were cooperating usefully with federal officials.[52]

Each New Deal agency operated differently, and federal-state relations under the NRA were not necessarily typical. Still, they were instructive. As proponents of the NRA pointed out, the model bills required no state expenditures and no substantial changes in administration. Unimpressed, most governors thought special sessions unnecessary while the NRA was popular, and imprudent when it was dying.

[49] L.W.C. Mather to Merton L. Emerson, January 17, 1935, Series 101 (Vermont File), *ibid.* See also Richard M. Judd, "A History of the New Deal in Vermont," unpublished doctoral dissertation, Harvard University, 1959, 103.

[50] Mark Merrell to Harry C. Carr, February 11, 1935, Series 101 (Virginia File), NRA Records. "State Recovery Legislation," February 11, 1935, Series 101 (Harriman Folder), NRA Records, contains a state-by-state survey.

[51] See Ernest L. Tutt to Sol Rosenblatt, March 5, 1935, Series 101 (Texas File); Anna Dickie Olesen to R. S. Beach, February 5, 1935 (Minnesota File); and Roy M. Brewer to Beach, May 10, 1935 (Nebraska File), Box 7940, all in NRA Records, for examples of attitudes reported in three states.

[52] A few governors considered calling regional conferences to recommend legislation to replace NRA after the Supreme Court decision. See especially efforts of Gov. Olin Johnston (S.C.) in letter to FDR, May 31, 1935, PPF 2361, Roosevelt Papers. See also OF 52, Roosevelt Papers for comments of other governors. Roosevelt, however, seemed unenthusiastic about state action, and governors, rather than trying to replace NRA separately, awaited further congressional action.

The noticeable lack of state enthusiasm was not fatal to the NRA—its weaknesses were its own. Yet the reluctance of states to cooperate revealed that they could and did remain somewhat independent of the supposedly all-powerful New Deal. It also exposed the impotence of the NEC, which had to sit by quietly and watch NRA personnel handle all negotiations.

Federal-state experiences in regional planning were almost as discouraging. Many New Dealers were vitally concerned with conserving and developing natural resources, and in 1934 the National Resources Board offered states the services of planning consultants provided that governors appointed volunteer planning boards. Governors were also asked to call for permanent state planning agencies, to provide space and staff, and to participate in regional planning activities.[53] Advertising its proposal, the resources board dispatched agents to meet the governors.

Their task was pleasant, and their reports to Washington enthusiastic. "My interview with Governor-elect [Olin] Johnston of South Carolina was entirely satisfactory," one wrote happily. "He will cooperate in securing planning legislation."[54] An interview with Alabama Governor Bibb Graves was equally harmonious. "He says he started state planning in his former administration, which started eight years ago, and will be glad to bring the matter before the Legislature."[55] By the end of 1934, 41 governors had set up state boards; by 1937 all had.[56] The New Deal, it seemed,

[53] Ralph B. Cooney, "Planning by the States," *New Republic*, xcv (July 20, 1938), 296-97.

[54] H. T. McIntosh to Harold Merrill, November 22, 1934, No. 1/442, Alabama (4), National Resources Planning Board Records (NRPB), Record Group 187, National Archives.

[55] H. T. McIntosh to Harold Merrill, November 22, 1934, No. 1/442, Alabama (4), NRPB Records.

[56] Cooney, "Planning by the States."

had dramatically advanced the cause of regional and state planning.

Appearances were deceptive. In fact governors cooperated superficially because the resources board provided financial help and cost states nothing more than office space. State boards served without pay, while money for engineering and planning came from federal relief funds. In 1937 states received some $1.8 million from the WPA for planning, while paying out practically nothing in return.[57] It was a neat example of federalism, with Washington giving the money and states joyfully and inexpensively cooperating.

Federal field men were not deluded. The Maryland board, an agent reported, "does not seem to be planning far enough ahead and . . . much of its planning is of a reactionary type. Social vision is lacking."[58] In Missouri the trouble was lack of time. "It has been found extremely difficult to schedule meetings, the Governor being chairman. Meetings have been the luncheon 'grab it and run' variety with little time for serious discussion and consideration of problems involved."[59] And the Kansas legislature refused to appropriate any funds whatsoever, leaving the state board in a precarious position. After 1935 its activity declined; in 1941 it was abolished.[60]

A careful federal report in 1938 summed up the situation. State planning boards, it began optimistically, "are winning for themselves a permanent place in State Govern-

[57] "The Future of State Planning," No. 445.5, Box 1070, 1938, NRPB Records.

[58] Report on Maryland, July 30, 1935, General Correspondence, Box 107, NEC Records. NEC agents followed developments in the field of planning in addition to their many other duties.

[59] Philip Elwood report on Missouri, January 31, 1938, No. 445.5, Box 1070, NRPB Records.

[60] James W. Drury et al., *The Government of Kansas* (Lawrence, 1961), 316-17.

ment, and are establishing working relations with other agencies." State participation was "not limited to any one section of the country, nor to the wealthier States; it is spread widely over the entire country." But the boards "have been groping, experimenting, feeling their way . . . there exists confusion." Worse, 15 states were appropriating no funds, and few others were offering more than token assistance. Recognizing that federal support might not last very long, the report admitted that planning boards were "precarious" in one-third of the states and "non-existent or relatively inactive" in another one-third.[61] Another appraisal in 1938 concluded even more unfavorably: "the whole state-planning movement represents but a surface ripple across the waters of public interest."[62]

Because regional planning, despite Roosevelt's interest, never enjoyed sizable financial support except through the separate Tennessee Valley Authority, it could hardly be called a major attempt at cooperative federalism. That states, preoccupied with other matters, failed to get excited about it, was understandable. Yet federal officials, including NEC men, had tried repeatedly to accelerate the movement on the state level and with noticeable lack of success.[63] As one disillusioned federal agent phrased it, "the element of idealism it seems, is essential and important. . . . This at once eliminates narrow sordid politics, graft and political chicanery, which must never be allowed to enter into the state planning movement."[64]

[61] "The Future of State Planning," 1-31. George B. Tindall, in *The Emergence of the New South, 1913-1945* (Baton Rouge, 1967), 587, finds southern planning boards pretty ineffectual.

[62] Cooney, "Planning." A slightly more optimistic view is in Jane Perry Clark, *The Rise of a New Federalism* (New York, 1938), 27-35.

[63] See efforts of NEC men, General Correspondence, Box 107, NEC Records.

[64] Elwood, "Status and Future of State and Regional Planning," January 21, 1938, No. 445.5, Box 1070, NRPB Records.

This judgment, while valid, was perhaps a trifle harsh. States were trying to find money in the 1930's, not to spend it: the depression was no time for the idealistic "frills" of long-range planning. Moreover, the New Deal had not worked entirely in vain; in Utah, federal assistance awakened the state plan board.[65] And it is arguable that the TVA educated state officials to the advantages of regional development. An assessment of federal-state planning in the 1930's must be largely negative, but it must also recognize how little had been done in the 1920's and estimate how much less might have been done in the 1940's and 1950's without the positive example of the New Deal.

An important New Deal concern was improving working conditions. The Department of Labor had long sought to persuade states to set minimum wages and maximum hours for women and children, and to pass anti-injunction laws and workmens compensation. When Roosevelt assumed office in 1933, federal efforts redoubled, and representatives from the NEC, NRA, and Division of Labor Standards lobbied tirelessly.[66] Such efforts facilitated advances during 1933. Ten states enacted laws reinforcing NRA code standards; 7 approved minimum wage laws for women and children (only 15 had done so before 1933); and 14 ratified the federal child labor amendment. Because only 6 states had done so between 1924 and 1932, this progress was especially encouraging.[67]

65 See Gov. Henry Blood Papers, Planning Board, Boxes 80, 90, 104 for evidence of the board's activity.

66 For NEC efforts see General Correspondence, Box 105, NEC Records; for Roosevelt's role see OF 91 and PPF 2422, Roosevelt Papers; and for the important part played by the Division of Labor Standards see Files 5-3 and 6-1, Boxes 34 and 48, Division of Labor Standards Records, Record Group 100, National Archives.

67 "Labor Laws and Court Decisions," *Monthly Labor Review*, XXXVIII (March 1934), 559-79; U.S. Dept. of Labor, *Growth of Labor Law in the United States* (Washington, 1962), 42.

Gains in the next three years were less spectacular, but the frontier continued to inch forward. Four more states approved the child labor amendment, making 24 in all, and 6 strengthened their existing child labor statutes. Two states enacted workmens compensation, making 46 states in all, and Connecticut's Republican legislature surprised progressives by setting a 48-hour maximum work week for women and children.[68] All but 2 states provided the matching funds necessary to participate in the United States Unemployment Service which had been created in 1933.[69] By 1936 the states had made "very substantial progress."[70]

But few authorities were foolish enough to assume that the battle was over. Even before 1936, state minimum wage laws exempted many occupations and provided scanty funds for enforcement. Then the Supreme Court struck down the New York law in 1936, destroying much of the progress that had been made. Large gaps also appeared in child labor legislation: as late as 1937, 7 states permitted 14-year-olds to work 11 hours per day, and 32 states allowed 16-year-olds to work in hazardous jobs.[71]

The drive for progressive labor law then accelerated. After his overwhelming victory in 1936, Roosevelt set out to fulfill

[68] Rowland Mitchell, Jr., "Social Legislation in Connecticut, 1919-1939," unpublished doctoral dissertation, Yale University, 1954, 402-04. For trends in 1935, "State Labor Legislation in 1935," *Monthly Labor Review*, XLII (January 1936), 121-39; and "Principal Labor Legislation Enacted in 1935," *Labor Information Bulletin*, II (September 1935), 2-4. For 1936, "State Labor Legislation of 1936," *Monthly Labor Review*, XLIII (December 1936), 1444-59.

[69] Harry R. Seymour, "National-State Employment Security Programs in the United States: Issues in Policy and Administration," unpublished doctoral dissertation, Syracuse University, 1962, 50, 242-44.

[70] Louise Stitt, "The Present Status of Minimum Wage Legislation in the United States," *Social Service Review*, X (March 1936), 109-16.

[71] Beulah Amidon, "Children Wanted," *Survey Graphic*, XXVI (January 1937), 10-15.

his promise of a national labor standards act. Federal agents in the states renewed their campaigns by passing around model bills.[72] New activist labor unions lobbied strenuously for "little Wagner acts" to guarantee the right of collective bargaining in intrastate disputes.[73] And the Supreme Court in 1937 not only validated the social security and Wagner acts but reversed itself on the constitutionality of state minimum wage laws. The outlook for progress in the states had never appeared so bright.

The results in 1937 were indeed remarkable. Four more states approved the child labor amendment, leaving it just 8 states short of ratification when the federal fair labor standards law made it unnecessary in 1938. Five other states passed new laws regulating child labor, and 5 more limited the working hours of men as well as women. Nine states strengthened existing hours legislation for women, and 12 either passed new laws or fortified old ones guaranteeing minimum wages for women and children. Most encouraging of all, 5 states, including such important industrial areas as New York, Pennsylvania, Wisconsin, and Massachusetts, advanced boldly by passing little Wagner acts.[74]

Liberals rejoiced at these gains. Wisconsin's little Wagner act went beyond the federal version by providing for state mediation and voluntary arbitration, thus protecting the public as well as the union. In its first nineteen months it heard 847 disputes, successfully mediated 588 of

[72] General Correspondence, Box 104, NEC Records, reveals federal interest in state labor legislation.

[73] Federal agents also assisted in the drive for little Wagner acts; Box 73, File 8-1, Division of Labor Standards Records.

[74] "State Labor Legislation, 1937," *Monthly Labor Review*, XLVI (January 1938), 132-65; Dept. of Labor, *Growth of Labor Law*, 240-41; Clara M. Beyer, "Major State Labor Legislation Enacted in 1937," *Labor Information Bulletin*, IV (August 1937), 5-8; and Paul Herzog, "The Labor Relations Acts of the States," *Annals of the American Academy of Political and Social Science*, CCXXIV (November 1942), 19-24.

them, settled 175 strikes and prevented 80 others.[75] And Pennsylvania, a stronghold of reactionary corporate interests prior to the depression, emerged in 1937 as one of the most progressive in the field of labor law. Besides approving a little Wagner act, it passed a minimum wage bill and a 44-hour week for women and children, improved its workmens compensation system, and adopted new regulations for industrial home work.[76]

Then the states retreated. A series of sitdown strikes in 1937 coincided with Roosevelt's hasty attempt to pack the Supreme Court. Conflict between craft and industrial unions divided labor's legislative voice, and in the fall of 1937 a sharp economic recession further embarrassed New Dealers. By early 1938 the reform spirit of the early 1930's had diminished, and chances faded for rapid new strides in labor legislation. With few state legislatures sitting in 1938, new progressive laws were scarce—including only 3 regulating working hours for women and children and 2 new state minimum wage statutes.[77]

Even these modest gains seemed gratifying in contrast to the fate of labor bills after conservative gains in the 1938 elections. Maine passed a minimum wage law, and several other states added mildly progressive amendments to keep pace with the federal law passed in 1938, but the outlook in most states was gloomy. One field man complained of North Carolina: "There must be a lot of educational work done in this State if we are to get anywhere with a State

[75] Rev. Thomas Blantz, C.S.C., "Francis J. Haas: Priest in Government Service," unpublished doctoral dissertation, Columbia University, 1968, passim.

[76] Richard C. Keller, "Pennsylvania's Little New Deal," unpublished doctoral dissertation, Columbia University, 1960, 263-76.

[77] "State Labor Legislation, 1938," *Monthly Labor Review*, XLVII (October 1938), 807-16; Arthur H. Reede, "Injury Compensation Rises Slowly," *State Government*, XI (April 1938), 71-74.

law."[78] Other agents were equally pessimistic, and as early as March 1939, the assistant director of the Division of Labor Standards wrote sadly that "the State legislatures, in almost every instance, are dominated by farmers and big business. Very little labor legislation will be enacted."[79]

Little Wagner acts fared even worse. The Pennsylvania legislature amended its law so as to benefit employers, and Wisconsin legislators repealed theirs. Minnesota and Michigan, not to be outdone, restricted unions.[80] One authority on labor law wrote in September that the "outstanding feature" of the 1939 sessions was the "tendency in several states to enact measures seriously restricting the rights of labor to organize and to bargain collectively."[81] Subsequent state laws in the 1940's were no less restrictive, as "little Taft-Hartley acts" moved onto the ground once occupied by the Wagner acts of 1937.

Compared to the laws passed in the 1920's, 40's, and 50's, the state labor acts of the New Deal years marked more of a break than a continuity. Federal agents in the states could be moderately proud of the gains which had been made before the reaction of 1939. Yet most of the significant progress occurred in a few legislative sessions operating under unusually liberal governors during the progressive year of 1937. Federal agents, however helpful in encouraging these ad-

[78] A. L. Fletcher to Verne Zimmer, July 19, 1938, Box 59, No. 12-0-15-4, Division of Labor Standards Records.

[79] Clara M. Beyer to Paul Sifton, March 20, 1939, Box 59, No. 12-0-15-4, *ibid.* See also Virginia Cook, "State Cooperation in Enforcement of the Federal Wage-Hour Law," *American Political Science Review,* XLVIII (September 1954), 721-37; and "Progress of State Minimum Wage Legislation in 1939," *Monthly Labor Review,* L (February 1940), 312-24.

[80] Sanford Cohen, *State Labor Legislation, 1937-1947: A Study of State Laws Affecting the Conduct and Organization of Labor Unions* (Columbus, 1948), 43-50.

[81] Charles F. Sharkey, "State Legislation on Labor Relations," *Labor Information Bulletin,* VI (September 1939), 10-11.

vances, were unable to save them from attack when the political climate changed in 1938. Federal guidance could abet state action, but it could hardly compel it, and as often as not it had little effect. By Pearl Harbor, the gap between state and federal labor law was widening, and standards in all too many states remained weak and poorly enforced.[82]

Roosevelt had been right in realizing the need of cooperative state action. But except for the ill-supported NEC, he himself spent relatively little time trying to coordinate the expanding bureaucracy in the states after 1933. The result was a host of differing field forces from the various agencies, working singlemindedly for their own ends.[83] It was not surprising that they failed to squeeze much money from hardpressed states or to stimulate state NRA's, planning, or labor law. That they had so little overall effect, however, revealed all too clearly that the New Deal, far from being a dictatorial blueprint, was more like an overused piece of carbon paper whose imprint on the states was often faint and indistinct.

Yet to reveal federal-state confusion in the 1930's is not to indict the New Deal. The pace of change was impossibly fast, and New Dealers had all they could do to minimize friction in Washington, let alone abolish it in the states. While more effort toward cooperative federalism might have prevented some conflicts, the sheer size and complexity of postdepression government in America have always per-

[82] See for instance Addison T. Cutler, "Labor Legislation in Thirteen Southern States," *Southern Economic Journal*, VII (January 1941), 297-316.

[83] Clark, *Rise of New Federalism*, 294, concludes that the devices of federal-state cooperation as of 1938 were "frequently complex, cumbersome, and unwieldy. . . . In their present development, they must be thought of as only tentative groping rather than carefully conceived and planned rational processes." She remained optimistic, however, adding that "the development of federal-state cooperation is a hopeful sign," 295.

plexed bureaucrats and experts in public administration. It is difficult to see how Roosevelt or any other magician could have worked wonders as early as the 1930's.

It is almost as unjust to blame the states. To be sure, some reactionary governors and legislators, branding federal interference as dictatorial or harmful, obstructed field men at every turn. Many others cooperated only superficially, evading national stipulations as much as possible while collecting federal funds. But just as many tried sincerely to cooperate, indeed to conform, failing because of lack of funds, a shortage of time, or insuperable obstacles in communication.

The barriers in the way of thoroughgoing cooperative federalism in the decades since 1930 have perhaps been beyond the capacity of public administrators to overcome. One continuing obstacle has been the essentially independent position of state politicians. Nominated by state parties largely free of national control, they enter office with few obligations to presidents or congressmen, and they stand or fall mainly because they satisfy or ignore state and local aspirations. Indeed, loud assertions of independence from Washington are sometimes a governor's prime political asset. Another barrier in the late 1930's was the absence of any clear mandate for liberal legislation on the state level. Had the voters insisted that state politicians toe the national line, even the relative autonomy of state politics might not have protected those who stood in Roosevelt's way. But no such mandate existed. In its absence governors and lawmakers naturally praised or obstructed the New Deal as political expedience seemed to dictate.

What an ironic situation! Even before 1933, the centralization of twentieth-century life had induced many reformers to prefer national to state solutions. But this nationalizing force was not irresistible: it could not refute states rights ideology or suppress the autonomy of state politics. Thus states lost potential as positive agents of reform at the same time that they retained a rather negative freedom from federal dictation. It is hardly surprising that federal-state relations have fallen somewhat short of the generous, harmonious liberalism which some reformers hoped for in their more optimistic reveries.

6. The Governors: Liberals, Conservatives, & Nobodies

PENNSYLVANIA Avenue offered a fascinating view of American federalism in the 1930's. But it was hazy and unreliable compared to the perspective from the states. For governors and state legislators, not Roosevelt, Walker, or Hopkins, made cooperative federalism either reality or a fatuous dream. Some cooperated enthusiastically with Roosevelt, others tolerated him, others were stubbornly independent. The result was great variety: the New Deal had not one but 48 milieus in which to operate.

A few strong-willed and politically powerful governors pursued policies conceived before the New Deal, influencing state affairs at least as much as Roosevelt and his field men were later able to do. In such states excitement was almost as great as in Washington.

One such governor was Floyd Olson of Minnesota. Reelected on a reform platform in 1932, he championed the cause of the poor and unemployed well before the Hundred Days began in Congress. Concerned over farm foreclosures, he declared a three-month mortgage moratorium in February 1933. He also outlined a progressive program which included unemployment compensation to be financed by employers alone, a strong state authority to handle unemployment relief, an increase in corporate income taxes, public ownership of utilities, and an appropriation of $2 million for relief.[1]

[1] George H. Mayer, *The Political Career of Floyd B. Olson* (Minneapolis, 1951), 122ff.

Uncooperative legislators made Olson's successes less striking than his requests. Afraid that unemployment compensation would drive industry out of the state, lawmakers rejected it. They also demanded stringent economies, reducing the state budget to the lowest level since 1921. But they did enact a moderately progressive income tax, outlawed yellow dog contracts and court injunctions against strikers, made a start toward statewide old age pensions, and set a maximum work week of 54 hours for women. They also passed Olson's relief plan.[2] The governor's proposals, while similar in some respects to those of the New Dealers, stemmed from a tradition of agrarian radicalism strong in the region and represented views held by the dominant wing of his Farmer Labor Party.[3]

Dissatisfied with the pace of progress, Olson began to speak more forcefully after 1933, and he terrified conservatives with his widely quoted remark early in 1934, "I am frank to say I am what I want to be. I am a radical." He then proceeded to approve a party platform featuring state ownership of utilities, mines, and transportation.[4] Even Lorena Hickok grudgingly gave him some credit. "Floyd Olson really is a remarkable man," she wrote Hopkins. "Sometimes when I'm talking with him, under the spell of his personality, I feel like a dirty dog for ever doubting him. The truth is that he is really an expert politician—a darned smart one."[5]

After 1934 Olson's star began to fade. Hurt politically by a truck strike, his party failed to capture the legislature in the 1934 elections, and during the 1935 session he wrangled with lawmakers over proposals for increases in relief

[2] *Ibid.*, 137-40.

[3] *Ibid.*, 154-56.

[4] *Ibid.*, 171.

[5] Hickok Report to Hopkins, December 10, 1933, Box 89, Hopkins Papers, Roosevelt Library, Hyde Park.

and income taxes. The legislature finally passed a sales tax, but Olson, refusing to surrender, vetoed it. An increase in property tax rates followed, infuriating conservatives, and the session dissolved in acrimony.[6]

Tragedy then dwarfed political troubles. Afflicted by cancer, Olson sank rapidly in 1936, dying in the summer before the election which might at last have given him the mandate to carry out sweeping reforms. His successor, Elmer Benson, was a progressive eager to carry out Olson's program. He exempted poor homesteads from general property levies, supported truckers in another strike in 1937, and earned the title of "Labor Governor Number One."[7] But Benson lacked Olson's personal force, and his party fell into factions.[8] In 1938, young, moderately liberal Harold Stassen captured the governorship for the Republicans, and the "most conservatively minded legislature in the memory of Minnesota politicians" turned the state to a new path.[9]

The legacy of the Olson years was mixed. Budget conscious legislators imposed the same kind of rigid economy which curbed progressive plans in other states. And partisanship severely damaged his ideals. Yet Olson's visions left their mark. As he said shortly before he died, "We haven't accomplished much in legislation. Something, of course—relief appropriations, mortgage moratoriums, and the like.

[6] Mayer, *Olson*, 260-71.

[7] A. I. Harris, "Benson: Labor Governor," *New Republic*, XCII (November 3, 1937), 360-62.

[8] Ivan Hinderaker, "Harold Stassen and Developments in the Republican Party in Minnesota, 1937-1943," unpublished doctoral dissertation, University of Minnesota, 1949, 8-13, assesses Benson and emerges with a somewhat unfavorable verdict. See also Harry Levin, "Divided Front in Minnesota," *Nation*, CXLV (October 2, 1937), 346-48.

[9] See *New York Times*, March 19, 1939, IV, 7, for the 1939 legislative session in Minnesota. See also Arthur Naftalin, "The Failure of the Farmer Labor Party to Capture Control of the Minnesota Legislature," *American Political Science Review*, XXXVIII (February 1944), 71-8; and Hinderaker, "Stassen," passim.

More important, the party has been an educational force in inculcating certain principles—collective bargaining, for example. . . . Then the principle of the government, as against private charity, caring for the unemployed and appropriating money for relief."[10]

Another independent spirit was Olson's neighbor, Philip La Follette of Wisconsin. Turned out of office in the Democratic landslide of 1932, La Follette and fellow progressive Republicans chafed under the rule of conservative Democrats in 1933 and 1934.[11] Disgusted with reactionary elements in the Republican party, and unwilling to undergo the biennial chore of waging expensive primary campaigns for GOP nominations, La Follette and his friends started an independent Progressive Party which swept to victory over divided opposition in 1934. La Follette then outlined an aggressive legislative program. Like Olson's, it owed something to the New Deal but more to the indigenous progressive spirit of the state during the La Follette dynasty.[12]

He was moderately successful in 1935. The legislature passed a little NRA, increased surtaxes on incomes and dividends, and approved an excess profits levy.[13] But these laws fell far short of his objectives. A combination of Democrats, Republicans, and dissident Progressives defeated a state Wagner bill, a mortgage moratorium plan, and a work relief program. It was a disappointing session for the many who regarded La Follette as a great hope of independent progressivism on the state level.

[10] Charles R. Welker, "The Farmer-Labor Party of Minnesota," *Nation*, CXLIV (March 20, 1937), 318-20.

[11] Charles H. Backstrom, "The Progressive Party of Wisconsin, 1934-46," unpublished doctoral dissertation, University of Wisconsin, 1956, 364ff.

[12] *Ibid.*, 1-60, 110-11.

[13] *Ibid.*, 350-52.

Like his father "Fighting Bob," La Follette did not surrender easily. Reelected in 1936 and given a somewhat more cooperative, though still divided, legislature, he forced through some of the most progressive state legislation of the decade. A regular session passed a little Wagner act and approved the Wisconsin Development Authority. This so-called little TVA successfully encouraged creation of public power plants. Still dissatisfied, La Follette called a special session in October 1937 and ran it so firmly that opposition leaders, shouting "Heil," stomped out of the chamber on one occasion. Another observer likened the session, which La Follette forced to sit six days a week, to a "small town carnival or riot." The result was a triumph for the governor: the legislature appropriated additional aid for schools and relief, enacted new progressive taxes, and approved a reorganization bill giving La Follette power to shuffle state departments subject to legislative veto.[14]

It was his last major victory. Republicans and conservative Democrats, furious at his high-handed tactics, shuddered when the governor, with Fascist-style fanfare, created a new National Progressive Party in the spring of 1938. Joining together, conservatives of both parties adopted the unusual tactic of agreeing upon Julius Heil, a conservative Republican businessman, as La Follette's 1938 opponent.[15] Heil swept to victory on a campaign of rigid economy and a promise, shortly fulfilled, of "wiping off the books" the little Wagner and development acts.[16]

[14] *Ibid.*, 354-63. See also "Wisconsin's 'Little TVA,'" *New Republic*, XCII (September 29, 1937), 202. Olson and La Follette were not the only independent governors in the region. A third was William Langer, an aggressively independent Republican who was governor of North Dakota, 1933-1935, 1937-1939. For a description of the "Langer Revolution" see Elwyn B. Robinson, *History of North Dakota* (Lincoln, 1966), 403-05.

[15] Backstrom, "Progressive Party," 308-10.

[16] For a critical view of Heil see Harvey W. Schwandner, "Wisconsin's

It was some time before progressivism recovered in Wisconsin, and "Phil's" undoubted excesses were partly to blame for the vehemence of the conservative reaction. Yet even Heil and his successors could not abolish some of the gains. La Follette, like Olson, proved that states, borrowing here and there from the New Deal, could function effectively.

A third independent governor was Paul V. McNutt of Indiana. Handsome, silver-haired, and ambitious, McNutt was a former national commander of the American Legion and was dean of the law school at Indiana University when he assumed the governor's chair in January 1933. Elected on an economy platform similar to so many others in 1932, he did not seem to be much different from his cost-conscious colleagues in other states.[17]

Indiana's legislative session of 1933, essentially complete before the New Deal began, was thus a surprise. McNutt was lucky to have a heavily Democratic legislature, and he drove it until his program emerged intact. A staunch advocate of economy, he pushed through a strong reorganization bill which compressed 169 departments into 8 and made most important state offices appointive by the governor. According to McNutt, it saved $2 million a year. To obtain revenue, McNutt, who earlier in his career had argued for a state income tax, succeeded in getting through

---

Problem Governor," *American Mercury*, XLII (November 1939), 272-75; also "Republican Test Tube," *New Republic*, XCIX (May 24, 1939), 62; Arnold Serwer, "Wisconsin's Business Administration," *ibid.*, CI (April 15, 1940), 501-02; and Harold F. Gosnell and Morris H. Cohen, "Progressive Politics: Wisconsin an Example," *American Political Science Review*, XXXIV (October 1940), 920-35. For the phrase "wiping off the books," see *New York Times*, January 22, 1939, IV, 10.

[17] Robert R. Neff, "The Early Career and Governorship of Paul V. McNutt," unpublished doctoral dissertation, Indiana University, 1963, 107-20.

a gross income tax. This levy caused retailers to pass costs to consumers and was hardly progressive, but it did secure revenue and enabled McNutt to turn a $3.4 million deficit into a $10 million balance in 1937.[18] No governor in 1933 had greater success in meeting the pressing budgetary problems of the day.

McNutt also sympathized with some of the progressive ideas of the early 1930's. Although he opposed compulsory social insurance, he induced lawmakers to pass an old age pension law, an act barring yellow dog contracts, and a statute prohibiting discrimination in public construction. Liberals applauded his appointments to the state public utility commission.[19] Later in 1933 he pledged his wholehearted support to the NRA, adding that "we have before us the opportunity of a century to enact needful social legislation, minimum wage legislation, legislation which will forever abolish the sweatshop."[20] Under his guidance Indiana later enacted a state NRA.

But McNutt was also an ambitious politician for whom state reorganization meant creation of a personal machine to be used in a quest for the presidency. He even instituted the so-called 2 percent club, composed of Democratic state appointees whom he induced to contribute 2 percent of their salaries to the party. By March 1933 he was undisputed head of a machine which he used primarily to forward his

[18] McNutt, "Enlargement of Executive Authority," *Proceedings of the Governors Conference of 1933*, 54-63. For sketches of McNutt see James Stevens, "Indiana's Magnificent McNutt," *American Mercury*, XII (August 1937), 430-37, and Joseph H. Friend, "Watch Paul McNutt," *Nation*, CXLVII (July 23, 1938), 86-8. A laudatory biography is I. George Blake, *Paul V. McNutt: Portrait of a Hoosier Statesman* (Indianapolis, 1966). Blake credits McNutt with achieving a $17 million surplus by 1937 (135-36).

[19] Neff, "McNutt," 148-79.

[20] *Proceedings of the 1933 Governors Conference*, 19-20. See also *Indianapolis Star*, January 11, 1933, 1.

own interests. Increasingly formal relations ensued between Washington and Indianapolis. McNutt later received a series of middle-rank federal jobs, but advanced New Dealers never accepted him as one of them.

McNutt's significance was not so much his position on an ideological spectrum as his forceful state leadership. Like other governors, he insisted that states should be important units of government. "The States," he said in 1935, "have the power and can exercise it without destroying their birthright. Government is not in and of itself something. It is for something. This is the time for action, the time to do our part."[21] It was to his credit that he fulfilled his declamations where other governors failed.

If independence characterized the reigns of Olson, La Follette, and McNutt, defiance was the word for Eugene Talmadge of Georgia. An outspoken reactionary, Talmadge affected the common touch and directed his appeal to the farmers who dominated state politics under an antiquated county unit system of representation. One of his first acts as governor was to build a barn and a hen-house near the official residence; sleep was impossible, he explained, without the bellowing of livestock and the cackling of chickens in his ear. Ever a shrewd politician, Talmadge used Negrophobia and states rights in a remarkably successful career which thrust him into constant conflict with the New Deal.

A devotee of drastic economy in government, Talmadge touched off bitter factional warfare in 1933 by reducing fees for auto license plates, costing the state highway department an estimated $3 million a year in revenue. Highly popular with poor rural constituents, this action infuriated both his political opponents in the highway department and the Federal Bureau of Roads, which demanded more state

[21] *Proceedings of the Governors Conference, 1935*, 65.

money as part of matching funds for road construction.[22] Blocked by opponents, he fired his enemies in the highway department, declared martial law, and dared Roosevelt to take the unpopular step of cutting off highway funds to Georgia. Unwilling to intensify human suffering, federal officials surrendered both in 1933 and in 1935 when Talmadge again challenged federal authority.[23] These were but two of the many times during the decade when federal power had to compromise with an uncooperative state administration.

Talmadge also bitterly fought federal "interference." A rugged, self-reliant man used to having his way, he rebelled instinctively against the presence of New Deal field men, especially those who seemed liberal in any way. Criticizing New Deal spending (while at the same time accepting it), he remarked in typical vein as early as April 1933, "We may have to live on blackberries and plums for a year or two, but we would get over that and be prosperous again if the government would absolutely quit lending money to finance farming."[24] Of the NRA he said later, "Any regulation of business—any of it—we object to it. We Governors object to them taking our sovereign rights; we object to them coming into the states to set up activities that we know are states rights."[25] His quarrels with AAA and other federal agencies were just as vehement.

Nothing incensed him more than relief officials. To get

22 For a pro-Talmadge article see Peyre Gaillard, "Georgia at Last Has a Good Governor," *American Mercury,* XXXII (June 1934), 241-45. For a detailed description of Georgia politics in the 1930's see Roy E. Fossett, "The Impact of the New Deal on Georgia Politics, 1933-1941," unpublished doctoral dissertation, University of Florida, 1960, 94-106. Reinhard Luthin sketches Talmadge in *American Demagogues: Twentieth Century* (Gloucester, Mass. 1959), 182-207.

23 Fossett, "Georgia Politics," 94-106.

24 Quoted in *ibid.,* 82.

25 *Proceedings of Governors Conference, 1935,* 69-71.

federal money he cooperated occasionally with Hopkins and the FERA. But when social workers tried to provide Negroes with decent relief wages and to replace reactionary county officials with trained personnel, Talmadge rebelled. Referring to one federal social worker, he charged that a "crabbed old maid" was running relief in Georgia.[26] He followed by harassing federal agents.[27] "Go into some of the courthouses," he told Roosevelt in 1934, "and see how many employees they have on the FERA and also find out if some of these are not about the richest ladies in town and a great majority of them foreigners from across the waters in England."[28]

Recognizing the popularity of the New Deal in Georgia, Talmadge acted more cooperatively while campaigning for reelection in 1934. "In silly desperation," he declaimed, "the opposition is endeavoring to make the people of Georgia believe that it is Roosevelt versus Talmadge. In Georgia it is Roosevelt and Talmadge."[29] But once elected, he reverted to form, and Hopkins finally federalized relief in April 1935. Already popular with conservative corporate interests for denouncing minimum wages and for lowering taxes, Talmadge proceeded to tour the state denouncing the WPA. He also participated prominently in the so-called Grass Roots conference in 1935, a gathering of the nation's most renowned reactionaries financed by the anti-Roosevelt Liberty League.[30]

Better to have kept quiet. Without New Deal assistance

[26] Allen L. Henson, *Red Galluses: A Story of Georgia Politics* (Boston, 1945), 106, 138.

[27] Report of FERA agent Alan Johnstone to Hopkins, January 19, 1935, No. 401.2-420, Box 66, FERA Records, Record Group 69, National Archives, Washington, D.C.

[28] Fossett, "Georgia Politics," 110.

[29] *Ibid.*, 123.

[30] *Ibid.*, 146-64. Henson, *Red Galluses,* 165-66.

Georgians would have been desperate, and they knew it. Tired of the increasing highhandedness of his administration, they decisively rejected his candidacy for the senate, and chose a liberal by a 2-1 margin in the 1936 gubernatorial primary. Although Talmadge remained in political eclipse for four years, he retained many thousands of well wishers who would return him to office in 1940. More important, he had demonstrated that a governor could pursue his own peculiar path, denounce the New Deal, and still benefit temporarily from its bounty. It was a formula that others would repeat more delicately for years to come.

Even strong-willed men with personal programs such as Olson, La Follette, McNutt, and Talmadge were not wholly independent of the New Deal. They had to heed its guidelines, rely on its financial support, and reckon with its popularity. For most of their gubernatorial colleagues of the decade the impact of the New Deal was somewhat more powerful. Conservatives as well as moderates were moved in varying degrees by the more liberal influence of Washington.

This spirit naturally affected Republicans less than others, and some rather blindly opposed federal programs. Republicans in New York and Connecticut, especially before the election of 1936, tied up the reform plans of Democratic Governors Lehman and Cross. Rhode Island Republicans were no less obstructionist until curbed by Democratic Governor Theodore F. Green in 1935. And Republican Harold Hoffman, New Jersey's governor from 1934 to 1937, incensed liberals by working closely with Democrat Frank Hague, the unsavory boss of Jersey City.[31] Essentially anti-union, Hoffman also blocked federal relief policy, refusing to cooperate with Hopkins or to seek state

[31] Dayton D. McKean, *Pressures on the Legislature of New Jersey* (New York, 1938), 138.

appropriations in accord with New Jersey's ability to pay. Suffering mounted, and in April 1936 distraught relief clients staged a sitdown strike in the legislative chamber. Unmoved, Hoffman replied: "People should support the government and not expect the government to support the people. Some persons have the idea that the government owes them a living. This has never been and never will be."[32] He then vetoed a bill to provide relief.

Other Republican governors were almost as conservative but expediently gave lip-service to progressive ideals. Thus Governor James Rolph of California declared in 1933 that the "economic depression is slowly but surely passing away under the leadership of a man who in the short space of five months has brought order out of chaos, happiness out of misery, prosperity out of a depression, and hope and courage to a depressed and suffering world."[33] His successor, Frank F. Merriam, though unsympathetic with most New Deal ideas, also professed his admiration for the national administration when he was faced with a difficult race in 1934. At election time all but the most foolhardy of Republicans soft-pedaled their opposition to the New Deal.[34]

A few Republicans went beyond lip-service to cooperation with Washington. One was Alfred M. Landon, governor of Kansas from 1933 until his nomination for the presidency in 1936. Although Landon favored economy in government—a pledge kept by slashing salaries, consolidating jobs, and making good use of federal money—he was no simple states rights Jeffersonian. He called a special session in October 1933 which brought the state into line with

[32] McAlister Coleman, "Hoffman of New Jersey," *Nation*, CXLIV (May 15, 1937), 559-61; and "The Education of Governor Hoffman," *ibid.* (February 27, 1937), 229.

[33] *Proceedings of the Governors Conference of 1933*, 6.

[34] For Merriam see H. Brett Melendy and Benjamin F. Gilbert, *Governors of California* (Georgetown, Calif., 1965), 381-93.

national relief policy. Cooperation, he discovered, paid off politically, for he was able to control much of the relief patronage.[35] He also put through a small but graduated income tax, abolished the poll tax, effectively regulated public utilities, fought (in vain) for ratification of the child labor amendment, and provided bankrupt farmers with a mortgage moratorium.[36] Although close with state funds for relief and education, Landon gave Kansas honest and humane government. Many Democrats of his time were considerably less advanced.

Another moderately liberal Republican was George D. Aiken of Vermont, house speaker in 1935 and governor from 1937 to 1939. Attracted to the humanitarian side of the New Deal, Aiken guided a state planning board and an old age pension system through the 1935 legislature. As governor he sought to identify himself with the poor farmer and working man, arguing that it was time for the party to "discard the tall hat and get itself a blue shirt."[37] Although opposed to federal power projects and critical of national "interference," Aiken was a key figure in the transition of Vermont from rigid conservatism to a mildly humane liberalism.

[35] Francis W. Schruben, "Kansas During the Great Depression, 1930-36," unpublished doctoral dissertation, UCLA, 1961, 223-41; *New York Times*, October 21, 1934, IV, 7.

[36] Morton Taylor, "Budget-Balancer Landon," *New Republic*, LXXXV (January 15, 1936), 272-74. Careful and favorable views of Landon are Donald R. McCoy, *Landon of Kansas* (Lincoln, 1967), 128-30, 165ff; McCoy, "The New Deal Through Alf Landon's Eyes," *Midwest Quarterly*, VI (Autumn 1964), 59-74; and McCoy, "Alfred M. Landon: Western Governor," *Pacific Northwest Quarterly*, LVII (July 1966), 120-26. In the latter article McCoy calls Landon "one of the nation's outstanding governors during the 1930's" (125).

[37] Richard M. Judd, "A History of the New Deal in Vermont," unpublished doctoral dissertation, Harvard University, 1959, 120ff, 209-15; R. L. Duffus, "Vermont Speaks Out for Thrift," *New York Times Magazine*, July 11, 1937, 8.

Even Connecticut Republicans, who were very slow to accept positive government during the tenure of Governor Cross from 1930 to 1938, moved toward the center before 1940. Raymond Baldwin, who had been a partisan house speaker earlier in the decade, captured the governorship in 1938 and continued to criticize the national administration. But he also reminded conservative businessmen that "they not only owe a duty to the stockholders in their companies but to the jobholders as well." And he asked the legislature for laws outlawing anti-strike injunctions and protecting labor's right to bargain collectively. Republican lawmakers responded to his first request and even passed a minimum wage bill covering men as well as women.[38] The GOP had traveled far indeed.

Other new Republican governors in 1939 reflected the same spirit. William H. Vanderbilt of Rhode Island forced through a much needed civil service law, added a tax on the gross income of public utilities, and enthusiastically endorsed federal relief and social security policy.[39] Leverett Saltonstall of Massachusetts, while no radical, accepted the New Deal and worked easily within its framework.[40] In Minnesota, Harold Stassen was far to the left of the right-wing Republicans who had controlled his party earlier in the decade. And even in New York, a stronghold of rural Republicanism, Thomas E. Dewey took charge of the party

[38] Rowland Mitchell, Jr., "Social Legislation in Connecticut, 1919-1939," unpublished doctoral dissertation, Yale University, 1954, 479-84. See also "The Republican Party: Up From the Grave," *Fortune*, xx (August 1939), 33-35, 86ff.

[39] *New York Times*, June 23, 1939, IV, 7.

[40] Joseph F. Dineen, "The New Yankee G.O.P.," *Nation*, CXLVIII (August 12, 1939), 168-71. A handful of liberal Republican legislators had enabled Gov. James Michael Curley to get through part of his welfare program as early as 1935. See Harold Gorvine, "The New Deal in Massachusetts," unpublished doctoral dissertation, Harvard University, 1962, 389-95.

in 1938 and began the task of bringing it to terms with the times.[41]

No Republican governor during the 1930's went so far as to cheer the New Deal. Partisanship, if nothing else, precluded that. And many Republicans continued to denounce Roosevelt well into the 1960's. Yet by 1940 the GOP leadership in many states had at least realized the wisdom of accepting rather than obstructing the reforms of the past seven years. That the New Deal could accelerate the growth of so-called modern Republicanism was testimony to its ideological impact especially in the eastern states.

The penetration of reform ideas was somewhat deeper in most Democratic states. One was New York under Roosevelt's former lieutenant governor, Herbert H. Lehman. An undramatic, eminently respectable banker, Lehman was a careful administrator and a warm advocate of social justice. He also benefited from a state constitution which gave him more power than most governors, from a tradition of strong gubernatorial leadership, and from an existing nucleus of state activism inherited from Roosevelt and Smith.[42]

Despite inequitable districting which gave conservative Republicans more strength than they merited, Lehman's steady leadership kept New York in the van of progressive states. In 1933 he secured a model minimum wage law for women and children and adequate funds for unemployment relief.[43] He also cooperated fully with Hopkins, appointing personnel of such quality that even Miss Hickok had

[41] Warren Moscow, *Politics in the Empire State* (New York, 1946), 75-82. For Republican party affairs earlier in the decade see Jewel Bellush, "Selected Case Studies of the Legislative Leadership of Governor Herbert H. Lehman," unpublished doctoral dissertation, Columbia University, 1959, 199-204; and Bellush, "Roosevelt's Good Right Arm: Lieut. Governor Herbert H. Lehman," *New York History*, XLI (October 1960), 423-43.

[42] Bellush, "Case Studies," 355-57.

[43] *New York Times*, April 11, 1933, 11.

to admit that "I found relief administration and adequacy so far ahead of what I had seen in other states that there just isn't any basis for comparison at all."[44] In 1934 the Republicans defeated his comprehensive labor program but failed to prevent passage of a stronger law regulating public utilities.[45] Voters also backed a $40 million bond issue for relief, maintaining the state's enviously high standards.

Lehman at last received a bare majority in both houses in 1935, and he pressed forward with more success. The legislature again refused to ratify the child labor amendment, but it sanctioned another referendum for a relief bond issue, increased workmens compensation, raised the compulsory school age from 14 to 16, and provided for jury trials in cases involving court injunctions against strikes.[46] Lawmakers also approved state standards meeting the spirit of the social security law, and in 1937 passed another minimum wage bill to replace the one invalidated in 1936 by the Supreme Court.[47] Throughout Lehman's administration from 1933 to 1943, New York was a leader in per recipient payments for relief, old age assistance, and other forms of welfare.

The reforms suffered from the reaction against the New Deal after 1937. Lehman, recognizing the wisdom of moderation, reflected the new temper in his annual legislative message of 1938: "Today our task is different. It is to safeguard those essential reforms and beneficial social advances

[44] Hickok Report to Hopkins, September 19, 1933, Box 89, Hopkins Papers.

[45] Russell McInnes, "New York Legislature Again Impedes a Progressive Governor," *National Municipal Review*, XXIII (July 1934), 383-88.

[46] *New York Times*, May 6, 1935, I, 8; Allan Nevins, *Herbert H. Lehman and His Era* (New York, 1963), 167. George Meany, then head of the New York A.F.L., later praised Lehman's labor policy. Lehman Oral History Project, Columbia University, II, 186-91.

[47] Nevins, *Lehman*, 191.

in behalf of the people of the State. We must solidify the gains made."[48] After barely beating Dewey in the election, he had to defend his record against an increasingly antagonistic legislature.[49] Advances in New York had come to a halt, but between 1939 and 1942 the most determined legislators could not turn back the clock. Although Dewey then assumed control, he made no effort to repeal the gains of the Lehman years. New York progressivism under Lehman was safe and unspectacular, but it was as humane as anywhere else in the nation; it was a little New Deal.[50]

Liberalism in Michigan was far less steady, somewhat less durable, and much harder to assess. Governed by Republicans from 1935 to 1937, the state had little chance to adopt a little New Deal until 1937. Then it did so with a flourish. Under the dynamic leadership of Governor Frank Murphy, who was personally ambitious and sincere in his solicitude for the working man, a Democratic assembly and an evenly divided upper house enacted a remarkable program.[51] It advanced the date for payment of unemployment compensation, liberalized old age assistance and workmens' compensation, increased appropriations for education and mental health, approved a civil service law, and sanctioned a referendum to abolish the township system of distributing

48 *New York Times*, January 9, 1938, IV, 10. To a friend he added, "I hope that the session may be a short one. I believe there are relatively few controversial matters to be taken up this year." Letter to Benjamin Cardozo, January 8, 1938, Lehman Papers, Columbia University.

49 Bellush, "Case Studies," 303-48. *New York Times*, May 21, 1939, 1.

50 Moscow, *Empire State*, 19-23.

51 For welfare activities see Arthur Dunham, "Public Welfare and the Referendum in Michigan," *Social Service Review*, XII (September 1938), 417-39. For Murphy's predecessor, see John P. White, "The Governor of Michigan as Party Leader: The Case of William A. Comstock," *Papers of the Michigan Academy of Science, Arts, and Letters*, XLII (1956), 179-94.

relief.[52] One scholar later called this session "a first step toward a Michigan New Deal," while Murphy himself hailed it as "the most notable contribution to the cause of social justice ever accomplished by a government of Michigan."[53]

Unfortunately for Murphy, his administration coincided with an outbreak of sitdown strikes in the auto industry. Determined to remain impartial, he refused to evict strikers from the plants and was accused by conservatives of succumbing to the CIO. Old-line Democrats also resented his civil service program and his unconcealed ambition, and school administrators objected to his habit of dipping into education funds to aid the unemployed. A Democratic faction split off in 1938, organized the so-called Constitutional Democratic Party, and nominated its own choice for governor. Though this candidate withdrew before election time, the break exposed party disunity, and Murphy lost his bid for re-election in November.[54] Defeated with him was a referendum for reorganizing state relief administration.

Murphy maintained a brave front, writing an ally in December, "If we are not prepared to receive blows while fighting for the people and then go on with the struggle we should never have been in the fight at the start."[55] But the election had signaled a sharp reversal in political sentiment.

[52] Richard D. Lunt, *The High Ministry of Government: The Political Career of Frank Murphy* (Detroit, 1965), 140-52.

[53] *Ibid.*; *New York Times*, July 11, 1937, 1.

[54] Samuel T. McSeveney, "The Michigan Gubernatorial Campaign of 1938," *Michigan History*, XLV (June 1961), 97-127; Philip La Follette, Elmer Benson, and Frank Murphy, "Why We Lost," *Nation*, CXLVII (December 3, 1938), 586-90; James K. Pollock and Samuel J. Eldersfeld, "Michigan Politics in Transition," *Michigan Governmental Studies*, No. 10 (Ann Arbor, 1942), passim; and J. Woodford Howard, "Frank Murphy and the Sit-Down Strikes of 1937," *Labor History*, I (Spring 1960), 103-40.

[55] Murphy to Emil Hurja, December 30, 1938, Hurja Papers, Roosevelt Library.

In February, Murphy was unable even to secure appointment of his candidate for Democratic state chairman.[56] And when the new Republican governor died in 1939, he was replaced by an eighty-year-old Bible teacher, who bragged, "I have a pipe line to God," but who had no sympathy for social reform.[57] While the short-lived little New Deal was not forgotten, it was some time before liberals regained control of the state and administered Murphy's laws in the spirit of their passage.

Georgia also struggled toward a little New Deal in 1937. Governor Eurith D. ("Ed") Rivers, chosen in the anti-Talmadge reaction of 1936, guided the legislature into the "bill passin'est session since Oglethorpe climbed out on Yamacraw Bluff."[58] It approved a free school textbooks law, guaranteed additional state support of schools, increased funds for public and mental health, and began a new era of cooperation with federal highway and relief officials. It crowned its achievements by approving a thorough reorganization of welfare distribution.[59]

These were impressive advances, especially in contrast to those of the Talmadge years. But Georgia, unlike New York and Michigan, was poor, and legislators, instead of enacting new taxes, reduced homestead and personal property levies. Seeking to prevent financial chaos, Rivers called a special session in the summer of 1937. It approved higher personal and corporate income taxes, and passed license plate and chain store levies. But these measures se-

[56] *New York Times*, February 19, 1939, 6.

[57] "The Republican Party: Up From the Grave," *Fortune*, XX (August 1939), 33-35, 86ff. See also William L. White, "The Middle West Drifts to the Right," *Nation*, CXLVIII (June 3, 1939), 635-38, and Hubert R. Gallagher, "Legislative Highlights of 1939," *National Municipal Review*, XXVIII (July 1939), 509-17.

[58] Henson, *Red Galluses*, 181.

[59] Fossett, "Georgia Politics," 220-37.

cured little revenue, and an ominous $6 million deficit remained at the end of 1938.[60]

From then on Rivers' fortunes faded rapidly. Returned to office in 1938, he called for a sales tax but was ignored by a faction-ridden legislature. He then attempted drastic economies, removing 400 employees from the state payroll. The savings were small, and the revenue crisis soon forced teachers to wait as much as two months for salaries. Discarding all political caution, Rivers then diverted some $2.5 million from the highway fund. When the highway commissioner refused to cooperate, Rivers deposed him and placed a guard around the commissioner's door to keep him out. Prolonged litigation followed which eventually resulted in defeat for the governor, political ammunition for his foes, and continued budgetary shortages.[61] By 1940 Rivers was finished politically, and Talmadge, calling for strict economy, swept to victory in a gubernatorial primary.[62]

Rivers' administration was one of the most advanced of its time in the South, and despite Talmadge's second triumph, it was not forgotten. In 1942 Ellis Arnall beat Talmadge and presided over a reform legislature which abolished the chain gang, lowered the age for voting to 18, and reduced politics in the school system.[63] But the Rivers years explained why poor rural states found it so difficult to enact little New Deals—they lacked money. If one side of progressivism was the right spirit, the other side was public

[60] *Ibid.*, 237-46.

[61] *Ibid.*, 261-69; *New York Times*, March 26, 1939, 7.

[62] Fossett, "Georgia Politics," 314.

[63] Cortez A. M. Ewing, "Southern Governors," *Journal of Politics*, x (May 1948), 385-409; Tarleton Collier, "Georgia: Paradise of Oligarchy," in Robert S. Allen, ed., *Our Sovereign State* (New York, 1949), 154-58; and Cullen B. Gosnell and C. David Anderson, *The Government and Administration of Georgia* (New York, 1956), 79.

funds, and the latter the state of Georgia did not have.[64]

The impact of reform in Pennsylvania was perhaps most dramatic of all. At first the pace was slow. Working hard for liberal legislation, Pinchot managed to secure more stringent regulation of public utilities and an old age pensions law. But a fiercely factional Republican legislature spurned his bills for minimum wages and maximum hours, child labor regulation, and unemployment compensation, and was stingy in appropriations for relief and welfare.[65]

Pinchot's Democratic successor in 1935, George Earle, was a socialite who had voted Republican until 1932. Minister to Austria in 1933-1934, he returned to enjoy the support of Roosevelt and of Pennsylvania's powerful Democratic boss, Joseph Guffey. Although cautious and unprepossessing, Earle was humane.[66] As he declared in his first legislative message, "My fundamental conviction is that life must be made more secure for those millions who by accident of birth are left at the mercy of economic forces." He continued, "You are asking, 'Where are we going? Where do

[64] Fossett, "Georgia Politics," 318-37, sums up the legacy of the Rivers years.

[65] M. Nelson McGeary, *Pinchot*, 376-77; Richard C. Keller, "Pennsylvania's Little New Deal," unpublished doctoral dissertation, Columbia University, 1960, 41-64. Pinchot credited Roosevelt, expressing his "very deep and genuine gratitude to the help given me by the Democratic leaders and followers in many a tight place." Pinchot to FDR, May 15, 1933, PPF 289, Roosevelt Papers.

[66] See Eugene Pharo, "Gov. Earle of Pennsylvania," *American Mercury*, XLIII (February 1938), 164-74; and Walter Davenport, "Pennsylvania—of All Places," *Colliers*, XCV (March 23, 1935), 10-11. For Miss Hickok's evaluation see Hickok to Hopkins, July 24, 1935, Box 89, Hopkins Papers. Earle, she said, was "determined to be governor of this state!" She added that he was "our type of man. I think he's pretty swell, myself. But, politically, he's a babe in arms. And it's Guffey you're dealing with." See also Edwin B. Bonner, "The New Deal Comes to Pennsylvania: The Gubernatorial Election of 1934," *Pennsylvania History* (June 1960).

you want to lead us?' . . . I answer that we are going, along with the rest of the nation to a new ground."[67]

Like Pinchot, Earle at first pleaded for more than he got. Though his lower house, composed largely of eager new Democrats, enthusiastically backed his proposals, the Senate was more cantankerous.[68] It had not been redistricted since 1921 and remained Republican by a margin of 31 to 19 in 1935.[69] Cooperating closely with Hopkins, Earle refused to pretend that the state could not afford more funds for relief and forced the senate to appropriate enough money to satisfy federal requirements. He also increased utility and corporate taxes and secured a stricter law regulating child labor. The senate rejected the rest of his program—proposals to improve wages, hours, and working conditions. In 1936 it refused to sanction state participation in the federal unemployment compensation plan, even though such stubbornness threatened to cost Pennsylvania $20 million in tax refunds.[70] In few states were Republicans so narrowly partisan.

The election of 1936 at last gave Earle the majorities he needed, and the result was perhaps the most productive state legislative session of the decade. Lawmakers passed a little Wagner act, curbs on company police, a voluntary labor mediation law, restrictions on unfair injunctions against labor, and a minimum wage for women and children. They abolished the poor law system of relief, enacted

[67] Keller, "Pennsylvania," 156.

[68] For Democratic legislators see Hickok to Hopkins, July 14, 1935, Box 89, Hopkins Papers. They were, she said, "young—that is, in politics—liberal, energetic. . . . They certainly are the 'down-unders.' They've managed to get rid of the party leadership that for years was subsidized by the Republicans. They're hopeful—too hopeful, I'm afraid."

[69] Keller, "Pennsylvania," 205-06.

[70] *Ibid.*, 219-22.

a milk control law, established a bureau of civil liberties, and approved a statute meaningfully regulating public utilities.[71]

Earle's program reflected the methodology as well as the spirit of the New Deal. Friendly with Roosevelt, he abjured the independent stance which even some of his liberal colleagues liked to feign on occasion. He worked closely with Washington officials such as Hopkins, used fireside chats to rally the people to his programs, and was frank to recommend warmly a state Wagner act and NRA. He even had a "little brain trust." One observer said Pennsylvania government operated "by ear" during the 1930's; another called him "the nation's Number One Carbon Copy of Franklin Delano Roosevelt."[72] Earle would have welcomed both descriptions.

Unfortunately for New Dealers, Earle fell victim to the mood which downed Murphy, Benson, and so many other liberals in 1938. Unable to succeed himself because of a constitutional ban against successive terms, he ran for the senate. But conservative resentment, revelations of corruption in his administration, and bitter intra-party feuding combined to drag him as well as the party's gubernatorial candidate to defeat.[73] The new governor, Arthur James, was a conservative judge, and one reporter called him "a throwback to the Penrose-Vare past."[74] He cut relief in half, encouraged corporations to work women until midnight, sacked the state civil rights bureau, and emasculated the little Wagner act. He also cut $1 million from the budget

[71] Bruce Bliven, Jr., "Pennsylvania Under Earle," *New Republic,* XCII (August 18, 1937), 38-40; Ralph M. Bashore, "Recent Labor Legislation in Pennsylvania," *Labor Information Bulletin,* IV (August 1937), 1-4; Keller, "Pennsylvania," 244-86.

[72] Keller, "Pennsylvania," 157; Pharo, "Governor Earle," 166.

[73] Keller, "Pennsylvania," 320-63.

[74] "The Republican Party," *Fortune,* 98ff.

of the public utility commission, slashed the staff of industrial inspectors, and revised workmens compensation benefits so drastically that they declined from a place among the nation's more generous states to a spot near the bottom. James had pledged to throw all of the liberal legislation of the past four years into a bonfire, and he did his best to keep the promise.[75]

But even James' rampant Republicanism could not extinguish the liberal fire of the past few years. He found it impolitic to sever relations with Washington, and soon he was working on fairly harmonious terms with PWA, WPA, and social security officials. Because hard times refused to vanish, he had to ask for an additional appropriation for relief in 1940, and he retained the tax structure.[76] James, however, learned, as did other conservatives elected in 1938, that it is difficult to change a system once it is in force. Like it or not, he would have found it difficult to contest an impartial judgment rendered in 1940: "Pennsylvania politics has been fundamentally altered during the past ten years. It will probably never revert to industrial feudalism of the Penrose days."[77]

Lehman, Murphy, Rivers, and Earle, while perhaps the most heralded little New Dealers of the day, were not the only Democratic chief executives to embrace the national program. In California, Culbert Olson, former campaign manager of the muckraker politician Upton Sinclair, captured the governor's chair in 1938 and called for a host of

[75] Burtt Evans and Samuel Botsford, "Pennsylvania After the New Deal," *New Republic*, CI (May 6, 1940), 599-601; and Kenneth G. Crawford, "Roosevelt and the Vital East," *Nation*, CXLVIII (September 2, 1939), 237-40. For bonfire remark see Keller, "Pennsylvania," 320.

[76] Keller, "Pennsylvania," 378-87.

[77] Harold F. Gosnell and William G. Coleman, "Political Trends in Industrial America: Pennsylvania as an Example," *Public Opinion Quarterly*, V (1940), 473-86.

progressive laws. Utah, guided by Senate President Herbert Maw, experienced a gentle increase in liberal legislation in 1937. Green of Rhode Island, governor from 1933 to 1936, began a Democratic trend which overthrew Republican domination and mildly liberalized state policy. And Texas, Oklahoma, and Alabama elected governors whose enthusiasm for the New Deal went beyond mere party loyalty.[78] Except in Utah, however, reform rhetoric outweighed accomplishment by a wide margin. Counting the moderate reforms of Rivers, the number of successful little New Deals was four. Adding independent progressives such as Floyd Olson and La Follette, the total rose to six.

In fact, neither New Dealers such as Earle, independents such as McNutt, nor reactionaries such as Talmadge were the rule in the 1930's. Most governors were nobodies—moderate, undramatic, yawn-inspiring men with legislative programs as pedestrian as they were unsuccessful. Considering that in 1937, the most liberal year, Democrats controlled governorships in 39 states and both legislative chambers in 34, the mediocrity of these administrations re-

[78] See Frank H. Jonas, "Utah: Sagebrush Democracy," Thomas Donnelly, ed., *Rocky Mountain State Politics* (Albuquerque, 1940), 28ff; *New York Times*, July 8, 1934, IV, 7 (Ala.); Jerome Mason, "Oklahoma's Fuller Life Salesmen," *American Mercury*, XLIII (January 1938), 68-76; Hart Stilwell, "Texas, Owned by Oil and Interlocking Directorates," Allen, ed., *Sovereign State*, 325-28; Ralph W. Steen, *The Texas Story* (Austin, 1948), 351ff; Erwin L. Levine, *Theodore Francis Green: The Rhode Island Years, 1906-36* (Providence, 1963), 149-88; Murray S. and Susan W. Stedman, Jr., "The Rise of the Democratic Party in Rhode Island," *New England Quarterly*, XXIV (1951), 329-41; *New York Times*, January 2, 1935, 1 (R.I.); and John D. Minton, "The New Deal in Tennessee, 1932-38," unpublished doctoral dissertation, Vanderbilt University, 1959. Minton concludes, 371, "It would not be wrong to say that the New Deal wrought a revolution in Tennessee." For the progressive efforts of Gov. Ernest W. Marland (D. Okla., 1935-1938) see Edwin C. McReynolds, *Oklahoma: A History of the Sooner State* (Norman, 1954), 368-76.

vealed convincingly that state governments were relatively impervious to national events.[79]

Many of these Democratic administrations were unsympathetic to what they called the folderol going on in Washington. One such governor was Davey of Ohio, another Johnson of Colorado. A third governor, Elmer Holt of Montana, was so suspicious of federal intentions that he smelled Communism. "It does seem to me," he wrote Farley in 1936, that "some departments of the administration are catering too much to the 'Red' element."[80] And W. Lee (Pappy) O'Daniel of Texas, who won the governorship in 1938 with a campaign featuring hillbilly music, the golden rule, and demagogic promises to the aged, was another whose alert attention to reactionary corporate interests mocked his seemingly progressive promises.[81]

One of the most overtly hostile Democratic governors was Homer A. Holt of West Virginia, whose anti-labor views brought him into intermittent conflict with Washington during his term from 1937 to 1941.[82] The chief question of the age, he said in 1939, is "whether we have a government or whether Mr. John L. Lewis is the govern-

[79] Governors during the decade are described in John A. Perkins, "American Governors—1930 to 1940," *National Municipal Review*, XXIX (March 1940), 178-84. For legislators see Henry W. Toll, "Today's Legislatures," *Annals of the American Academy of Political and Social Science*, XCV (January 1938), 1-10. In 1937, Toll pointed out, there were 1,210 Democrats in state senates, only 476 Republicans. There were 3,821 Democrats in lower houses, and only 1,613 Republicans.

[80] Holt to Farley, September 11, 1936, Farley Correspondence, Box 6, Democratic National Committee Files, Roosevelt Library.

[81] Seth S. McKay, *W. Lee O'Daniel and Texas Politics, 1938-1942* (Lubbock, 1944), passim; Steen, *Texas Story*, 354ff. Another was Guy Park of Missouri (1933-1937), the ineffectual handpicked candidate of the Pendergast machine. See Dorsett, *The Pendergast Machine*, 95-100.

[82] For remarks about Holt see John Fenton, *Politics of the Border States* (New Orleans, 1957), 83-99.

ment of this country."[83] In 1939 he refused unemployment compensation to miners who were unable to work because of a shutdown by the operators.[84] He also objected to welfare in general, and the "double dealing" WPA in particular.[85] Holt's four years, added to the earlier term of Kump from 1933 to 1937, failed to bring progressivism to West Virginia and left the poverty ridden state at odds with the Democratic party in Washington.

Of all these conservative Democrats, Charles E. and Clarence D. Martin, the governors of Oregon and Washington (they were not related), most thoroughly disgusted liberals. Charles E. of Oregon, a hardheaded former general, incensed progressives by demanding that Roosevelt fire Frances E. Perkins—"that miserable Secretary of Labor of his."[86] He added that he would like to "kick the pants off the National Labor Relations Board," denounced the fair labor standards act, and vigorously attacked Ickes for trying to introduce public power to Oregon. New Deal relief policies, he added, were creating a "nation of softies."[87] Less outspoken, Clarence D. of Washington, according to one liberal congressman, was "not a friend of the Administration, though he is a Democrat in name. He conducts himself in a manner similar to that of General Martin, Governor of Oregon. . . . He is very unpopular with organized labor and with old age pensioners."[88] Only Republican support in a

[83] Holt to Jennings Randolph, May 5, 1939, Holt Papers, Box 2, University of West Virginia Library, Morgantown.

[84] *Ibid.*, Box 2.

[85] Holt to Edwin Watson, October 12, 1939, *ibid.*, Box 1.

[86] *New York Times*, December 26, 1937, IV, 10.

[87] *Ibid.*, October 13, 1935, II, 2. See also Richard L. Neuberger, "Ballot Poison for Labor," *Nation*, CXLVII (October 29, 1938), 444-46. For attitudes of Oregon Democrats toward Martin see OF 300, Box 106, Roosevelt Papers.

[88] Rep. John M. Coffee to Farley, October 25, 1938, OF 300, Box 107, Roosevelt Papers.

1936 primary saved him from defeat in his attempt for renomination, and liberals had to tolerate him until 1940.[89]

It is revealing that so many Democratic governors hostile to the New Deal reached office in the supposedly liberal 1930's. Some, such as Johnson and Martin of Washington, owed their initial success in part to the Democratic sweep of 1932, and their later triumphs to personal color or adept political management. Others, especially in the South, reflected the ambivalent feelings of influential constituents toward the New Deal. Still others, like O'Daniel, offered progressive programs and then turned about once they were in power. Men such as Davey campaigned as cooperative Democrats, rode into office on the party label, and stayed until their camouflage wore off. And all these men profited from a basic fact of American politics: state parties were independent of national control.[90] Neither Roosevelt nor his most astute political advisers could dictate the choice of state candidates.

The anomaly of conservative governors in the 1930's has other explanations. As analysts of voting behavior have suggested, ideology and even self-interest have often been less important than partisan loyalties or the attractiveness of candidates as reasons in forming the preference of the

[89] Mary McCarthy, "Circus Politics in Washington State," *Nation*, CXLIII (October 17, 1936), 442-44; "Politics on the West Coast," *Fortune*, XXI (March 1940), 41ff. See also Earl Pomeroy, *The Pacific Slope* (New York, 1965), 243-51, for brief accounts of the Martins and other Western governors. It is interesting that Pomeroy finds so little difference in the political climates of the 1920's and 1930's that he lumps them together under the heading of "politics of fundamentalism."

[90] For the rolc of state parties in American politics, see William Nesbit Chambers and Walter Dean Burnham, eds., *The American Party Systems: Stages of Political Development* (New York, 1967). Burnham brands American parties as cases of "arrested development" (277), for they have resisted a nationalizing trend which has broken down other state-local institutions.

voters.[91] Thus it is probable that some low income Democrats ignored self-interest and voted for people like Talmadge because of the stronger pulls of partisanship and local color. At any rate, it is obvious that many voters found it easy to ignore ideological considerations and to back candidates of widely differing points of view at the same time.

Another fact of American politics in the 1930's—or at any time—is that off-year state elections attract fewer voters than presidential contests.[92] Because the most regular voters tend to be people of wealth and high status,[93] it is probable that many low income citizens who supported Roosevelt in presidential years did not bother to vote at all in state elections. Their apathy allowed more conservative and upper income groups to control nominations and to play larger roles in elections as well. It would be a mistake to exaggerate this tendency into a law of politics, but it is certainly pos-

[91] Angus Campbell et al., *The American Voter* (New York, 1960), 110-15.

[92] For figures on voting in state elections, often difficult to find, see the *World Almanac and Book of Facts*, 1941 (New York, 1941), 769-812. My calculations from these figures indicate that approximately 14 percent fewer votes were cast in non-Southern gubernatorial races in 1934 than had been cast in these same states in races for governor (or for president if no gubernatorial contests occurred) in 1932. A similar drop-off took place in non-Southern races for governors in 1938, as contrasted to the vote in 1936. The drop-off in voting in one-party states was usually much larger. It is also true, however, that many states conducted gubernatorial elections only in presidential years; in these states the total vote for state office was almost as high as that for president. For a brilliant article on trends in voting turnout in the twentieth century see Walter Dean Burnham, "The Changing Shape of the American Political Universe," *American Political Science Review*, LIX (March 1965), 7-28. He notes not only the extent of drop-off in non-presidential elections, but the low turnouts generally in twentieth century America.

[93] Campbell, et al., *American Voter*, 189-94.

sible that state conservatism, like national liberalism, owes something to these basic aspects of voting behavior.

Ranged against these uncooperative governors were a few who sympathized with the New Deal but pursued cautious, moderate policies for political or temperamental reasons. John C. R. Ehringhaus of North Carolina, governor from 1933 to 1937, tried to adopt a program of social welfare and labor reform, but textile interests opposed ratification of the child labor amendment, and most of his other proposals became lost in a struggle over the state sales tax.[94] The scene of sharp factionalism reflecting sectional differences within the state, North Carolina did not prove especially fertile soil for New Deal ideas.

Another circumspectly liberal Democrat was Wilbur Cross of Connecticut, a hardy and popular governor from 1931 to 1939. Anxious to relieve human suffering, he was at the same time hostile to activist elements in the CIO and distressed by trends in federal spending. He was also fond of asserting states rights, and once went so far as to declare, "I associate largely with Republicans and when I come down to the fundamentals of government I find but little disagreement. We all stand for the rights of the state against federal government control."[95] Confronted by well-organized Republican opposition in the legislature and by sharp intraparty dissension, he was not adept enough as a party leader or inspiring enough as a speaker to put across a comprehensive program.[96] Cross led Connecticut away

[94] Puryear, *Democratic Party Dissension*, 185-97.

[95] W. Duane Lockard, "The Role of Party in the Connecticut General Assembly, 1931-51," unpublished doctoral dissertation, Yale University, 1952, 172.

[96] Rowland Mitchell, Jr., "Social Legislation in Connecticut, 1919-1939," unpublished doctoral dissertation, Yale University, 1954, 471. Also Joseph I. Lieberman, *The Power Broker: A Biography of John M. Bailey* (Boston, 1966), 58, 103-04, for a similar view of Cross.

from the indolence of the Republican machine of the 1920's but not far enough to enact a little New Deal.

Most Democratic administrations of the decade were neither suspiciously conservative nor cautiously liberal—they were practical and uninspired. Preoccupied with state events and more often than not hampered by party factionalism, they accepted as much New Deal aid as they could get, and contented themselves with praising the virtues of the Democratic party at election time. They looked on the New Deal less as a means of liberalizing state policy than as a way of keeping themselves in power. They cooperated with Roosevelt's program, but made little effort to sell it.

Three such states were Maine, Illinois, and Iowa. The New Deal—and the depression—worked political wonders in all three, destroying Republican monopolies and helping Democratic administrations take control. But in all three states the possession of power encouraged Democratic factionalism, forcing governors to deal with politics, not policy. "Legislation would be much simpler in Iowa if there was one good political boss," a federal agent complained. "There is no leadership. The legislature is divided into numerous factions on tax questions and these factions are not split along party lines."[97] In Illinois, Governor Henry Horner, a professed supporter of the New Deal, was too busy fighting the Democratic machine in Chicago to accomplish much on the legislative front.[98] And in Maine a Democratic congressman complained justly in 1936: "The Democratic organization is the poorest since 1928. . . . The chief and fundamental weakness is that the

[97] T. J. Edmonds to Hopkins, February 2, 1934, No. 406-420, Box 97, FERA Records, National Archives.

[98] Don E. Chamberlain, "Illinois, The New Look," in Allen, ed., *Sovereign State,* 190; Harold F. Gosnell, *Grass Roots Politics* (Washington, 1942), 93-96.

Maine Democratic candidates cannot bring themselves, as a unit, openly and emphatically, to say they are for Roosevelt and his policies."[99]

Democratic parties in Kentucky and Louisiana distressed progressives even more. Factionalism was so prevalent in Kentucky that Ruby Laffoon, governor from 1931 to 1935, dared do little more than make Mae West a Kentucky Colonel and solicit friends by means of a liberal pardon policy. When he left the state for a day, Albert (Happy) Chandler, lieutenant governor and leader of the opposing faction, assumed control and obtained a primary law enabling him to contest Laffoon for the governorship in 1935. Chandler won, but dissension continued. Under his reign Kentucky replaced an unpopular sales levy with mild income and luxury taxes, but the state prized economy above all else and remained among the most frugal in appropriations for relief and welfare. Such was the nature of the "Kentucky New Deal" under Chandler, who persistently professed his sympathy with the national administration while doing relatively little in the state to prove it.[100]

Louisiana politicians also sounded more progressive than they acted. Huey Long's dictatorship produced lasting educational and highway improvements but it was no more

[99] Rep. Edward C. Moran to Farley, August 11, 1936, Farley Correspondence, Box 4, Democratic National Committee Records. Also Paul W. Ward, "Will Maine Go Democratic?" *Nation*, CXLIII (September 5, 1936), 263-64; and Dane Yorke, "The Democratic Comedy in Maine," *American Mercury*, XXXII (August 1934), 494-96. Such Democratic states in the 1930's also included Colorado, Nebraska, Wyoming, and Missouri. Indeed, the politics of these states seemed to differ little from those of the 1920's, perhaps because economic conditions were poor in both decades. See Carl Ubbelohde, *A Colorado History* (Boulder, 1965), 296-306; James C. Olson, *History of Nebraska* (Lincoln, 1955), 318; T. A. Larson, *History of Wyoming* (Lincoln, 1965), 463-67; and Duane Meyer, *The Heritage of Missouri: A History* (St. Louis, 1965), 636-43.

[100] Fenton, *Politics in Border States*, 27-29; *New York Times*, July 4, 1937, IV, 10.

partial to organized labor than other southern states, and it weakened the mothers' pension law. Its supposedly progressive income tax was in fact moderate, and the bulk of revenue came from consumer levies on tobacco and gasoline.[101] Following Long's assassination in 1935, his machine dropped into the hands of a group "interested in getting wealth, not sharing it."[102] After swearing that Louisiana would never have a sales tax, Long's heirs put through a so-called luxury tax in 1936 which, by covering essential consumer items, in fact violated their pledge. After 1937 the machine fell a victim of its greed, forcing the governor to resign in 1939 and leaving a trail of corruption.[103] Far from trying to oust the party chiefs in the years after Long's death, federal officials dropped charges of tax evasion against them (opponents called Roosevelt's change of heart the second Louisiana Purchase) and accorded them political recognition until 1939.

The variety in state policy during the 1930's was perplexing. Why were some administrations progressive, others mediocre, others reactionary? More puzzling, why did states such as Georgia and California swing so sharply from one extreme to another while other states plodded routinely along worn-out paths?

Political scientists have provided useful if tentative answers. Using such indices as percent of state revenues derived from death and gift taxes, average educational expenditures per pupil, and average payments per recipient of a host of welfare programs, they have ranked states according to their generosity in providing social services. Turning then to external factors such as the degree of party competition,

[101] Allen P. Sindler, *Huey Long's Louisiana: State Politics, 1920-56* (Baltimore, 1956), 104-05.

[102] Allan Michie, "Huey Long's Heritage," *Nation*, CXLVIII (July 29, 1939), 120-23.

[103] *New York Times*, July 2, 1939, IV, 7.

voter turnout, percentage of urban residents, and per capita income, they have generalized cautiously about the types of states most likely to approve advanced social legislation.

Their findings are suggestive.[104] For one thing, states generous with services tend to be urban and to enjoy relatively great voter participation. In the 1930's, these were states such as Michigan, New York, and Pennsylvania, where large numbers of city dwellers were flocking to the polls for the first time to support Democratic candidates. Indeed, some correlation exists between little New Deal states in the 1930's and the percentage rise in voting turnout between 1928 and 1940. These increases ranged from 52 percent in Michigan and 43 percent in New York to 3 percent in Kentucky, 10 percent in Arkansas, 12 percent in Nebraska, and similar low percentages in many other rural states relatively unaffected by the somewhat urban orienta-

[104] See the especially useful analysis in Richard E. Dawson and James A. Robinson, "Inter-party Competition, Economic Variables, and Welfare Policies in the American States," *Journal of Politics*, XXV (May 1963), 265-89. See also Thomas R. Dye, "State Legislative Politics," and Austin Ranney, "Parties in State Politics," in Jacob and Vines, *Politics in the American States.* The most ambitious effort to isolate key variables is Dye, *Politics, Economics, and the Public: Policy Outcomes in the American States* (Chicago, 1966). He concludes that the key to generous state services, 1954-1964, is "economic development," a rubric including degree of industrialization, urbanization, wealth, and level of education. Other variables, including apportionment, party competition, voter turnout, and partisanship, were less relevant. See esp. 7-21, 22-45 (for method), 285-93. His exhaustive findings confirm more intuitive judgments. Whether they are valid for earlier decades remains undemonstrated. Moreover, Ira Sharkansky, in "Government Expenditures and Public Services in the American States," *American Political Science Review*, LXI (December 1967), 1066-77, shows that "money is not everything"—that the quality of state personnel and the overall political culture should also be considered in evaluating state services. Until Dye's findings are found inapplicable to the 1930's, however, I am willing to regard them as at least highly suggestive.

tion of the New Deal.[105] Low status residents in most rural southern and plains states, it seems, continued to stay at home on election day, giving less liberal politicians and voters a chance to dominate the picture. Urban, industrial states, on the other hand, were more likely to support New Deal reforms because more of their voters were going to the polls to support candidates promising liberal state services.

Consistent interparty competition also characterizes states with generous social programs. Indeed, the correlation between the degree of party conflict and urbanism has ordinarily been high in state politics, for rural states have generally lacked the socioeconomic diversity which stimulates competing groups to form stable political parties. Thus it is not surprising that few one-party states achieved reform records in the 1930's, and it is certainly relevant that Indiana, Michigan, and Pennsylvania, all relatively progressive in the 1930's, had changed from Republican fiefdoms in the 1920's to domains of political warfare. The closer the conflict, the more likely each party was—and is—to provide the social services necessary to outbid the opposition.[106]

[105] Percentages computed from statistics in Bureau of Census, *Historical Statistics of the United States from Colonial Times to 1957* (Washington, 1960), 686-87. The correlation was far from perfect. Thus Oregon and Washington showed percentage increases in voting, 1928-1940, of 54 and 59 percent respectively without much noticeable increase in progressive services. Generally, however, the urban Mid-Western and Eastern states showed the greatest increases in voting (usually more than 40 percent) and the most noticeable shifts in political ideology (if not legislation). It is also worth mentioning that these increases in voting turnout, though often considerable, were not revolutionary when contrasted to the much higher turnouts of the 19th century. See Burnham, "Changing Shape of American Political Universe."

[106] For a most useful historically oriented article on the effect of party competition see Richard E. Dawson, "Social Development, Party Competition, and Policy," in Chambers and Burnham, eds., *American*

But the *sine qua non* of state progressivism seems to have been per capita wealth. Those states which had broad tax bases were able to provide more generous social services than those which did not.[107] Of course, variations in policy existed among states of comparable wealth: Ohio and Illinois were less progressive in the 1930's than Wisconsin and New York. Moreover, it is true that many poor states strained to do a good job, collecting greater percentages of wealth in taxation than the rich states.[108] But the unemployed worker cared about actual services, not effort, and his chances of receiving meaningful assistance in a rich state like New York were much better than in Alabama, Mississippi, or Vermont.

These findings, though careful, cannot account for variations among states of similar socioeconomic character. Why

---

Party Systems, 203-37. Those states which became dramatically more competitive politically in the 1930's were those which previously had been dominated by the GOP. These included Illinois, Ohio, Indiana, Pennsylvania, Wisconsin, Connecticut, Michigan, Montana, Massachusetts, Oregon, Washington, and New Jersey. Most (but not all) became more progressive in tone and policy during the 1930's. Dawson concludes, however, by stressing that the degree of party competition was not so important a variable as per capita income in creating the base necessary for progressive legislation. It is also true that measures of party competition vary, that too much competition can stifle innovation, and that parties can be very competitive at the polls while agreeing in their approach to issues—and vice versa. For a relevant article see Joseph A. Schlesinger, "The Structure of Competition for Office in the United States," *Behavioral Science,* v (July 1960), 197-200.

It may be relevant that most Southern states became *less* competitive during the 1930's, for the simple reason that Roosevelt happened to be a Democrat. Republicans, sensing fertile ground in 1928, were shattered in the South during the New Deal period. The trouble with stressing this line of reasoning, however, is that the New Deal increased competition along ideological lines *within* the Democratic Party in some Southern states—the struggles of Rivers and Talmadge provide the clearest example.

107 Dye, *Politics,* 285-93; Dawson, "Social Development," 237.

108 Hansen and Perloff, *State and Local Finance,* 29.

did Wisconsin and Minnesota elevate men such as La Follette and Olson, while Iowa and Illinois did not? Why were there not more men such as Rivers in gubernatorial chairs in the South? Why did Pennsylvania and New York enact reform legislation while New Jersey and Maryland remained under GOP control for much of the decade?

While no single answer solves this riddle, several clues point the way. Tradition was one.[109] Wisconsin, Minnesota, and New York all had experienced reform administrations prior to the 1930's, and even Pennsylvania, landmark of reaction in the 1920's, had twice been ruled by Pinchot. New Jersey, on the other hand, had for some years endured uninspired bossism, and Maryland had passed more than a decade under the businesslike conservatism of Governor Ritchie. Ohio and many other states had undergone periods of reform in the past, but these had been relatively weak in the state house and dormant through most of the 1920's.

Ironically another simulant to change in the 1930's was the reverse: a heritage of especially inefficient or reactionary government. Much of Rivers' support came from politicians alienated by Talmadge's disruptive conservatism. In California Olson's success at the polls in 1938 was partly the result of uninspired Republican rule. And Frank Murphy was able to capitalize on the mediocre record of the many who had preceded him. If a progressive heritage was one cause of forward-looking administrations, a reactionary experience was sometimes the other.

[109] Another term for tradition might be "political culture," a concept now being applied to state politics by political scientists. See Sidney Verba, "Conclusion: Comparative Political Culture," in Lucian Pye and Verba, *Political Culture and Political Development* (Princeton, 1965), 512-60; and Samuel C. Patterson, "The Political Cultures of the American States," *Journal of Politics*, XXX (February 1968), 187-209.

Perhaps the indispensable ingredient was the governor himself. If Lehman, Murphy, Earle, and Rivers enjoyed anything in common, it was admiration for the New Deal. Able, forceful men with enough political skill or luck to reach the state house, they shared sympathy for the deprived and faith in the resources of state government. All were able to accomplish meaningful reforms in the face of inequitable legislative districting and factionalism because they believed in state-sponsored reform and because they had the political finesse to show lawmakers the way. Too many of the nobodies—the Chandlers and Daveys—were politicians first and policy-makers second.[110]

State administrations in the 1930's were unquestionably different from those of the previous decade. There were many more Democrats, much more reliance on federal funds, and a perceptible growth in awareness of the need for positive government. Yet factionalism rather than party discipline, patronage rather than policy, practicality rather than progressivism remained the dominant themes of the decade. Not the Earles and the Olsons but the nobodies characterized state administrations of the New Deal years.

While the unedifying character of many state administrations in the 1930's disturbed some liberals, most were neither surprised nor outraged. For Theodore Roosevelt and Wilson had drawn many of them to Washington before the 1920's, and the New Deal accelerated the migration, draining the states of reformers, and only rarely—as in the case of Murphy—sending them back to positions of power in the states. Confronting a national problem and scrambling desperately for funds, the progressives who remained at

[110] This argument does not mean to suggest that a few key men alone shaped events, but rather that the men—and their ideas—should not be ignored in a discussion of objective factors. Obviously, a host of these objective factors helped them reach positions of responsibility in the first place, and facilitated their plans of action once in power.

home had to content themselves with raising the banner of federal-state cooperation in order to implement the *national* programs which had become facts of life under the New Deal. These state leaders, indeed, were really shadow-boxing with issues decided in Washington.[111] Given the increased centralization of modern economic life, it would have been surprising if they had had the power—let alone the will—to do otherwsie.

111 Tindall, *Emergence of the New South*, 641-49, discusses briefly but wisely the careers of a few Southern governors in the 1930's, and his description of their "shadow-boxing" is used here.

7. States, Patronage, and Politics

FEDERAL field men claimed to know how to impose the New Deal on the states: "give the good guys the jobs, the bad guys the gate." With nearly 150,000 jobs to fill in the first two years, they argued, the administration need not have relied so much on idle threats of cutting off funds: they could have turned over patronage to their friends. The result would have been smoother federal-state relations and the creation of 48 dependably liberal Democratic parties. Only these could have transformed state governments into bastions of progress.[1]

Whatever the soundness of this advice, few federal agents were happy with Roosevelt's patronage policy as it existed, especially in the early days of the New Deal, when bureaucracy mushroomed alarmingly. In some states, they complained, agencies were too ready to cooperate with Republicans. "It is common talk," Miss Hickok wrote concerning North Dakota in 1933, "that no one save a Hoover Republican can get a job." Democrats, she said, "were not so cheerful . . . they are bitter, decidedly bitter."[2] Another agent objected to job dispensing in Montana. "It is becoming a positive mania," she wrote, "this 'taking care' of the Republicans, and the reports to my office from the separate counties is that the county organizations are almost in open revolt on the subject."[3]

[1] For an excellent study of Democratic party affairs see "The Democratic Party," *Fortune*, XI (April 1935), 62-68, 133ff.

[2] Hickok to Hopkins, November 6, 1933, Box 89, Hopkins Papers, Roosevelt Library, Hyde Park, N.Y.

[3] Mrs. Edith Buttey to Mary Dewson, December 27, 1933, OF 300,

Other observers objected to the kind of Democrats getting the jobs. "Missouri gave Roosevelt his second largest majority," Senator Harry Truman bragged to Democratic National Chairman James A. Farley in 1936. But, he added, "when the patronage was handed out the people who control things in the party in this State were not recognized. . . . It is rather discouraging to say the least."[4] And the complaints of Democratic liberals in North Dakota as late as 1938 echoed Miss Hickok's observations in 1933. One county chairman wrote: "If this election [of 1938] showed a weakness in the Democratic Party, . . . it was largely due to lack of cooperation by Federal Agencies. Men at the head of these agencies . . . did nothing to promote the Democratic cause. This could be expected because the best jobs in many instances were given to job hunters (convenient Democrats)."[5] Similar criticisms reached Farley throughout the decade, especially after the 1938 election when many politicians blamed such "convenient Democrats" for party difficulties.

A partisan Democrat sensitive to complaints of Republican interference, Farley occasionally reminded his cabinet colleagues of the importance of Democratic appointments. But Ickes and Wallace were former progressive Republicans interested less in politics than results, and Hopkins was more concerned with dispensing money quickly and honestly

---

Womens Division, Democratic National Committee Records, Roosevelt Papers, Roosevelt Library. Many similar letters exist in OF 300 (Election Forecasts and Analyses, 1938), Box 107, Roosevelt Papers. For a case in reverse—appointment of a Texas Democrat to head the WPA in Republican Vermont—see Richard M. Judd, "A History of the New Deal in Vermont," unpublished doctoral dissertation, Harvard University, 1959, 288-93.

[4] Truman to Farley, August 28, 1936, OF 300, Farley Correspondence, Box 5.

[5] S. G. Nagel to Farley, December 23, 1938, *ibid.*, Box 106.

than with examining the political backgrounds of relief administrators. Because these three men cleared many of the important field jobs, state politicians often failed to get their hands on the pork.

Too intelligent to fight with cabinet heads, Farley turned to other expedients. One of his first concerns was to play fair with politicians seeking federal jobs for constituents in Washington. He wrote Frank Walker in 1933 that "one of the common practices of Democratic State leaders is to go from one Department to another in an attempt to locate positions for persons from their States. They always try to keep confidential the number of places they have located in each Department so that they will not be prevented from getting many more places in other Departments."[6] Farley then asked Walker and other officials to send him master lists of appointments. His watchfulness succeeded in reducing favoritism, and after 1933 politicians complained less often of discrimination.

The more challenging task remained of distributing federal patronage in state field operations. Ticklish enough for any administration, Farley's chore expanded with the depression: one observer estimated that ten people pleaded for each of the 150,000 jobs to be filled between March 1933 and March 1935.[7] To solve the problem Farley and his aides devised a plan. Jobseekers, they decided, should first get endorsements from county chairmen or congressmen. The national committee would then select its men, basing choices on ability and on the attitude of supplicants toward Roosevelt before the 1932 convention. To enable congressmen and county chairmen to appear helpful to all applicants, Farley even worked out a procedure by which en-

[6] Farley to Walker, September 27, 1933, Case 14 (Farley Folder), Walker Papers, Notre Dame University, South Bend, Ind.

[7] "The Democratic Party," *Fortune*, 62ff.

dorsers could give sincere recommendations on pink paper, *pro forma* backing on white. Congressmen and county chairmen could then show neglected applicants their rave notices (on white paper) and refer them to Farley and his committee.[8] Farley's plan promised to reward able Roosevent men and to satisfy all but the most narrowly partisan of organization Democrats.

It did not work. For one thing, there were too many jobs to be filled, and neither Farley nor any single committee could hope to oversee them all. For another, Farley did not control patronage flowing from men like Hopkins and Ickes. For a third, endorsers, as one observer put it, were "as undiscriminating as poppy girls at a Legion ball."[9] Pressed by jobless constituents, county chairmen heartily recommended all but the blackest Republicans, and under the emergency conditions of the time it was impossible for job dispensers to sift the wheat from the chaff.

Perhaps the most formidable barrier to systematic patronage was the same as had blocked earlier administrations: existing state machines could not be ignored. Farley had to think twice before challenging such satraps as McNutt of Indiana, Boss Frank Hague of New Jersey (a Democratic national committeeman), Governor Martin of Oregon, or the Byrd machine in Virginia. Strongly entrenched in their states, these men were invulnerable to threats of loss of patronage. Had Roosevelt and Farley attempted to fight them, the result would have been more harmful to New Deal programs—at least in the short run—than it would have been to the bosses. More concerned until 1937 with practical results than with long-term party realignment, Roosevelt let Farley negotiate with the bosses, many of whom were hardly New Dealers. Thus, Hague, Martin,

[8] *Ibid.*
[9] *Ibid.*, 135.

and Byrd managed to get their share of jobs without noticeably promoting reform. "The Democratic machine of the early thirties," one critic observed accurately, "is in no remarkable way distinguishable from the political machines, Republican or Democratic, which have preceded it. It is not, that is to say, a device which the United States Patent Office would look upon with interest. Aside from certain improvements in the timing gears giving it a continuing, instead of a spasmodic, action, and the quite unexampled enthusiasm . . . of its promoter, it is a dead ringer for earlier and all too familiar models."[10]

If Roosevelt's experiences in boss-controlled states were frustrating, elsewhere they were painful. In some states he had to decide whether to support disunited and conservative Democrats or a well-organized, more liberal opposition party. In others he had to choose between an uncooperative Democratic administration and its more progressive but relatively powerless factional opponents within the Democratic Party. In others he found not one but two, three, or four Democratic parties, each demanding spoils instead of social welfare. How much easier it would have been to deal with 48 machines, each with its price but—more important—each able to turn out little New Deals when the price was met!

Those few states with viable liberal alternatives to the Democratic Party worried the national administration most deeply. One was New Mexico, where Senator Bronson Cutting had constructed a potent Republican organization by 1933. Though Cutting's men had enacted little forward-looking legislation, they represented the state's progressive

[10] *Ibid.*, 63. Also McAlister Coleman, "Hague's Army Falls Back," *Nation*, CXLVII (November 26, 1938), 557-60. For Farley's close relations with the Pendergast machine of Missouri, see Dorsett, *The Pendergast Machine* (New York, 1968), 104-07.

elements. By contrast, Democrats were a collection of factions, each controlled by county bosses. Few doubted that New Mexico's best hope for a little New Deal in 1933 lay with Cutting's progressive Republicans.[11]

Unwilling either to break with Cutting or to pick sides among Democrats, Roosevelt tried to remain neutral. But from the start Farley deplored the idea of a progressive Republican-Democratic coalition in New Mexico, and supported Democratic regulars instead. Democratic Governor Arthur Seligman, who had benefited from such a coalition, complained incessantly of Farley's actions. "The National Administration," he wrote on one occasion, "has certainly been giving us a good drubbing."[12] In another letter he asked a friend to pay his "compliments" to Farley's friends, and to "continue to give them the devil. Some of these appointments are absolutely unbelievable, ridiculous and incredible."[13] Meanwhile, Seligman noted anxiously, regular Democrats like Congressman Dennis Chavez were profiting from Farley's largesse and "hauling off left and right ignoring the organization entirely."[14]

Seligman's death in September 1933 did not end the fighting; on the contrary, it sharpened as time approached for Cutting's reelection contest in 1934. Some state Democrats urged the party to endorse Cutting in return for Republican help on other offices. Others, led by Chavez, refused. Once rid of Cutting, they reasoned, Democrats would get

[11] A survey of New Mexico politics is Thomas Donnelly, "New Mexico: An Area of Conflicting Cultures," in Donnelly, *Rocky Mountain State Politics*, 238-47. He stressed Democratic factionalism. So does Warren A. Beck, *New Mexico: A History of Four Centuries* (Norman, 1962), 311-12. Beck, however, is critical of Cutting.

[12] Seligman to Antoinette Funk, July 25, 1933, Seligman Papers, New Mexico State Archives, Santa Fe.

[13] To Edgar F. Puryear (Cutting's secretary), July 13, 1933, *ibid.* See also Seligman to Farley, July 15, 1933, PWA Folder, *ibid.*

[14] Seligman to Funk, June 10, 1933, *ibid.*

all the patronage. As time for the state convention of 1934 approached, they moved ever closer to naming Chavez as their candidate.[15]

The issue remained in doubt until convention day. The attitude of Democrats, Governor A. W. Hockenhull wrote, is a "question . . . everything is a guess at this time."[16] But at this point Farley arrived and conferred with Chavez and his friends. Cutting anticipated the result. "Jim Farley has been here," he wrote his mother, "and consulted entirely with my enemies. I think there is no chance to do anything with the Democrats, even if I felt disposed to. It will be tough making an alignment with the Old Guard Republicans, and I may get beaten in the process, but God knows it will not be much deprivation to be out of public office."[17]

His fears were justified. Preferring party gain to Cutting's progressivism, Democrats nominated Chavez, and Cutting responded by seeking the support of conservative Republicans whom he had so often scorned in the past. The result in November was disputed, and Cutting, flying back to Washington after defending his case, crashed to his death. The tragedy crippled progressive Republicanism in New Mexico and left a dissension-ridden Democratic Party in power for the remainder of the decade.[18] Never entirely at ease with Roosevelt, Cutting might not have supported the New Deal after 1934, and it is not at all certain that he could have imposed reform candidates on the decentralized

[15] *New York Times*, July 15, 1934, IV, 6.

[16] Hockenhull to Vance Johnson, July 7, 1934, Hockenhull Papers, New Mexico State Archives, Politics-Miscellaneous 1933-1934 Folder.

[17] Cutting to Mother, July 19, 1934, Box 11, Cutting Papers, Library of Congress, Washington, D.C.

[18] Republicans were as faction ridden. See Charles B. Judah, *The Republican Party in New Mexico: A Challenge to Constructive Leadership* (Albuquerque, 1949), 10-15.

maze which passed for state politics. But in letting Farley support Chavez, Roosevelt traded the possibility of a more progressive New Mexico for the likelihood of control by Democrats concerned with patronage instead of policy. Neither alternative was a happy one.

Roosevelt's dilemma in Minnesota was even more perplexing. Here the Democratic Party was considerably less progressive than Olson's Farmer Laborites and badly divided. One faction headed by national committeeman Joseph Wolf was willing to back Olson for the governorship in 1932 if Olson would support the Democratic national ticket. Another more conservative group led by state chairman Joseph Moonan had endorsed Smith in the 1932 Democratic national convention and strongly opposed a deal with a man so unpredictable as Olson. Anxious to work with strength. Farley heeded the advice of the Wolf faction and made no effort to aid Moonan's Democratic gubernatorial candidate in 1932. In return, Olson supported the Roosevelt ticket.[19] A similar arrangement worked in 1934.[20] By 1936, the Democratic Party was so dispirited that its nominees withdrew in favor of a coalition with the Farmer Laborites. Disgruntled Moonanites suffered in silence or bolted to back Republicans.[21]

Relations between New Deal Democrats and Farmer Laborites, while friendly, had never been perfect. Olson strongly opposed Roosevelt's domestic allotment plan for agriculture, and the president distrusted Olson's ambition, describing him as "Olson, playing for Olson all the way through—everything is for Olson."[22] Always the partisan

[19] G. H. Mayer, *The Political Career of Floyd Olson* (Minneapolis, 1951), 99-112.

[20] *New York Times*, October 7, 1934, IV, 6; November 11, 1934, IV, 7. Also Mayer, *Olson*, 238-41.

[21] *New York Times*, October 4, 1936, 1; October 6, 1936, 10.

[22] Seligman and Cornwell, *New Deal Mosaic*, 13.

Democrat, Farley was even more eager to create a more united state Democratic party.[23] But so long as Olson, and later Benson, supported the national ticket, Farley sided with Wolf in promoting coalitions.[24] It was a mutually profitable arrangement, and one which worked to the best interests of progressivism in Minnesota.

It did not last. By 1938, the Moonan faction had gained many adherents who asked resentfully why their party should be so powerless during the days of Democratic success in other states. When Wolf again supported Benson in 1938, many Democrats revolted and backed Stassen, hoping to destroy the Farmer Labor dynasty and leave Roosevelt with no choice but to support Democrats. As Moonan wrote, "Democrats throughout the State have resented the manner in which patronage has been handled. The ignoring of local organizations for six years by Joe Wolf has been resented . . . the old-line Democrats were angry about the situation and voted for Stassen to be sure Benson would lose."[25] For this and other reasons Benson was defeated, and the Farmer Labor party was never again so powerful.

These complicated relations left an uneven legacy. The loose Roosevelt-Olson alliance helped both men at the polls, and it enabled Olson to promote reform in the state. But it enfeebled Democrats, many of whom hotly resented the New Deal. When the reaction came in 1938, it left Republicans as the dominant force. Farley tried to woo Farmer Laborites, but it was an arduous task. Not until the late 1940's would a strong and liberal Democratic Party emerge from the doldrums of the New Deal years.

[23] State Democrats pleaded with Farley for help. See George F. Sullivan to Farley, August 6, 1936, OF 300, Farley Correspondence, Box 5.

[24] *New York Times*, October 10, 1937, IV, 9. The article referred to state Democrats as "orphans."

[25] Moonan to Farley, November 25, 1938, OF 300, Box 105.

Roosevelt's hardest choice was in Wisconsin, home of the La Follettes and of an uninspired and illiberal Democratic Party. Albert G. Schmedeman, Democratic governor from 1933 to 1935, was particularly uncooperative. Visiting him in 1933, Miss Hickok was disgusted to find him terrified of radical attack. He was "afraid to go home," she reported to Hopkins. "I told him he'd better come on out here with me, and I'd protect him. . . . He just gave me a dirty look."[26] Roosevelt, sharing her opinion, called him "just a plain weak sister."[27] During his administration Schmedeman incensed progressives by removing David Lilienthal from the public utility commission, demanding regressive taxes, and cutting educational expenditures.[28] As the 1934 campaign approached, Philip La Follette, running again for governor, hoped that Roosevelt would promote the progressive cause by ignoring Schmedeman. Democrats, longing for the president's all-important backing, assumed that he would support the party ticket.

Once again Roosevelt tried to squirm out of the situation by taking a middle course. Silent until a visit in August, he proceeded to endorse for reelection Senator Robert La Follette, Jr., Phil's older brother. But for Phil, Roosevelt had nothing to say, and during the rest of the campaign Phil La Follette carried the progressive attack with little help from Washington.[29]

Election results left both sides annoyed. Though Philip La Follette won, his margin was only 13,000, compared to his brother's 217,000. Because he had praised some aspects

[26] Hickok to Hopkins, November 10, 1933, Box 89, Hopkins Papers.

[27] Seligman and Cornwell, *New Deal Mosaic,* 13.

[28] Louis Adamic, "La Follette Progressives Face the Future," *Nation,* CXL (February 20, 1935), 213-15.

[29] Charles H. Backstrom, "The Progressive Party of Wisconsin, 1934-46," unpublished doctoral dissertation, University of Wisconsin, 1956, 266-68.

of the New Deal, he resented Roosevelt's silence. Old-line Democrats were even angrier, arguing that the president's support of Robert La Follette, Jr., had helped the entire Progressive Party ticket, dragging state candidates to defeat. Sulking, these Democrats joined with Republicans to block reforms in the 1935 legislative session. As Leo Crowley, the party's patronage minded chief, reported, "the State Democratic leaders and a large portion of the rank and file are in a very bad frame of mind." Roosevelt, he added, seemed to have "turned down the Wisconsin Democrats for the Progressives."[30] Equally sour, Democratic Senator F. Ryan Duffy added in 1936 that "a number of Democrats are incensed with the President because of the many overtures and gestures toward the Progressives. . . . I don't mind saying that I had one devil of a time trying to keep the organization lined up for the President, in view of the hundreds of circumstances which are so aggravating to the Democrats in Wisconsin."[31]

Instead of heeding such complaints, Roosevelt edged closer to the La Follettes. Though he continued to channel some patronage through Duffy and Crowley, the Progressives also received a large share.[32] Reciprocating, the La Follettes supported Roosevelt in 1936. In the 1937 session Roosevelt aides helped Progressives organize the state legislature.[33]

It was a loose but profitable partnership—until 1938. By this time many Democrats so hotly resented their treatment from the New Deal that they joined in naming Republican Julius Heil as La Follette's November opponent for gover-

[30] Crowley to Marvin McIntyre, August 5, 1935, PPF 1004, Roosevelt Papers.

[31] F. R. Duffy to Farley, August 20, 1936, Box 10, Democratic National Committee Records, Roosevelt Library.

[32] Backstrom, "Progressive Party," 278-80.

[33] *New York Times*, January 10, 1937, 1; January 14, 1937, 46.

nor. Capitalizing on the conservative trend of 1938, Heil won easily, and La Follette never again held public office. Robert La Follette, Jr., managed to keep his Senate seat in 1940, but his political strength ebbed during the war years, and by 1946 the Progressive organization was so weak that he felt obliged to run as a Republican. In a primary he lost to Joseph R. McCarthy.

As in Minnesota, Roosevelt's agile maneuvers had paid off, both to himself and—temporarily—to the La Follettes. But again he had sacrificed state Democrats. One complained angrily in 1938: "It seems to me necessary to revert to the 1932 election to find the cause [of our troubles]. . . . We had elected a Senator, several congressmen, a governor, various state officers and had a substantial control of the Legislature, but for some reason or other the Democratic Party in the Nation seemed to feel that the Progressives of Wisconsin were more Democratic than the Democrats. . . . Then we came to the campaign of 1934, when President Roosevelt . . . saw fit to pat the La Follette boys on the back, which gesture was interpreted as a slap in the face by the Democrats." By 1938 it was "impossible even to get assistance enough from people to circulate hand bills, arrange for town meeting halls . . . there was only a skeleton organization to put on only a half-hearted campaign."[34] This Democrat and others could not understand why the president had not built up the state party, rewarding liberals and exiling the spoilsmen, instead of negotiating a temporary treaty with the undependable La Follettes.

Whether Roosevelt dealt wisely with Cutting, Olson, and La Follette was debatable. By working with friendly Democratic leaders, he would have strengthened state parties—and possibly liberalized them at the same time. Such a pol-

[34] Francis T. Golden to Farley, December 13, 1938, OF 300, Box 107, Wis.

icy certainly would have left Wisconsin and Minnesota with more healthy Democratic organizations when the third parties collapsed after 1938. But in working with the progressive elements in Wisconsin and Minnesota he enabled them to enact more liberal legislation than he could probably have obtained from the divided, job-conscious Democrats. Moreover, the result in New Mexico proved that even large doses of patronage could not abolish existing factions or make "convenient Democrats" into liberals. For all his power and popularity, the fact remained that Roosevelt, like presidents before him, was unable to rearrange existing state political patterns.

Wisconsin, Minnesota, and New Mexico were exceptions. Outside of a few Republican strongholds, the remaining states went Democratic during the Roosevelt landslides of the decade. The president's dilemma here was not to pick between unprogressive Democrats and liberal alternatives, but to encourage those Democratic factions most likely to promote the aims of the New Deal.

On the surface this task did not seem difficult—all New Dealers had to do was to reward friends and punish enemies. In practice it was extraordinarily complex. To begin with, Democratic factions unsympathetic with national policy dominated many states. One was Ohio, where a liberal branded Governor Davey as "a complete traitor to, not only himself but the entire Democratic Party. . . . We would not vote for him as dog catcher, let alone anything else."[35] Another was Maine, where Democrat Louis Brann, governor from 1933 to 1937, played along with conservatives rather than risk defeat in his traditionally Republican state.[36] Massachusetts was a third: James M. Curley, gover-

[35] S. D. Taylor to Farley, December 9, 1938, OF 300, Box 106, Ohio. See also Hickok to Hopkins, October 10, 1935, Box 89, Hopkins Papers.

[36] *New York Times*, August 11, 1935, II, 2; April 16, 1936, 17.

nor from 1933 to 1936, proclaimed Roosevelt's virtues but embarrassed New Dealers by appointing party hacks to key positions and running the state for political gains.[37] And in Idaho, Governor C. Ben Ross maintained his position in the state house from 1933 to 1938 less by cooperating with the New Deal than by using the office to advance his own career.[38]

Ever practical, Roosevelt handled each situation according to its dictates. Davey, who was defiant, became *persona non grata* well before 1938, and received little important federal patronage. Brann and Ross, less objectionable, managed to retain official favor, but had to share patronage with more liberal elements. Curley also collected a few jobs, but only because other Democratic factions were also at odds with the New Deal. Roosevelt spurned him during his contest for the Senate in 1936, and Henry Cabot Lodge, Jr., his opponent, ran away with the election.

Roosevelt's tolerance of uncooperative factions irritated some liberals. When Republicans gained at the polls in 1938, one columnist proclaimed that the election should "persuade Roosevelt that the local Democratic machines which have flourished under his Administration are liabilities, and that the work of spreading the gospel is not a proper mission for gorillas."[39] But it is hard to see what

[37] Louis M. Lyons, "Jim Curley and His Gang," *Nation*, CXLII (April 29, 1936), 540-42. See esp. Harold Gorvine, "The New Deal in Massachusetts," unpublished doctoral dissertation, Harvard University, 1962, 515-24.

[38] For the bitterness of one anti-Ross Democrat see Allen Denman to Farley, December 12, 1938, OF 300, Box 104. Another Democrat called Ross "one of the most asinine persons I have ever come in contact with so far as appreciation of an organization . . . is concerned." Cited in Michael P. Malone, "C. Ben Ross and the New Deal in Idaho," unpublished doctoral dissertation, Washington State University, 1966, 81.

[39] Paul Y. Anderson, "What the Election Means," *Nation*, CXLVII (November 19, 1938), 527-29.

else Roosevelt and Farley could have done. To have driven such elements from state parties would have been time-consuming and—witness his abortive purge in 1938—most likely unsuccessful. It was easier to accommodate these groups than to brawl with them.

With men like Davey, Ross, and Curley, Roosevelt at least knew where the power lay. All too often, however, he confronted states with two or more Democratic factions, none of which was firmly in control or likely to promote progressivism if it should gain it. It was in these states that federal agents complained most loudly. A WPA director in North Dakota wrote that the Democratic Party "has never been a resourceful organization and it is not now, with the caliber of men who head it. These men are all good Democrats, well meaning, but they have interested themselves more in patronage possibilities of the game than in any intelligent effort to build up the party."[40] Frank Murphy of Michigan, surveying party politics before his race in 1936, found an even more chaotic picture. "The confidence of the people," he wrote, "has been almost irretrievably impaired by political ineptitude of party leaders, frequent discord of party sensibilities, bitter dissension within the ranks and finally the trial and indictment of party leaders in Detroit for fraud."[41]

Factionalism was certainly not new to state politics. It had thrived for decades and flourished in one-party states or those without competitive parties.[42] Elsewhere, as in New

[40] Thomas H. Moodie to Farley, July 21, 1936, Box 7, Democratic National Committee Records.

[41] Murphy to Hurja, March 3, 1936, Box 14, Hurja Papers, Roosevelt Library. For other states see "Democratic Party," *Fortune.*

[42] For the relation between party faction and party competition see Austin Ranney, "Parties in State Politics," Jacob and Vines, *Politics in the American States,* 88ff; and Key, *American State Politics,* 124, 201-02.

York, Illinois, and California, intraparty dissension reflected sharp ethnic and geographical differences. These kinds of factions would persist well after the New Deal was gone.[43]

But the politics of the 1930's may even have sharpened these divisions. Because the period was so propitious for Democrats, they battled all the more fiercely for the spoils of office. As Miss Hickok complained, "in each of these states you have *one or more* of the boys trying to build up Tammany organizations overnight, with plenty of opposition from other Democrats, while the Republicans piously hold their noses! And the President, if he isn't actually dragged into it, is left without any organization, or any spokesman."[44] The clawing for office sometimes created new, liberal factions; more often, it merely intensified the greed of office seekers.

As if this bickering were not enough, factionalism often increased when one or another bloc managed to capture the state house or legislature. Instead of uniting and sharing the newly won prizes, Democrats tended to divide into one or more "out" and "in" groups. The "outs," seeking to ingratiate themselves with the national administration, complained that the "ins" were reactionary. The "ins," not to be outdone, accused the "outs" of obstructing the New Deal. Too often each side was interested only in destroying the other.

Roosevelt's reactions to such Democratic disagreement varied as widely as the factional patterns. Where he was lucky enough to find both strength and a measure of liberalism in the same faction, he tried to assist it. In New

[43] Lobbyists were especially active in factional states. See Harmon Zeigler, "Interest Groups in the States," in Jacob and Vines, *Politics in the American States*, 116-22.

[44] Hickok to Hopkins, November 3, 1935, Box 89, Hopkins Papers. This was very clear in Idaho. See Malone, "C. Ben Ross," 64-65, 80-81, 131-32.

York, he backed Lehman openly against Tammany Hall, with which he had already fought while governor. In Georgia he supported Rivers against Talmadge, and in Michigan and Pennsylvania he helped to nominate Murphy and Earle and worked closely with their administrations.[45]

In most other states he was less fortunate. Illinois trapped him in a struggle between the Chicago machine and downstate Democrats led by Henry Horner, governor from 1933 to 1941. The dispute, which some described as a battle between a corrupt urban machine and a more progressively inclined governor, was really a power contest between two opponents, each of whom pined for recognition from Washington. Remembering the Chicago organization's opposition to Roosevelt in 1932, Farley at first channeled patronage through Horner. Chicago leaders then concentrated on proving their indispensability. After winning a landslide election in 1935, they made their point, and Farley became more amenable to their suggestions.[46]

But Farley could not banish bad feeling, and in 1936 the Chicago group opposed Horner's renomination. To the surprise of many, Horner won the primary, and the Chicago leaders then tried to take over his campaign. Horner stubbornly resisted. "It is difficult to understand just why any Democratic candidate would act so independently," a Chicago leader grumbled to Farley. "We are honestly striving

[45] Roosevelt's role in New York, his home state, was especially important. For his successful efforts to persuade Lehman to run for reelection in 1936 see letter to Lehman June 29, 1936, PPF 93. He pointed out that Lehman was needed to promote the New Deal in New York and added, "And I have not talked over the *political importance*. To do that would help neither of us, yet of course that *is* important, too." (Italics his.) For his role in Michigan see Richard D. Lunt, "Frank Murphy's Decision to Enter the 1936 Gubernatorial Race," *Michigan History*, XLVII (December 1963), 327-34.

[46] "The Kelly-Nash Political Machine," *Fortune*, XIV (August 1936), 47-52, 114ff.

to promote genuine harmony, but his actions in every way and the suspicious attitude he displays at times hamper our efforts seriously."[47] Just what he expected Farley to do about it was not clear.

Horner easily defeated his Republican opponent in 1936, but his victory failed to heal the upstate-downstate division. Although Democrats controlled both houses of the legislature, intraparty dissension disrupted the 1937 session. In trying to accord equal recognition to both groups, Roosevelt and Farley had labored valiantly to make friends with Democrats of all persuasions. However, they satisfied neither side, and the two groups fought as bitterly in 1940 as they had in 1932.

The growth of factionalism in Pennsylvania was more disastrous for the New Deal because it seemed so unnecessary. Dominated by conservative Republicans in the 1920's, the state swung strongly to the Democratic column as a result of the depression, the New Deal, and the effective if job-conscious leadership of the Democratic boss, Senator Joseph Guffey. A practical politician, Guffey coolly recognized the potential electoral power of a party program appealing to the underprivileged, and he gladly welcomed new elements who joined the party out of enthusiasm for the New Deal. By 1937 Pennsylvania was solidly Democratic, and in Earle it had a governor who got results. Farley worked easily with the Guffey-Earle organization, and federal-state relations seemed harmonious.

Success brought squabbling. Since Earle was ineligible for a second term in 1938, the state committee met to nominate him for the Senate. But it then defied John L. Lewis, head of the powerful United Mine Workers, by refusing

[47] Edward J. Kelly to Farley, July 24, 1936, Farley Correspondence, Box 2, Democratic National Committee Records. Also Horner to Farley, July 20, 1936, *ibid.*

to endorse Lieutenant Governor Thomas Kennedy (a UMW vice president) for the governorship. Guffey, also unhappy, joined Lewis to support Kennedy against the convention's nominee, Charles A. Jones. When the mayor of Philadelphia decided to oppose Earle for the Senate nomination, Lewis and Guffey backed him as well. To add further confusion, the former attorney general proceeded to air charges of corruption against the Earle administration and to run for the governorship himself.[48]

Farley, who had recently enjoyed pleasant relations with the Pennsylvania Democrats, squirmed in the middle as all groups sought his blessing. At first he affected neutrality, arguing—as he consistently did in such cases—that primaries were strictly state matters. But it was difficult to stay wholly impartial, and he finally compromised. On the day before the primary he backed Earle for the Senate and Kennedy, Lewis's man, for governor.[49] His attempt to straddle at this late date pleased no one.

All sides suffered. Earle and Jones won in the primaries: Farley had backed one winner, one loser. But Republicans, sensing victory, resolved their differences and nominated a staunchly conservative slate. Both Earle and Jones went down to defeat in November, and the GOP clamped a hold on the state house until the mid-1950's. As much as anything else, the cause of Republican success was Democratic dissension, which Farley had been powerless to prevent.[50]

Nothing more clearly revealed the limits of presidential political power in the states than California in 1934. The lackluster Republican administrations of Governor James Rolph, who died early in 1934, and of his successor, Frank

[48] Guy V. Miller, "Pennsylvania's Scrambled Politics," *Nation*, CXLVI (May 14, 1938), 555-58.

[49] Richard C. Keller, "Pennsylvania's Little New Deal," unpublished doctoral dissertation, Columbia University, 1960, 290-315.

[50] For revealing letters see OF 300, Box 106, Pa.

F. Merriam, convinced Democrats that the state house would at last be theirs. Led by patronage dispenser J.F.T. O'Connor, comptroller of the currency, Democrats set out to find a candidate acceptable to the party's numerous splinter groups. In George Creel, a Democratic regular who had been Wilson's wartime director of public information, they thought they had found their man.

Upton Sinclair, former socialist and writer of the muckraking novel *The Jungle,* upset their plans. Running on a platform which promised to End Poverty In California (EPIC), Sinclair challenged Creel for the Democratic nomination, appealing strongly to California's many aged and indigent. Roosevelt found himself dragged into a hot contest by partisans of both sides eager for his support.

Again the president was unable to change events. An appeal by one Democrat was especially revealing. "The Democrats here are all fighting among themselves," he wrote Roosevelt. "No leadership—but just leaving themselves wide open for *any* party that might have a semblance of an organization. . . . Frankly, you are the only one who could save the situation." Roosevelt passed the letter to his friend and political advisor, Louis M. Howe, who in turn gave it to Farley. "You are running California," Howe told him. "What will I tell this man?" Farley had to admit his weakness. "I don't know what to say to you, Louis, except to pass the letter back to you and write him and say you will call the matter to my attention. It is a terrible mess but how we are going to be able to do anything, I don't know."[51]

He was indeed unable to "do anything." Despite Creel's pleas for endorsement, the national administration stayed

[51] H. R. Keefe to Roosevelt, June 22, 1934; Howe to Farley, June 29, 1934; Farley reply, July 2, 1934, in OF 300, Box 16.

out of the struggle, and Sinclair won the primary.[52] But instead of ending the dispute, his victory intensified it, for many Democrats, Creel included, eventually refused to endorse him. Some switched to Merriam, who suavely responded by stating that he was "heartily in accord with Roosevelt's recovery policies."[53] Others appealed again to Roosevelt and Farley to dissociate themselves from a wild man who they claimed would discredit the Democratic Party in California.

Trapped again, Roosevelt and Farley insisted that they did not interfere in state contests. Thus they endorsed Sinclair only indirectly by permitting other cabinet members to say favorable things about him. But as the campaign progressed, Sinclair alienated more Democrats, and it seemed wise not to identify themselves too closely with his prospects. At the last moment, O'Connor conferred with Merriam and advised key Democrats to aid the Republican ticket. Merriam, he explained, would treat them well.[54] For this and other reasons Sinclair lost in November and returned to writing novels.

The election did not end party warfare. Sinclair's supporters, led by campaign manager Culbert Olson, continued to beseech Farley for recognition. More conservative Democrats, led by Creel and Senator William G. McAdoo, demanded that Olson be ignored. "I think you have made a grave error in identifying your Administration so conspicuously . . . with the Sinclair and Epic movements in California," McAdoo wrote Roosevelt in December 1935. "If you want the delegation from this state, and if you want the electoral vote of this state in 1936, it is your friends here,

[52] See Creel to Marvin McIntyre, August 13, 1934, OF 300, Box 12.

[53] Ronald E. Chinn, "Democratic Party Politics in California, 1920-56," unpublished doctoral dissertation, University of California, Berkeley, 1958, 101.

[54] *Ibid.*, 102-11.

the real Democrats, who carried the state in 1932, before the Epics were born, who can win, and not the Epics or any other group or combination."[55]

When Olson won the gubernatorial primary of 1938, he finally eclipsed the McAdoo faction. Roosevelt and Farley, while regretting Olson's old age pensions plank, endorsed his candidacy.[56] It was too late. Though Olson won in November, he faced determined Republican opposition as well as sniping from his own Democratic lieutenant governor. His administration failed to accomplish most of the liberal goals which it had so optimistically proposed.[57]

Political patterns in Illinois, Pennsylvania, and California were far from identical. The Illinois conflict featured a nonideological urban machine and a stubborn, rurally based governor. The Pennsylvania battle involved two pro-New Deal groups with support in urban as well as rural areas. In California, ideology played a stronger role, with one group to the left of the New Deal, the other to the right. These states were also not typical. Most southern states lacked potent urban machines such as those in Illinois or New York, the progressivism which was evident in Pennsylvania, and the ideological division which characterized California. The Rocky Mountain states, large and decentralized, presented still different political patterns. Unfortunately for New Dealers, party organization in the states followed no blueprint which would have enabled them to adopt a consistent plan of counteraction.[58]

[55] McAdoo to Roosevelt, December 21, 1935, PPF 308.

[56] Chinn, "Democratic Party," 113-18.

[57] See Robert E. Burke, *Olson's New Deal for California* (Berkeley, 1958), passim.

[58] For factionalism in other states see various chapters in Donnelly, *Rocky Mountain State Politics*; Key, *Southern Politics in State and Nation*; Fenton, *Politics of the Border States*; John Gunther, *Inside U.S.A.* (New York, 1947); and the state studies mentioned in the bibliography. Also OF 300, Election Forecasts and Analyses 1938, Roose-

But the intraparty feuding in these three states—and in most others as well—did share some common features. It showed that Roosevelt and Farley, far from wishing to impose their candidates on states, were often dragged into Democratic disputes against their wishes. The bickering also exposed the essentially self-serving methods of factional leaders trying to convince Farley of their eternal loyalty to Roosevelt.

Above all, these cases revealed the inability of the national administration to prevent factions from arising or to coerce them into line. Roosevelt inherited a downstate-upstate division aggravated by ethnic differences in Illinois. To have taken sides might have temporarily sustained one group but would not have erased a fact of state politics. In Pennsylvania his choice was again limited, for both antagonists could claim with some justification to represent the New Deal. Had he backed one side, he would have encouraged the other to wave the flag of states rights. Indeed, this is what happened when he sought to purge his enemies in 1938. In California, his option was most restricted of all. Once Sinclair emerged as the nominee, the president had the unenviable alternative of backing a Republican or supporting a radical Democrat at war with the regular party organization. Small wonder that he preferred to stay out of state politics.

Some observers then and later judged Roosevelt's dealings with state politicians and delivered an unfavorable verdict. Often, it seemed, he vacillated, unwilling to lend his support to Democratic groups loyal to the New Deal. Thus he weakened progressive Democrats in Wisconsin and Minnesota, played along with bosses such as Hague of New

---

velt Papers; and Farley Correspondence, 1936, in Democratic National Committee Records. These collections are excellent sources for state politics, esp. in 1936-1938.

Jersey, tolerated spoilsmen such as Curley, and refused to stifle bickering in Illinois and Pennsylvania. The sad result, they declared, was that Democratic parties remained as uninspired, as patronage-conscious, and as dissension-ridden as ever, creating an ever-growing gap between a reformist national administration and 48 unimaginative states. Worse, they insisted, Roosevelt missed an unparalleled opportunity to create ideologically oriented parties, to make Democrats the spearhead of liberalism, leaving Republicans as the anchor of conservative (and minority) opposition.[59]

Such critics base their case on little but wishful thinking. While chances for party realignment did seem auspicious in the mid-1930's, they faded later in the decade when New Deal ideas lost some of their hold on the voters. Moderate Democrats, despite their respect for presidential electoral magic, balked at jumping the safe tracks of party regularity laid out by the dominant state machines. Roosevelt might indeed have tried harder than he did to destroy the more arrogantly independent state organizations. But as the purges of 1938 indicated, the odds were long and the chances for ultimate success distinctly limited. Roosevelt's failure to liberalize Democratic parties stemmed not from timidity or from lack of vision, but from a weak hand in the first place. As he well knew, state politicians held too many aces.[60]

[59] Perhaps the best-known apostle of party realignment for this period is James McGregor Burns, in *Roosevelt: The Lion and the Fox* (New York, 1957). Indeed, the gospel of logical parties has attracted many political scientists. See "Toward a More Representative Two-Party System: A Report of the Committee on Political Parties of the American Political Science Association," printed as a supplement to the *American Political Science Review*, XLIV (September 1950).

[60] It is arguable that state politicians *ought* to hold the aces, and specifically that a decentralized party structure facilitates intergovernmental collaboration. A nationalized party system, according to this

Roosevelt's detractors also underestimated the continuing force of laissez-faire thinking and of the skilled interest groups sustaining it in the cozy legislative corridors of the decade. These anti-New Deal lobbyists especially hated progressive taxation, industrial labor unions, and costly welfare laws which might drive industry out of state. Challenged by the reform ideas of the early 1930's, they retreated temporarily. But their case endured, especially on the state level, for legislators had no desire to pass laws which would disturb potent corporate interests at the core of their tax bases. From this perspective, Roosevelt's inability to create strong liberal parties in the states seems the result not of inept political management but of the continuing strength of traditional American beliefs in self-help, the inherent virtues of hard work, and the benevolent character of business enterprise.[61]

Attitudes have remarkable staying power, and such was the case in the 1930's. Even the disastrous economic changes could not destroy decades of obeisance to the ideal of limited state activity. Thus the depression years pre-

view, would remove power and responsibility from the states. See Morton Grodzins, "American Political Parties and the American System," *Western Political Quarterly*, XIII (December 1960), 974-98. Less optimistic about the results of decentralized parties are David B. Truman, "Federalism and the Party System," in Aaron Wildavsky, ed., *American Federalism in Perspective* (Boston, 1967), 81-109; and Rufus Davis, "The 'Federal Principle' Revisited," *ibid.*, 3-33. Many of the articles in this useful recent collection devote considerable attention to the role of parties in a federal structure.

[61] The strength of an ideology in any society is of course difficult if not impossible to quantify, but the weakness of reform ideology in the 1930's was revealed above all by its remarkably short career in Congress, from 1933 to 1937. For a case study stressing the continuation of old ideas see Robert and Helen Lynd, *Middletown in Transition: A Study in Cultural Conflicts* (New York, 1937), passim. Also remarks and citations in Chapter One for stress on the strength of business values in American society.

served older ideologies at the same time that they witnessed sharp (if transitory) changes in the economy.[62] That a practical, pluralistic America should have failed to adopt an ideologically oriented party system in the 1930's is hardly surprising. That it could not nourish a dominant progressive party is all the more understandable in a business society.

[62] The literature on the "newness" of the 1930's is already large. For an excellent article stressing continuity in the 1930's see Richard S. Kirkendall, "The New Deal as Watershed: The Recent Literature," *Journal of American History,* LIV (March 1968), 839-52.

8. Federalism in the Style of the 1930's

NO TWO people, it seemed, agreed on the New Deal's impact on the states during the 1930's. Friendly observers spoke of a "new federalism," a potentially cooperative relationship enriched by matching funds.[1] Others, conceding the blessings bestowed by the national administration, countered that the New Deal was discriminatory—that some states basked in the warmth of presidential friendship while others shivered outside in the cold. Conservatives perceived not a generous father but an autocratic Leviathan. "We are all beginning to look to Uncle Sam to be Santa Claus," one Democratic governor complained in 1935. "I think the toughest problem that we as governors have is to stay away from it if we can."[2] And liberals, reflecting a fourth view, disagreed sharply on all counts, maintaining that federal timidity was stranding the nation in the miasmatic conservatism of the 1920's. "Since 1930," one critic charged in 1949, "state government has dismally failed to meet responsi-

[1] For a guardedly favorable view of federalism in this period see Jane Perry Clark's *The Rise of a New Federalism.* Daniel J. Elazar is more optimistic in *The American Partnership: Intergovernmental Cooperation in Nineteenth Century United States.* He argues that "cooperative federalism was the rule in the nineteenth century as well as in the twentieth. . . . What has changed is the routinization of shared procedures." (337). See also Morton Grodzins, *The American System: A New View of Government in the United States* (Chicago 1966), ed., Elazar. Grodzins views the period 1913-1948 as the "triumph of cooperative federalism." 41-57.

[2] David Sholtz (Fla.), *Proceedings of the 1935 Governors Conference,* 37. A sketchy study of Sholtz is Merlin G. Cox, "David Sholtz: New Deal Governor of Florida," *Florida Historical Quarterly,* XLIII (October 1964), 142-52.

bilities and obligations in every field. . . . The federal government has not encroached upon state government. State government has failed."[3]

Various improvements in state government during the decade seemed to support defenders of the thesis of cooperative federalism. One was administrative efficiency. Eleven states passed reorganization statutes during the decade, making a total of 26. Many others, acting in piecemeal fashion, removed administrative control and financial responsibility from the archaic local units which had formerly dominated the field.[4] It was no accident that the home rule movement languished in the 1930's: states seemed better answers than counties or towns to the economic problems of the era.[5]

A related development was the expansion of the merit system in the late 1930's. One authority remarked in 1939 that "the past two years have probably seen more progress in the field of public personnel administration than any previous period in our national history." Five states, the first since 1920, passed workable statutes in 1937, and 6 others applied the merit system to various departments, most often in the realm of public welfare.[6] The trend toward state merit systems, revived after a lapse of more than fifteen years, continued steadily if unspectacularly through the 1940's, 50's and 60's.

[3] Robert S. Allen, ed., *Our Sovereign State* (New York, 1949), xxix.

[4] John A. Perkins, "American Governors—1930 to 1940," *National Municipal Review*, XXIX (March 1940), 178-84; Lynton K. Caldwell, "Perfecting State Administration," *Public Administration Review*, VII (Winter 1947), 25-36; and Leonard D. White and M. Harvey Sherman, "The Governors March On," *State Government*, XIII (October 1940), 195-97, 206ff.

[5] George C. Benson, *The New Centralization: A Study of Intergovernmental Relations in the United States* (New York, 1941), 117-21.

[6] G. Lyle Belsley, "The Advance of the Merit System," *State Government*, XII (January 1939), 7-8, 18ff.

These laws were not always comprehensive, and they passed for varied reasons.[7] Some governors, facing factional opposition, sponsored merit systems to protect their followers.[8] Others promoted civil service because dispensing patronage for so many desperate jobless was a political liability, not an asset. In still other states civil service reform and administrative reorganization sprang from the need to cut excess jobs from the public payroll. Moreover, many governors hotly resented federal stipulations calling for merit appointments under the social security system—what one governor branded "the blow at state sovereignty through the club of federal grants."[9] In this sense, federal-state disagreement over methods of appointment sometimes offset gains in efficiency. But the New Deal can take some credit for the improvements which were made. Its insistence during the lifetime of the FERA on a single state agency for welfare and its later requirement in 1939 of civil service procedures in social security stimulated administrative efficiency in the states.

The New Deal also hastened the spread of social legislation, some of which reached the statute books in the little New Deal states. And even in the majority of states where little immediate effect was visible, it transformed the nature of argument. Before the New Deal, states rights re-

[7] Joseph A. Schlesinger, "The Politics of the Executive," in Jacob and Vines, *Politics in the American States*, 216.

[8] Henry A. Ritgerod, "Arkansas Abandons the Merit System," *National Municipal Review*, XXVIII (April 1939), 296-98; H. F. Alderfer, "Centralization in Pennsylvania," *ibid.*, XXVII (April 1938), 189-96; Benson, *New Centralization*, 73-74.

[9] Gov. Homer Holt (D.-W. Va.) to Gov. Julius Heil (Wis.), January 26, 1940, Holt Papers, Box 3, University of West Virginia Library, Morgantown. This box contains many revealing letters from governors supporting Holt's protests against the civil service amendment to social security and against the Hatch Act regulating state primaries and elections.

mained a vital if negative dogma which enabled people like Byrd of Virginia and Ritchie of Maryland to achieve national prominence. Even Brandeis and Roosevelt had stressed a more affirmative version. But in showing what positive government could do, the New Deal forced politicians to recognize that states rights without state activism must perish. As Governor Olin Johnston of South Carolina warned his colleagues in 1935, "There has been a continuous decrease of state powers because . . . the states have not used them, and the people wanted government. If a government does not measure up to its responsibility by the exercise of its powers . . . the powers will not be there . . . they will be exercised by the mobs, by the rabble, or something. . . . It is God's and nature's law."[10] Even conservatives readily understood this logic.

The Roosevelt years also altered—conservatives said warped—state political patterns. Appealing to previously ignored groups, the New Deal stimulated increases in political participation in many states.[11] Most of these new voters were underprivileged—Negroes, unemployed, unskilled workers, immigrants. They tended to vote Democratic in national elections and in so doing to force both parties in competitive states to promise more liberal services.

The New Deal cannot take all the credit for this development. Although voter participation did increase during the decade, the trend had already begun with the nomination of Smith in 1928. Moreover, uninspiring, job-seeking Democrats all too often cashed in on Roosevelt's electoral magic without in any way selling progressive ideas on the state

[10] *Proceedings of the 1935 Governors Conference*, 77.

[11] Lester Milbrath, "Political Participation in the States," in Jacob and Vines, *Politics in the American States*, 38ff. For the impact of national policy on voting trends in individual states see Fenton, *Politics in the Border States*; Gosnell, *Grass Roots Politics*; and Joseph P. Harris, *California Politics* (Stanford, 1955), 9ff.

level. But even though few states enacted significant reforms in the 1930's, the trend started in 1928 and accelerated by the New Deal spurred many politicians in both parties to listen to long-silent urban voices. In this sense, the New Deal did indeed promote, however slowly and accidentally, the spread of urban programs in the states.

Above all, the combination of national policy and depression forever transformed federal-state relations. Take, for instance, the governor of 1925: he could expect a few congressional dollars for highways, agricultural extension work, and vocational education. If he was a Republican —and most were—he traveled to Washington once or twice a year to confer with the president and be photographed for the home folks. Otherwise he expected little, and worried still less about the bickering on Pennsylvania Avenue.

His successor in 1940 inhabited a different world. While purely intrastate matters continued to dominate the governor's time, national policy intimately affected the economic health of his state and his own political future. Like it or not, he usually played along with the New Deal, and if he too often refused to press for progressive reforms, he was even less likely to reject the matching money which his constituents found so appealing. Partly because of federal activism, the American state of 1940 spent more, taxed more, and provided much more than it had two decades before. And three decades later its importance had grown even further, following many of the same guidelines and policies on grants that had been established from 1933 to 1940.

Whether the New Deal was discriminatory, as many governors have maintained ever since, is difficult to determine. Some statistics suggest that it was. A state-by-state comparison of federal tax incidence and federal aid in 1940 revealed wide variations. Delaware residents, ranking first in per capita tax incidence with a figure of $172, ranked 40th in aid with $22.24 per capita. New Yorkers, third in tax incidence

($82), received only $18 per capita in aid, for a ranking of 47th. Conversely, many states with low tax incidence ranked high in amounts of federal aid. Mississippians, last in taxes at $10 per capita, got $37 per capita in aid, a ranking of 18th. And North Dakotans, ranking 39th in taxes (with $21) stood third in aid at $79 per capita. Residents of sparsely populated western states tended to pay less in federal taxes than they received in benefits. So did southerners. Inhabitants of the urban East and the Middle Western states seemed to suffer.[12] With figures like these, it is not surprising that some New England governors complained about throwing their tax money west and south.

Federal aid procedures contributed to these variations. Western states ranked unusually high in aid per capita because of grants for conservation and agriculture, and because the matching formula for highways favored states with large areas. And they tended to pay lower taxes partly because much of their land was publicly owned; indeed, they complained constantly of losses in revenue caused by tax-exempt federal holdings within their borders.[13] Urban states, on the other hand, received less per capita for farms, conservation, and highways. And the formula for the assistance of the aged, blind, and dependent, by setting limits to federal contributions, also tended to discriminate unintentionally against the needy in the richer urban states.

But these figures distort the truth. Variations in tax incidence stemmed from variations in per capita income not from federal favoritism. Residents in wealthy states paid more per capita, not because Roosevelt wanted to spread their money around but because they had more to pay. Urban states had large numbers of needy—numerically many more than elsewhere—but they also had many more

[12] *Federal State and Local Fiscal Relations*, 78th Cong., 1st Sess., Sen. Doc. 69, 219-25.

[13] Donnelly, *Rocky Mountain State Politics*, 3ff.

who could pay federal taxes. Thus it was natural that tax incidence was highest in the wealthier states of the urban East and Midwest.

Perhaps the fairest way to judge New Deal grants-in-aid policy is to note the amount per state of federal per capita grants. From such a perspective, poorer states were most justified in complaining, for they were also those with the least per capita aid. Federal grant policy was more concerned with securing state participation than with discovering the extent of need. Indeed, Roosevelt made little effort to equalize wealth by state or region, or even to establish a minimum state payment for various kinds of welfare. Far from being deliberately discriminatory, New Deal aid policy perpetuated the existing imbalance between rich and poor states in America.[14]

Conservative critics seemed to have other tenable arguments. Compared with the 1920's and 1940's, states were more friendly to organized labor than many businessmen desired. States also stiffened regulation of public utilities. And despite the scarcity of funds, public spending for services multiplied after the crisis of 1930-1934; those reactionaries who wanted as little government as possible were not at all pleased. Most galling to states-righters, the New Deal cornucopia led states to fit their spending and tax policies to federal stipulations. Governors would no longer enjoy the freedom of action in finance which they had had before the depression.

But liberals were also unhappy, justifiably so. Though

[14] See Bureau of Census, *Federal and State Aid, 1941* (Washington, 1943), 30-36, for revealing comparative statistics on aid to states. Also Maxwell, *The Fiscal Impact*, 397-403. The variations by states remained much the same in the early 1960's. See *Congress and the Nation, 1945-1964: A Review of Government and Politics* (Washington, 1965), 1388-89.

labor legislation in some states was more progressive than in the 1920's, it was short lived, and after the sitdown strikes of 1937 a reaction set in, halting further gains. In a short time state right-to-work and criminal syndicalism laws appeared with alarming frequency. The record of the states in relief spending was equally disappointing. Despite some advances in administration, social workers were less optimistic in 1940 than they had been a few years earlier. Especially disheartening were the scanty state contributions for general relief. Because the WPA let states provide for unemployables, and because the federal formula for aid to aged, blind, and dependent children required no minimum state contribution, the needy in many areas fared almost as badly as they had in the early days of the depression. And although all states cooperated with the unemployment compensation program, few surpassed the niggardly minimum requirements.

State financial policy also veered to the right during the decade. While a few progressive income and corporate taxes reached the books, the most striking trend was the sales tax movement. Because states were already seeking new sources of revenue before 1930, such a development would probably have occurred anyway, but federal policy accelerated it. Increased income levies passed in the Hoover and Roosevelt administrations forced states to turn elsewhere, and the insistence by New Dealers that states contribute a share to welfare costs intensified the search. Far from "soaking the rich," states remained as regressive in raising revenue as they had been in the past.

The New Deal was not only unable to force progressive labor, welfare, and tax policies on the states, but one may question whether it inspired those gains which were made. Did the New Deal deserve credit for the advances in labor law—or was the organized political power of the CIO more important? Did federal policy awaken some states to their welfare responsibilities, or did the depression leave them no choice? And why did a few states tighten public utility regulation—because the New Deal set an example, or because the conduct of some utility executives was so flagrant? Were state policies of the 1930's the result of federal guidelines or of economic necessity?

The New Deal was certainly important; try to imagine what states would have done without money and exhortation from Washington. Yet it is equally hard to understand the occasional advances in state legislation in the 1930's without recognizing that they occurred in a time of crisis. Localities alone simply could not provide for relief, education, and highways, and the states had begun to stumble into the breech even before Roosevelt inaugurated the New Deal. The centralization of American life was forcing the states to assume local functions. Nothing since that time has reversed this invincible trend.

The liberal critics have the strongest case. While state activity expanded in the 1930's, the change was far from dramatic: indeed, the growth in state services in the 1950's and 1960's has been much more impressive. The New Deal produced neither federal dictation, a completely cooperative federalism, nor a new state progressivism. Instead, it helped create a rather flat mixture of achievement, mediocrity, and confusion. For all the supposed power of the New Deal, it was unable to impose all its guidelines on the autonomous 48 states.

The causes of this mixed record defy simple explanation, but perhaps the most obvious was the limited nature of positive state action prior to the depression. Scholars have shown that the states contributed materially to nineteenth century economic development, that they preceded the national government in regulating corporations, and that they often served as laboratories of social reform.[15] But neither the states nor the federal government prior to 1929 had been forced to provide costly welfare programs, countercyclical spending, or legislation beneficial to organized labor. Since these were staples of the new progressivism of the 1930's, it was not surprising that state leaders, like many New Dealers, were slow to adopt them. And given the inexorable centralization of modern life, it is clear that the national government was better equipped to handle economic problems by 1933.

Lack of funds provided a second difficulty. Even before the crash, real estate and personal property taxes—until then the chief sources of state and local revenue—had proved burdensome, and states tried to pay for the enormously expensive task of road building in the 1920's by issuing bonds. When the depression struck so quickly, it caught the states in unsound financial positions, which they sought to escape—first, through drastic economies and then, through regressive taxes. Chastened by this experience, many legislators shunned costly progressive services wherever they could.[16]

Timing also worked against activists. The reform impulse of the 1930's, unlike that of the progressive era, was national in origin and limited in duration. Pressed for funds early in the depression, the states awaited federal action. But because many key New Deal measures affecting states—social security, the Wagner act, and fair labor standards—passed in or after 1935, and because the Supreme Court did not sustain them until 1937 or later, the states enjoyed no certain constitutional mandate before then. After all, the

15 See Sidney Fine, *Laissez Faire and the General Welfare State* (Ann Arbor, 1964), 19ff, 353ff; and Elazar, *The American Partnership*.

16 Edna Trull, "Resources and Debts of the Forty-Eight States," *National Municipal Review*, XXVII (June 1938), 293-98.

court had invalidated the NRA in 1935 and state minimum wages in 1936. When the Supreme Court finally did make its "switch in time that saved nine" in 1937, resentment against the CIO, distrust of Roosevelt, and hostility toward heavy government spending began to disperse the more activist mood of 1933 to 1935. Despite these drawbacks, some states did manage to accomplish a good deal, especially in 1937. For most others the time was too short.

Existing institutions presented another obstacle. Just as courts blocked the New Deal, so they interfered with new reform programs in the states. Outdated constitutions obstructed the financing of new services.[17] State legislatures were still full of ill-prepared, ill-experienced, and poorly paid men, chosen according to district lines which remained inequitable in 41 state senates and 36 assemblies. In most of these states, districting favored rural lawmakers, many of whom denounced the urban liberalism and bureaucracy of the New Deal.[18] While one critic exaggerated when he called the state legislatures the "bawdy houses of state gov-

[17] B. U. Ratchford, "Constitutional Provisions Governing State Borrowing," *American Political Science Review*, XXXII (August 1938), 694-717.

[18] Several important articles deal with these problems. See David O. Walter, "Reapportionment and Urban Representation," *Annals of the American Academy of Political and Social Science*, CXCV (January 1938), 11-20; Charles W. Shull, "Reapportionment: A Chronic Problem," *National Municipal Review*, XXX (February 1941), 73-79; Walter, "Representation of Metropolitan Districts," *ibid.*, XXVII (March 1938), 128-37; and Charles S. Hyneman, "Tenure and Turnover of the Indiana General Assembly," *American Political Science Review*, XXXII (February and April 1938), 51-67, 311-31. For individual states see Mona Fletcher, "Wanted: Experienced Legislators," *National Muncipal Review*, XXX (May 1941), 268-74 (Ohio); Moscow, *Politics in the Empire State*, 166-67; and William T. R. Fox, "Legislative Personnel in Pennsylvania," *Annals of the American Academy of Political and Social Science*, CXCV (January 1938), 33-39.

ernment," it was true that they were not especially edifying spectacles in the great majority of states.[19]

Political bickering played a large role in blocking progressive state legislation. In some states Republicans were the culprits, but this was to be expected. More distressing —and more common—was the feuding among Democrats who controlled both state house and legislature. Serious enough in more stable times, this dissension may even have grown in the 1930's when younger, activist New Dealers challenged old-line leaders, and when Democrats of all persuasions swarmed after the prizes of office so suddenly dangled before them. Farley and Roosevelt were no more able to discipline these unruly groups than Hopkins was able to coerce states into line on relief spending.

What could the Roosevelt administration have done to ensure a more profound and lasting impression on state policy and politics? Very little. The limited nature of predepression progressivism was not the fault of the New Deal, nor was the financial chaos of many states in the early 1930's. Indeed, federal aid to states, which increased from $220 million in 1932 to $2 billion in 1935, rescued state finances from chaos.[20] Obstacles raised by state courts, inequitable districting, and state constitutions were also beyond federal control.

Coercion was not the answer. Men such as Farley and Hopkins realized only too well that politicians were easily offended, and that to charge in, as Roosevelt finally did in his purge of 1938, would invite resentment and defeat. Thus Farley tried to avoid intraparty battles, endorsing all Democratic nominees, conservative, moderate, or liberal. Hopkins was equally cautious. As he said of Democratic fighting in Delaware, "I am not disposed to do any-

19 Allen, ed., *Sovereign State,* xxxi.

20 H. J. Bitterman, *State and Federal Grants-in-Aid* (New York, 1938), 142. This total included relief spending.

thing in this administrative jam. I think it is up to Delaware. I am disposed to let them stew in their own juice."[21] Had all New Deal agencies consistently bolstered progressive groups in every state, it is conceivable, if unlikely, that they could have accelerated the liberalization of the state Democratic parties. But in many states, factions did not even divide along ideological lines; in others there was more than one potentially progressive clique; and in still others, as in California, the left wing seemed unpredictable, not progressive. Even where a reformist bloc clearly existed, it was often a minority: to have supported it would have infuriated the ruling group with whom Roosevelt had to deal, causing more harm than good.[22] Farley, Hopkins, and others were wise to treat politicians with gentle care.

This is not to say that New Dealers did all they could. Some ignored state affairs, others carelessly appointed hostile personnel, still others too timidly endorsed entrenched machines. The lack of coordination among federal agencies, while not always avoidable, so distressed Roosevelt that he himself regarded administration as his weakest point.[23] And some of the federal formulas for matching grants encouraged stinginess and distortion in state budgets.

But the most striking feature of federal-state relations during the 1930's was not the failure of New Dealers, but the

[21] Hopkins telephone conversation, April 19, 1934, Box 93, Hopkins Papers.

[22] A case in point was Ohio, scene of a 1934 senatorial primary between Democratic governor George White and former governor A. Victor Donahey, a conservative. At the last minute a third candidate, Rep. Charles West, entered the lists, backed (or so it seemed) by federal officeholders directed from Washington. The result? Donahey won, giving Roosevelt a conservative Senator to contend with for six years; White was bitter, referring to Farley's "dictatorship"; and West finished badly, contributing not at all to the New Deal in Ohio. See White to John Scheide, July 3, 1934, Personal Correspondence, White Papers, Ohio Historical Society, Columbus, Ohio.

[23] Louis Brownlow, *A Passion for Anonymity* (Chicago, 1962), 392.

limits in which they had to operate. Time was short, courts hostile, state institutions obstructive, and political parties too often concerned with patronage instead of policy. Above all, state reformers faced the same potent forces which eventually brought the New Deal to its knees: the durable appeal of materialistic, pro-business ideology and the stubborn resistance to a strong central government, be it in Washington, Albany, or Carson City. For all the apparent nationalism of the 1930's, states rights and strict constructionism remained remarkably healthy. Indeed, the system of federalism itself, far from serving as a flexible medium for change, revealed itself—in Canada as well as the United States—to be better suited to preserving diversity than to encouraging strong and coordinated national action.

Considering these limitations, the liberal critics, though essentially correct, might have been more understanding. By working with instead of against the status quo in the states, Roosevelt managed to avoid pitched battles; if the result was not gloriously cooperative federalism, neither was it chaos. Indeed, for all his faith in state experimentalism, Roosevelt wisely worried rather little about the peccadillos of states, for he recognized that congressional legislation was the best answer to the problems of the modern age. Compared to the national government, the states lost authority in the 1930's—and they have regained very little since.[24] But their loss was not the fault of Roosevelt, Hopkins, Farley, or the most nationalistic ideologues of the New Deal. They have slipped—relatively—because the states alone, for good or ill, have lacked the potential to solve the problems of urban, mid-twentieth century America.

[24] For state activity since the 1930's see *Congress and the Nation*, 1377-78. Civil expenditures (excluding defense, foreign policy, space, and debt services) of the federal government have increased eight-fold in the period from 1938 to 1963; of states and localities, seven and one-half-fold.

A Bibliographical Essay

AS the footnotes reveal, this study required research in archival sources as well as in specialized literature in the fields of economics, political science, and public administration. It also necessitated consulting unpublished dissertations and manuscripts for information concerning affairs within individual states. The *New York Times, New Republic, Nation, American Mercury, Fortune, Review of Reviews,* and many scholarly journals also proved essential. Listed below are some but not all of the most valuable sources, magazine articles excluded. For the latter as well as for other less useful sources see the footnotes.

Archives

A wealth of material exists in the National Archives in Washington, D.C. Among the richest collections are the FERA records (Record Group 69), the NRA Records (RG 9), the records of POUR, Hoover's commission for unemployment relief (RG 73), and those of the National Emergency Council, housed in the Office of Government Reports (RG 44). All contain reports and correspondence easily accessible and arranged by states. Also revealing were the records of the Division of Labor Standards (RG 100); the Social Security Board (RG 47); and the National Resources Planning Board (RG 187). These files also include some boxes arranged by states.

Also consulted at the National Archives were records of other New Deal agencies. Among these were Soil Conservation (RG 114), PWA (135), RFC (234), Public Housing (196), Farmers Home Administration including the Farm Security Administration (118), and WPA (housed with

FERA in 69). Not so systematically organized, these proved less rewarding and were time-consuming sources.

The Franklin D. Roosevelt Library at Hyde Park, New York is a second mine of archival material for the period. Valuable here in giving insights to relief policies were the Harry Hopkins Papers, particularly the reports in Box 89 from Miss Lorena Hickok. The records of the Democratic National Committee, especially James A. Farley's correspondence by states in 1936; and OF 300, particularly "Election Forecasts and Results, 1938," were very helpful in assessing political relations with the states. Roosevelt's Personal Files (PPF) and Official Files (OF) filled in many gaps; excellent indices guide the researcher to the right places in these voluminous files. Also consulted at Hyde Park were the papers of Aubrey Williams, Hopkins' aide; Emil Hurja, Farley's assistant; and John Carmody, a New Deal planning official. The Williams papers include an unpublished manuscript, "The New Deal—A Dead Battery," which provides colorful insights into relief problems.

Other private papers are scattered about the country. The Frank Walker manuscripts at Notre Dame University in South Bend, Indiana, contain interesting correspondence concerning the National Emergency Council, and the voluminous Gifford Pinchot collection at the Library of Congress in Washington, D.C., includes some important letters. Also at the Library of Congress are the papers of Theodore F. Green, Rhode Island's governor from 1933 to 1936; Sen. Bronson Cutting of New Mexico; and Sen. William McAdoo of California. The latter two collections contain some revealing political correspondence.

The Alfred M. Landon papers at the Kansas Historical Society in Topeka are rich in material. Disappointing are the Gov. Wilbur Cross (Connecticut) papers at Yale University Library, New Haven, and the Gov. Paul McNutt

(Indiana) papers at the Indiana State Library in Indianapolis. At the Ohio Historical Society in Columbus are the collections of three Ohio governors, George White, Martin Davey, and John Bricker. The Davey and Bricker papers are rather thin, but the White collection contains a few revealing letters. The Gov. Guy Park (Missouri) papers at the University of Missouri Library, Columbia, contain little helpful material. The Gov. Herman Kump (West Virginia) papers at the West Virginia University Library in Morgantown are a useful source, as are the Gov. Homer Holt (West Virginia) papers, also at this library. The Herbert Lehman letters at the Columbia University Library are large but circumspect; an oral history collection concerning Lehman, also at Columbia, is more useful.

A western trip enabled me to visit state archives in Colorado, Utah, and New Mexico; all have assiduously collected gubernatorial papers. In Denver are the collections of governors Teller Ammons and Edwin Johnson. The Ammons papers are largely official; the Johnson manuscripts are voluminous and important. The George Dern papers at Salt Lake City are extensive, but relatively uninformative for the period of his governorship from 1929 to 1933. The papers of his successor, Henry Blood, are also large, but lack the straightforward letters which can tell so much. The records of New Mexico governors A. W. Hockenhull and Clyde Tingley, housed at the state archives in Santa Fe, are only occasionally helpful; neither is very large. The collection of Gov. Arthur Seligman, however, compensates in frankness for what it lacks in bulk; it provides a sketchy guide to the ruthless character of New Mexico politics.

For many other gubernatorial collections I relied upon unpublished doctoral dissertations which used archival sources with various degrees of success. The dissertations listed below were very helpful in filling gaps in the states of Vermont, Massachusetts, Connecticut, Pennsylvania, Indiana, Georgia, California, Wisconsin, and Idaho.

Materials available at the Herbert Hoover Library in West Branch, Iowa, proved worthwhile, though much less so than those at the Roosevelt Library. These included correspondence and reports relating to the Bureau of Roads, the RFC, and unemployment. The records of the Council of State Governments at the University of Chicago are unfortunately thin, although an unpublished interview with social worker and administrator Frank Bane was of some value.

These varied collections, while necessary for such a study as this, suggest why the realm of state affairs has received so little attention from historians. Distressingly few states have made it a practice to preserve systematically the records of key agencies. Fewer still have made a concerted effort to gather the papers of governors or other key politicians. And few newspapers during the 1930's provided thorough and analytical coverage of state politics. These deficiencies present formidable hurdles to the scholar interested in past comparative politics or even in charting the course of one state during this period. But they are not insurmountable, and the diligent scholar can benefit from scanning the *Monthly Checklist of State Publications, Library of Congress* (Washington, 1910——). For an excellent guide to state manuals and blue books containing state election statistics—an exceedingly important area for the scholar concerned with past comparative politics—see Walter Dean Burnham, *Sources of Historical Election Data: A Preliminary Bibliography* (East Lansing, 1963).

Documents and Government Publications

The list of government documents published during the depression years is endless. But a few summaries provide shortcuts to the scholar in this field. Among the most valuable are *Federal, State, and Local Fiscal Relations*, 78th Cong., 1st Sess., Sen. Doc. 69 (Washington, 1943); Bureau of Census, *Historical Statistics on State and Local Finance, 1902-53* (Washington, 1955); *ibid., Revised Summary of State and Local Finances in 1942* (State and Local Special Studies, No. 26, 1948); *ibid., Federal and State Aid, 1941* (Washington, 1942); *Book of the States, 1935* and *1937* (biennial publication by Council of State Governments); Department of Labor, *Growth of Labor Law in the United States* (Washington, 1962); and *5th Annual Report of the Social Security Board* (Washington, 1941).

Other important publications are Department of Commerce, Rowland Haynes, *State Legislation for Unemployment Relief from Jan. 1, 1931 to May 31, 1932* (Washington, 1932); Public Works Administration, *America Builds, The Record of the PWA* (Washington, 1939); Works Projects Administration, *Final Report on the W.P.A. Program, 1935-43* (Washington, 1946); and Theodore Whiting, *Final Statistical Report of the F.E.R.A.* (Washington, 1942). The Census Bureau also published annual reports on state finances during most of the depression years; these provide more detailed information for one-year periods. *Congress and the Nation, 1945-1964: A Review of Government and Politics* (Washington, 1965), is a mine of information on federal-state activity since World War II.

Unpublished Dissertations

Owing to the paucity of published material on individual states, unpublished doctoral dissertations proved necessary. Among the most comprehensive are Richard M. Judd, "A History of the New Deal in Vermont," Harvard University, 1959; Roy E. Fossett, "The Impact of the New Deal on Georgia Politics, 1933-1941," University of Florida, 1960;

Charles H. Backstrom, "The Progressive Party of Wisconsin, 1934-46," University of Wisconsin, 1956; James F. Wickens, "Colorado in the Great Depression: A Study of New Deal Policies at the State Level," University of Denver, 1964; Rowland L. Mitchell, Jr., "Social Legislation in Connecticut, 1919-39," Yale University, 1954; Ronald E. Chinn, "Democratic Party Politics in California, 1920-56," University of California (Berkeley), 1958; Arthur H. Benedict, "Federal Centralization Through Congressional Legislation, 1924-39," Ohio State University, 1948; Richard C. Keller, "Pennsylvania's Little New Deal," Columbia University, 1960; and Michael P. Malone, "C. Ben Ross and the New Deal in Idaho," Washington State University, 1966.

Others of considerable value are Walter D. Lockard, "The Role of Party in the Connecticut General Assembly, 1931-51," Yale University, 1952; Ivan H. Hinderaker, "Harold Stassen and Developments in the Republican Party in Minnesota, 1937-43," University of Minnesota, 1950; William M. Griffin, "The Impact of Federal Grants-in-Aid on Certain Aspects of Texas State Government," University of Texas, 1959; Sidney Baldwin, "The Farm Security Administration: A Study in Politics and Administration," Syracuse University, 1956; Samuel J. Astorino, "The Decline of the Republican Dynasty in Pennsylvania, 1929-34," University of Pittsburgh, 1962; Francis W. Schruben, "Kansas During the Great Depression, 1930-36," University of Southern California, 1961; Jewel Bellush, "Selected Case Studies of the Legislative Leadership of Governor Herbert H. Lehman," Columbia University, 1959; Robert R. Neff, "The Early Career and Governorship of Paul V. McNutt," Indiana University, 1963; Harold Gorvine, "The New Deal in Massachusetts," Harvard University, 1962; and Paul L. Simon, "Frank Walker: New Dealer," Notre Dame University, 1965.

A Bibliographical Essay

Secondary Works

The number of books by economists and political scientists in the realm of state government and politics is very large, but a few proved of special relevance. Among these are W. Brooke Graves, *American State Government* (Boston, 1941), a still readable survey; and V. O. Key, Jr., *American State Politics* (New York, 1956), a pathbreaking analytical treatment of trends in state politics. Older works are H. J. Bitterman, *State and Federal Grants-in-Aid* (New York, 1938); and George C. Benson, *The New Centralization: A Study of Intergovernmental Relations in the United States* (New York, 1941). Two books dealing with state institutions are Joseph A. Schlesinger, *How They Became Governor: A Study of Comparative Politics, 1870-1950* (East Lansing, 1957); and the imaginative study of freshmen legislators, James D. Barber, *The Lawmakers: Recruitment and Adaptation to Legislative Life* (New Haven, 1965). Three indispensable recent books are Herbert Jacob and Kenneth Vines, eds., *Politics in the American States: A Comparative Analysis* (Boston, 1965); William N. Chambers and Walter D. Burnham, eds., *The American Party Systems: Stages of Political Development* (New York, 1967); and Thomas R. Dye, *Politics, Economics, and the Public: Policy Outcomes in the American States* (Chicago, 1966). It is often said that historians need to consult other disciplines; these books, full of excellent insights drawing upon quantitative evidence, are testimony to the wisdom of such advice.

Three books of special interest in probing the question of changes in American federalism are Jane Perry Clark, *The Rise of a New Federalism* (New York, 1938); Morton Grodzins, *The American System: A View of Government in the United States*, ed., Daniel Elazar (Chicago, 1965); and

Elazar, *The American Partnership: Intergovernmental Cooperation in the Nineteenth Century United States* (Chicago, 1962). Perry is careful but optimistic about the potential for intergovernmental cooperation, while both Elazar and Grodzins exaggerate the degree of agreement past and present. One of many journalistic but nonetheless useful critiques of states is Robert S. Allen, ed., *Our Sovereign State* (New York, 1949). A useful collection of articles dealing with federalism here and abroad is Aaron Wildavsky, ed., *American Federalism in Perspective* (Boston, 1967). The Canadian experience with federalism is excellently described in *Report of the Royal Commission on Dominion-Provincial Relations, Book I, Canada, 1867-1939* (Ottawa, 1940).

Economists have provided essential studies on various aspects of intergovernmental finances. A Keynesian account is Alvin H. Hansen and Harvey S. Perloff, *State and Local Finance in the National Economy* (New York, 1944); and a readable and accurate brief survey is Frederick Mosher and Orville F. Poland, *The Costs of American Governments: Facts, Trends, Myths* (New York, 1964). James Maxwell has written two careful works, *The Fiscal Impact of Federalism* (Cambridge, Mass., 1946), and *Financing State and Local Governments* (Washington, 1965). Solomon Fabricant, *The Growth of Governmental Activity in the United States Since 1900* (New York, 1952) is also relevant. When these authorities cited differing figures—which was disconcertingly often—I turned to the indispensable source of historians, the Census Bureau's *Historical Statistics of the United States, Colonial Times to 1957* (Washington, 1960), and to the other special studies by the Census Bureau mentioned above.

For somewhat more specialized areas of state government focusing on the 1930's see Arthur E. Buck, *Reorganization of State Governments in the United States* (New York, 1938); Leslie Lipson, *American Governor: Figurehead to Leader* (Chicago, 1939); Josephine Brown, *Public Relief, 1929-39* (New York, 1940); Donald Howard, *WPA and Federal Relief Policy* (New York, 1943); Neil Jacoby, *Retail Sales Taxation: An Analysis of Economic and Administrative Problems* (Chicago, 1938); Sanford Cohen, *State Labor Legislation, 1937-1947: A Study of State Laws Affecting the Conduct and Organization of Labor Unions* (Columbus, 1948); Arthur Altmeyer, *Formative Years of Social Security* (Madison, 1966); and Roy Lubove, *The Struggle for Social Security* (Cambridge, Mass., 1968). For an especially valuable work reprinting with wise comments the record of meetings of the National Emergency Council from 1933 through 1935 see Lester Seligman and Elmer Cornwell, eds., *New Deal Mosaic: Roosevelt Confers with His National Emergency Council* (Eugene, Ore., 1965).

Studies of individual states and politicians for this period are not so numerous as they might be. Some works, however, do exist. A few are Robert Burke, *Olson's New Deal for California* (Berkeley, 1958); Bernard Bellush, *Franklin D. Roosevelt as Governor of New York* (New York, 1955); M. Nelson McGeary, *Gifford Pinchot: Forester-Politician* (Princeton, 1960); Erwin L. Levine, *Theodore Francis Green: The Rhode Island Years, 1906-1936* (Providence, 1963); Elmer Puryear, *Democratic Party Dissension in North Carolina, 1928-1936* (Chapel Hill, 1962); and William E. Leuchtenburg, *Flood Control Politics: The Connecticut River Valley Problem, 1927-50* (Cambridge, Mass., 1953).

In addition, the following studies have been made: Allen P. Sindler, *Huey Long's Louisiana: State Politics, 1920-52* (Baltimore, 1956); J. Joseph Huthmacher, *Massachusetts People and Politics, 1919-33* (Cambridge, Mass., 1959);

George H. Mayer, *The Political Career of Floyd B. Olson* (Minneapolis, 1951); Allan Nevins, *Herbert H. Lehman and His Era* (New York, 1963); Dayton D. McKean, *Pressures on the Legislature of New Jersey* (New York, 1938); Richard D. Lunt, *The High Ministry of Government: The Political Career of Frank Murphy* (Detroit, 1965); Seth S. McKay, *W. Lee O'Daniel and Texas Politics, 1938-1942* (Lubbock, 1944); Gerald D. Nash, *State Government and Economic Development: A History of Administrative Policies in California, 1849-1933* (Berkeley, 1964); Donald R. McCoy, *Landon of Kansas* (Lincoln, 1966); Lyle W. Dorsett, *The Pendergast Machine* (New York, 1968); and Keith L. Bryant, Jr., *Alfalfa Bill Murray* (Norman, 1968).

Regional studies include V. O. Key, Jr., *Southern Politics in State and Nation* (New York, 1949); John H. Fenton, *Politics in the Border States: A Study of Political Organization and Political Change Common to the Border States—Maryland, West Virginia, Kentucky, and Missouri* (New Orleans, 1957); Thomas Donnelly, ed., *Rocky Mountain State Politics* (Albuquerque, 1940); Earl Pomeroy, *The Pacific Slope* (New York, 1965); Howard Odum, *Southern Regions of the United States* (Chapel Hill, 1936); and George B. Tindall, *The Emergence of the New South, 1913-1945* (Baton Rouge, 1967). All are excellent and most useful works.

State histories run the gamut from travelogues to anecdotal surveys, and all too few give much consideration to recent politics. A few books with suggestive bibliographies do exist, however. Among these are Charles H. Ambler and Festus P. Summers, *West Virginia: The Mountain State* (New Jersey, 1958); Duane Meyer, *The Heritage of Missouri: A History* (St. Louis, 1965); Elwyn B. Robinson, *History of North Dakota* (Lincoln, 1955); Warren A. Beck, *New Mexico: A History of Four Centuries* (Norman, 1962);

Seth S. McKay and Odie B. Faulk, *Texas After Spindletop* (Austin, 1965); Rupert N. Richardson, *Texas: The Lone Star State* (New Jersey, 2nd edn., 1958); Edwin C. McReynolds, *Oklahoma: A History of the Sooner State* (Norman, 1954); Arrell M. Gibson, *Oklahoma: A History of Five Centuries* (Norman, 1965); Herbert S. Schell, *History of South Dakota* (Lincoln, 1961); and William F. Zornow, *Kansas: A History of the Jayhawk State* (Norman, 1957). Helpful sketches of California governors, with suggestive bibliographies, appear in H. Brett Melendy and Benjamin F. Gilbert, *The Governors of California: Peter H. Burnett to Edmund G. Brown* (Georgetown, Calif., 1965). Two recent works offering an historical dimension on testing findings in comparative politics are Jack E. Holmes, *Politics in New Mexico* (Albuquerque, 1967); and Alan L. Clem, *Prairie State Politics: Popular Democracy in South Dakota* (Washington, 1967). It is a pity that the list is not three times longer: that it is not testifies to the great amount of work which may profitably be begun in the field of state history.

Index